DISCARDED

Rousseau, Nature,
and the
Problem of the Good Life

Laurence D. Cooper

Rousseau, Nature, and the Problem of the Good Life

The Pennsylvania State University Press
University Park, Pennsylvania

Library of Congress Cataloging-in-Publication Data

Cooper, Laurence D., 1962–
    Rousseau, nature, and the problem of the good life / Laurence
D. Cooper.

        p.   cm.
    Includes bibliographical references and index.
    ISBN 0-271-01922-0 (cloth : alk. paper)
    ISBN 0-271-01923-9 (pbk. : alk. paper)
    1. Rousseau, Jean-Jacques, 1712–1778.   2. Philosophical
anthropology—History—18th century.   3. Philosophy of
nature—History—18th century.   4. Political science—History—18th
century.   I. Title.
    B2138.M3   C66   1999
    194—dc21   98-50149
                                                        CIP

It is the policy of The Pennsylvania State University Press to use acid-free paper for
the first printing of all clothbound books. Publications on uncoated stock satisfy the
minimum requirements of American National Standard for Information Sciences—
Permanence of Paper for Printed Library Materials, ANSI Z39.48-1992.

To Vicki

elle plaît chaque jour davantage–Emile V:410

Contents

Preface

The philosophy of Jean-Jacques Rousseau is famous—some would say infamous —for its apparent contradictions. At some places it appears radically individualistic; at others, just as radically collectivist. In some works Rousseau rhapsodizes about nature or love and emerges as a founder of Romanticism, while in others he speaks the harder language of austere virtue and so seems a modern Stoic. And there are other paradoxes as well. Indeed, so manifold and so pronounced are these contradictions that they have led to an astounding array of conflicting interpretations. Perhaps no other philosophical corpus—and almost certainly no other corpus as systematically coherent as Rousseau's —has been subject to so many contrary readings.[1] Rousseau has been variously tagged as a revolutionary, a conservative, a protototalitarian, and a progressive —and these designations only cover his political thought.[2] The psychological, anthropological, and aesthetic aspects of his thought are equally subtle and have given rise to their own interpretive controversies.

But if the most problematic of Rousseau's paradoxes stem from the conflicting character of his solutions, the most significant is found in his basic diagnosis of the human condition. The greatest paradox in Rousseau's work is the

1. Rousseau insisted that his thought was a systematic whole whose many contradictions are resolvable. (See *Dialogues* III:211–14.) It should be noted at the outset that I accept his claim, even if many others do not. The most convincing argument for the truth of Rousseau's claim is made by Arthur M. Melzer in *The Natural Goodness of Man: On the System of Rousseau's Thought* (Chicago: University of Chicago Press, 1990). It is my hope that the present work will, among other things, shed further light on the truth and meaning of Rousseau's claim.

2. For a sense of the breadth and persistence of the interpretive controversy surrounding Rousseau's works, see Guy H. Dodge, ed., *Jean-Jacques Rousseau: Authoritarian Libertarian?* (Lexington, Mass.: D. C. Heath, 1971). See also the bibliographical surveys in Asher Horowitz, *Rousseau, Nature, and History* (Toronto: University of Toronto Press, 1987), 3–26, and Peter Gay's introduction to *The Question of Jean-Jacques Rousseau*, by Ernst Cassirer (Bloomington: Indiana University Press, 1954), 17–24.

contrast between his exculpatory claim that man is naturally good and his damning insistence that man is wicked and mean. Few have argued *either* side of this paradox as strenuously as Rousseau, let alone both sides. The significance of this paradox has little to do with the difficulty it presents to Rousseau's readers. Indeed, as veteran readers of Rousseau know, the paradox is not all that difficult to resolve, for what is exculpated and what is indicted are two separate things—namely, nature and man, respectively. It is nature that is good. To say that man by nature is good is to say that man *was* good while he remained natural. Today, no longer natural, he is corrupt and corrupts all he touches. As Rousseau puts it at the start of book I of *Emile*, "Everything is good as it leaves the hands of the Author of things; everything degenerates in the hands of man" (37). Among the things that have degenerated in the hands of man, he explains, is man himself.

Rather, the contrast between natural goodness and human degradation is so significant because in it is contained the whole grim logic of man's lot as Rousseau sees it. That logic might be expressed as follows. Man is sorely in need of redemption, yet the very corruption that has put him in such dire need prevents him from successfully developing a solution. An attempt at a solution, being of his own making, would surely fail: "everything degenerates in the hands of man," or as Rousseau puts it in the *Second Discourse*, "the vices that make social institutions necessary are the same ones that make their abuse inevitable" (172–73). Humanity, it would seem, is hopelessly lost, its vision so blurred by corruption that it can never hope to find its way out of the morass in which it has placed itself.

But perhaps things are not quite as bleak as this logic would suggest. After all, man may be fallen, but nature is not—indeed, it is wholly good. If we could discover a way to be guided by nature, we just might find a road out of our present misery. Surely whatever hope we have, if any, lies in nature.

And so it does, except that there are two problems. The first, a practical problem, is that man would seem bound to foul whatever solution nature might offer up to him. It is hard to imagine that he who causes everything he touches to degenerate would not botch this too, especially given that he failed to hew to nature's way the first time. This is no small difficulty, though perhaps we may be granted license for a certain optimism nonetheless. Perhaps by adopting a nature-based solution, man would be returning to nature, at least in part, and so would cease to cause everything he touches to degenerate. Perhaps, if he were to follow a path laid out by nature, he could avoid the effects of his blurred vision and find his way back to health; perhaps he could even find his way *up*, to a new healthfulness. True, he strayed from nature once

before, but that was before he had fully developed his reason—and before anyone had been able to explain what is at stake and what nature really is, as
Rousseau now has done.

To the second problem, however, there is no such easily imagined solution.
That problem is as forbidding as it is simple: nature, as Rousseau conceives it, is
not teleological. It does not comprehend ends. Consequently, it does not prescribe any particular way of life for human beings once they have departed from
their original state. In short, it lays out no path. To be sure, it offers certain
consolations. Some are able to admire nature's harmony and take a certain joy
in doing so.[3] And the wise among us can even find a measure of freedom
through studying nature: they can recognize the unnaturalness of certain passions and liberate themselves, at least partly, from their stranglehold.[4] But
these are only palliatives, not solutions. As Rousseau sees it, no one has yet
found in nature a comprehensive solution to the human problem. No one has
been able to derive from that pure source a prescription for impure humanity.[5]

No one, that is, prior to himself. For this is exactly what Rousseau purports
to have done. He offers a broad range of prescriptive thought, and there is no
part of that thought that does not in some essential way take its bearings from

3. Rousseau believed that modern men and women, though permeated by unnatural tastes and
impulses, could still appreciate at least some of nature's beauty. He expected that readers would
respond to his evocative descriptions of natural beauty and it was not a mistake to do so. Indeed, he
seems to have been a major force in inspiring a new sensibility. Toward the end of his life and con-
tinuing after his death, a new page was turned in European cultural history. The literary classes began
to discover the beauty of the countryside, the charm of rustic life, and the voluptuous pleasure of
freely expressing one's feelings. Pristine nature, once lightly regarded, came to mean something good
and pure, and Rousseau, the man of nature, came to be hailed as a prophet. For a fascinating and succinct discussion of Rousseau's place in this new cultural regime, see Simon Schama, *Citizens: A
Chronicle of the French Revolution* (New York: Alfred A. Knopf, 1989), 150–62.

4. Rousseau allows that "true philosophers," motivated in part by a love of order, can free themselves from many illusions and unnatural passions. In this they maintain a closer proximity to nature
than either false philosophers, who are motivated merely by the desire for distinction, or ordinary
individuals. But even these true philosophers, of whom Socrates would seem to have been the truest
of all, cannot free themselves totally from unnaturalness. Although motivated in part by the love of
order and the dispassionate love of truth, they are also motivated by pride: they take pleasure in comparing themselves to others. And while their pride is more natural than the vanity that motivates
most human activity and all false philosophy, it is still unnatural and hence an infringement of natural freedom. For Rousseau's praise of true philosophers, see *Narcissus* 102–7, and *FD* 63. For more
on Rousseau's estimation of Socrates, see Chapter 4, below, "*Amour-Propre*'s Ambiguity." See also
Julie IV-12:402–3 and IV-7:351–52, in which Wolmar is presented as a true philosopher.

5. Others, of course, such as Aristotle, had claimed to derive ethical and political principles
from nature. But since their understanding of nature was to a significant extent teleological, their
prescriptions are rejected by Rousseau as invalid. For more on the contrast between Rousseau's
understanding of nature and Aristotle's, see Chapter 3, below, "Between Aristotle and Hobbes,
Between Plato and Freud."

nature. Much—indeed, most—of his prescriptive thought is not offered for direct, practical use (he would certainly challenge our self-appropriated license for optimism). But he insists on its theoretical validity, and he bases his claim for that validity on the grounds that his "prescriptions" would lead to the replication of natural goodness.[6] Although nature is nonteleological and thus would seem to tell us little about how we ought to live once we have left our original state, Rousseau coaxes some rather substantial answers from it after all. How he does so, and what these answers are, is the essential subject of this book.

My purpose is twofold. First, through an exploration of his treatment of nature, I hope to improve our general understanding of Rousseau's thought. Although nearly all readers would agree that nature holds a central place among Rousseau's ideas, there is confusion as to what nature actually means for Rousseau, and there is considerable disagreement over the role it plays in his thought. My intent is to clarify Rousseau's meaning and to establish the role— as I see it, the preeminent role—that nature plays, not only in his diagnostic thought but also in his constructive or prescriptive thought. I shall offer a new interpretation, one that differs significantly from those expounded by other scholars. The focus of Rousseau's thought about nature is the soul: it is on the basis of their inner state that individuals are judged to be natural or unnatural. Yet if naturalness is in the first instance a psychological notion, it nevertheless has enormous political implications. Nature is the source of all of Rousseau's moral and political standards. Thus my inquiry, if successful, will lead to a more complete understanding not only of Rousseau's philosophical anthropology but also of his political thought.

My second purpose goes beyond Rousseau scholarship per se and concerns one of the larger issues of political philosophy. Rousseau presents us with an opportunity to consider whether it is possible to derive moral and political standards from a nonteleological understanding of nature—and, if it is possible, with what effects.

Early modern philosophers, including political philosophers such as Hobbes, repudiated classical teleology and adopted a rather low understanding of what is natural to human beings. Instead of referring to virtue and self-perfection, as it had for Aristotle, nature now came to refer, most of all, to the desire for self-preservation. The natural ceased to be a distant and difficult end toward which to strive and became instead a firm and accessible base on which to build. And

---

6. Regarding Rousseau's practical intention, see Melzer, *Natural Goodness of Man*, 252–82.

it *was* built upon, not only in theory but also, to a significant extent, in practice. A new social order began to emerge in Europe, an order based on the theories of liberal (and protoliberal) figures such as Locke and Hobbes. Whatever the differences between them, these theories were constructed upon a shared insight. A successful political and social order, it was believed, must be built upon and must reinforce the desire for self-preservation, for no other passion can be enlisted so reliably and effectively into the service of peace and security. In accordance with this insight, liberal theory and a newly emerging liberal politics validated the pursuit of rational self-interest and encouraged the pursuit of comfortable self-preservation; they promoted commerce and commerce-friendly virtues and so produced a new world.

Although he sympathized with much of the motivation behind liberal political philosophy (namely, the desire to tame religious fanaticism and aristocratic vainglory), Rousseau detested this new world. He saw in its ethos a prod toward selfishness and exploitation and an undermining of all but the coldest and most cruel of social bonds. In place of fanaticism it put complacency; in place of vainglory, pettiness of soul. In short, he saw the world produced by modern politics, the world whose leading human type was the bourgeois, as a further, disastrous step away from natural goodness. And he recognized that this step had its source in the modern reconceptualization of nature. As bad as the old world may have been, at least it had believed in the naturalness of the sublime. The new world, shorn of this faith, was running headlong, even eagerly, into degradation—and it would continue to do so unless it found a way to believe once more in the naturalness of the sublime.

In *Emile* and elsewhere, Rousseau sets out to solve this problem. He does so by articulating an original, dual-level understanding of nature. At one level Rousseau actually extends the modern tendency to truncate the realm of the natural. In the *Second Discourse* he defines nature in such a way as to deny the naturalness of virtually every characteristic that we customarily regard as distinctively human. Only the most primitive, submoral aspects of our being are held to be natural. All the rest—not only sublimity but also language, reason, sociability, and sensibility—are held to be unnatural. But at another level Rousseau vastly enlarges the compass of nature, and enlarges it "vertically," as it were. He introduces a distinction between "what is natural in the savage state" and "what is natural in the civil state." And while the former is limited to the primitive, to the merely physical, the latter, it turns out, comprehends the very highest human capacities and possibilities. Few human beings are as sublime or as highly developed—mentally, morally, aesthetically, and spiritually—as either Emile or the solitary dreamer of the autobiographical writings;

and both of these figures are explicitly presented as "natural men." Clearly, nature has once again been redefined. With his dual-level conception, Rousseau has found a way to assert the naturalness of the sublime even while remaining true to the modern scientific naturalism that had denied the naturalness of the sublime.

Nevertheless, even if Rousseau radically redefines nature, he still does not return to a teleological understanding of it. His acceptance of modern scientific naturalism prevents him from returning to anything like an Aristotelian conception of nature. Even if nature yields moral and political standards, it does not specify a single end for civilized man. Even if nature once again comprehends the sublime, it does not prescribe any particular way of life. The prescribing is left for the philosopher, for Rousseau.

When nature was thought to be teleological, the job of the moral and political philosopher was to investigate it. Nature would yield substantial answers in response to interrogation, or so it was thought.[7] When nature has been discovered not to be teleological, however, the philosopher who wishes to find in it the ground for a noble human type must do more than interrogate. He must be more creative. Rather than expect answers to his questions, he must develop proposals of his own and then test them against nature. Nature remains the final arbiter, but it merely nods, as it were, rather than speaks. No longer a source of positive guidance, it is at most a touchstone.

Doubtless this complicates the philosophical enterprise. Those who would base a high human type and an understanding of the good life on a nonteleological conception of nature proceed at a serious disadvantage compared to their teleologically minded predecessors. But at least that disadvantage isn't fatal—so, at least, Rousseau purports to show. And for a world that seeks a moral and political lodestar but that largely continues to reject classical teleology, any disadvantage that is less than fatal ought to be tolerable. And any philosophical corpus that makes a serious claim to have surmounted this obstacle ought to be given considerable attention.

---

7. I am well aware that there was nothing simple about this enterprise, that is, that for the best of classical philosophy, nature was not *simply* teleological—that, rather, it encompassed origins as well as ends, and bodily needs and impulses as well as spiritual goals; that the tension between these things constituted a tension within nature itself; and that because of this internal tension, the ends prescribed by nature could serve as practical ends only in the most indirect and oblique (not to say utopian) of senses. Still, however distant and even impractical these ends may have been, they *were* ends, and they did arise from nature. For valuable discussions of the ways in which Aristotle's conception of nature was not simply teleological, see Michael Davis, *The Politics of Philosophy: A Commentary on Aristotle's* Politics (Lanham, Md.: Rowman and Littlefield, 1996), esp. 7–8, and Mary P. Nichols, *Citizens and Statesmen: A Study of Aristotle's* Politics (Lanham, Md.: Rowman and Littlefield, 1992), 14–19.

Acknowledgments

This book has benefited from the contributions of many people, beginning with my teachers at Duke University, where it started out as a doctoral dissertation. Ruth Grant supervised the project from its inception and offered constructive advice throughout the dissertation process. I am particularly grateful for her gentle insistence that I spell out some things that needed to be spelled out and for her unwavering confidence in the value of the undertaking. Michael Gillespie offered extensive and very helpful comments on the initial proposal and the final dissertation draft. He also taught me much about modern political philosophy, as did Thomas Spragens.

Christopher Kelly read and responded to drafts of each chapter as it was written. I am grateful for his thoughtful responses to my arguments and for the benefit of his expertise, which was my surest check against glaring interpretive error. Arthur Melzer read the whole of my manuscript and raised challenging questions that made me more deeply aware of the complexities of Rousseau's thought. Jeff Reno undertook the tedious task of converting my manuscript from a computer language of the forgotten past to one of the present.

Much of my work on this book was facilitated by the generous financial support of the Symposium on Science, Reason, and Modern Democracy at Michigan State University and by the moral and intellectual support of its directors.

Parts of Chapter 4 appeared as "Rousseau on Self-Love: What We've Learned, What We Might Have Learned," in the *Review of Politics* 60:4 (1998). My thanks to the publisher for permission to reprint.

Finally, it is a great and long-awaited pleasure to acknowledge those to whom I owe the most: my parents, Hyman and Ann Cooper, for their support and confidence throughout the years of my education; my wife, Vicki, for her loving and sustaining presence; and my sons, Ben and Aaron, who came along late in the making of this book but in time to confirm, delightfully, that Rousseau was indeed onto something with his principle of natural goodness.

Abbreviations

Full bibliographical information on the following works by Rousseau can be found in the References.

d'Alembert	*Letter to M. d'Alembert on the Theater*
Beaumont	*Jean-Jacques Rousseau citoyen de Genève à Christophe de Beaumont, archevêque de Paris*
Bordes	*Preface of a Second Letter to Bordes*
CG	*Correspondence générale de Jean-Jacques Rousseau*
Confessions	*The Confessions*
Corsica	*Constitutional Project for Corsica*
Dialogues	*Rousseau, Judge of Jean-Jacques: Dialogues*
Emile	*Emile, or on Education*
FD	*First Discourse*
Fragments	*Fragments politiques*
Julie	*Julie, or the New Heloise*
Languages	*Essay on the Origin of Languages*
Last Reply	*Last Reply by J.-J. Rousseau of Geneva*
LM	*Lettres morales*
Narcissus	*Preface to Narcissus*
OC	*Oeuvres complètes*
PE	*Discourse on Political Economy*
Reveries	*Reveries of the Solitary Walker*
SC	*On the Social Contract*
SD	*Second Discourse*

Introduction

Rousseau and the Question of the Good Life

What is the best way of life? What ends should one pursue, and how should one pursue them?

One who would put the question of the good life to Rousseau must be prepared for a peculiar response. For one thing, Rousseau endorses not one but three very different kinds of lives. Sometimes he praises the life of the true citizen, at other times the life of what he calls "the natural man living in the state of society," and at still other times the life of solitary reverie and contemplation. Other philosophers, to be sure, had suggested that different ways of life are indicated for different individuals. But only with Rousseau does the notion arise that there is more than one valid substantive ideal. Unlike any of his predecessors, Rousseau proposes that man has available several valid goals—several divergent but equally valid paths—and not just different degrees of realizing the same goal.

Consider, by contrast, the Socratic tradition. Certainly the members of that tradition did not advise the same sort of life for everyone. The Socratic tradition saw the philosophical life, which it held to be the highest and the most human of lives, as the province of the few. The majority was seen as unfit for that best but most demanding of lives. Nevertheless, all individuals would flourish to the extent they could partake of the single good for man: reason. All ways of life were to be measured by the extent to which they partook of this good. And the different ways of life prescribed for different individuals (on the basis of different dispositions and capacities) could be seen as occupying different places on a single scale defined by that single good. The philosophic life was held to be the purest form of the life of reason and hence the best life, but other ways of life, including the political life and even a life lived in accordance with good laws, could also partake of reason and hence could also be fulfilling, even if only to a lesser degree. Rousseau, on the other hand, allows for three different scales defined by three different substantive goods. The exemplary citizen, "the natural man living in the state of society" (*Emile* III:205), and the solitary dreamer exemplify three highly divergent but equally valid versions of the good life; they stand atop separate but equally valid scales. For reasons that will later become clear, none of these ideals lies within the practical reach of modern men and women. But that counts little against the fundamental point. For Rousseau, human nature is such that any one of three very different ways of life, defined by three very different substantive goods, can lead to its fulfillment.

But the multiplicity of good lives is only one factor complicating Rousseau's answer to the question of the good life. Another factor is that he answers the question only indirectly. Although he does dispense a variety of specific practical advice, ranging from breast feeding (a good thing) to urban life (a very bad thing), he never proposes either a code of conduct, or a set of principles of action, or even a catalog of virtues. He has written no *Ethics*. Rather than provide guidance for conduct, he addresses the *sources* of good conduct—which is to say, the circumstances favoring the development of a healthy soul. This holds true for each of the three varieties of the good life. Instead of offering a guide to good citizenship, Rousseau articulates the principles and institutions of a worthy republic, on the apparent premise that it is only the formation of such a republic that can lead to good citizenship. Without the right laws and institutions, no set of principles or rules and no amount of exhortation will suffice to produce good citizens. Instead of offering a set of principles for those who would be natural men in the state of society, he describes and explains the education of such a man; he writes an *Emile* rather than an *Ethics* on the premise that the only way to achieve a high degree of naturalness amid civilization is to be reared in a very particular way. Once corrupt passions have taken root in the soul, there is little that can be done to subdue them; only the prevention that comes with good education can do much good.[1] Instead of detailing the steps needed to become capable of enjoying solitary reverie, he describes the idiosyncratic development of the one person whom he knows to have achieved that end, namely, himself. He goes to great lengths to underscore his uniqueness and hence, by implication, the improbability that anyone will follow after him. It would be incorrect to characterize Rousseau as a determinist, but he clearly believes that character is destiny and that character is formed, for the most part irreversibly, by social, political, and even material circumstances.[2]

Rousseau does not directly answer the question of how one should live. Instead, he addresses the question of what one should be and how one might become what one should be. The focus of his moral and political thought is the education of the soul. Even when he gives practical advice for individual use— as, for example, in the *Lettres morales*—his emphasis is on achieving the right setting rather than on establishing specific rules or principles of conduct. Parts of the *Lettres* do indeed read like a handbook, but a handbook for enjoying rustic simplicity rather than what we might normally expect from "moral letters."

For these reasons, among others, putting the question of the good life to Rousseau is a complicated affair.[3] Nevertheless, it is precisely this question that drives the following inquiry. The chapters that follow present an interpretation of Rousseau's thought on the content and basis of the higher possibilities —or, more precisely, the *better* possibilities—available to human beings. Because Rousseau's position on this question is tripartite, my interpretation takes account of all three versions of the good life. (My emphasis, however, is on the life of "the natural man living in the state of society," the version exemplified

1. The *Lettres morales* represent a partial, but only a partial, exception to this statement. By following the advice given in the *Lettres*, one can take a few steps toward naturalness. But one will still fall far short of Emile's naturalness. And even those steps have more to do with where to place oneself than with what to do.

2. Rousseau at one time planned to write an entire book on the moral effects of material circumstances. This book, which would address the influence of specific forces (climate, diet, light, noise, and so forth) on character, was to have been called "La morale sensitive, ou le matérialisme du sage." The project is discussed at *Confessions* IX:343–44.

3. Among the other factors that make Rousseau's answer to the question of the good life a complicated one is the unsystematic way he presents his philosophical system. Not only does he seem to contradict himself by proposing one solution in one work and another in another work, he seems to criticize in one work the solution put forth in another. For example, his severe critique of social man as such in the individualistic and "naturalistic" *Second Discourse* would seem to include, by implication, the austere ancient republics that he admires and that he elsewhere praises.

by Emile, since that version is by far the most relevant to most modern people.)[4] Because Rousseau's treatment of this question concentrates on character, or the soul, so does my interpretation.

To judge from the hundreds of serious studies of his life and works, the world would not seem to lack for books on Rousseau. Yet for all the scholarly attention, Rousseau's thinking on the problem of the good life—that is, his thinking on the development of a healthy soul—has been only minimally explored. Surprisingly few scholars have commented on this all-important question. For that matter, only a handful have written about *Emile*, which, besides being the work in which Rousseau's understanding of the soul is most fully related, is also the one Rousseau considered "his greatest and best book" (*Dialogues* I:23). (A recent bibliography lists only nine works on *Emile*, compared with forty-two on the *Social Contract* and thirty-two on the *Discourses*.)[5] What's more, much of what *has* been written on this subject, most notably on the matter of nature, has been marred by serious misunderstanding. To correct this misunderstanding would be a step toward a fuller, more useful interpretation of Rousseau.

Rousseau, Nature, and History

Rousseau's high regard for nature is obvious and widely acknowledged. Less obvious, though, is his view of nature's relevance to civilized men and women.

4. That "the natural man living in the state of society" is the most relevant of Rousseau's three theoretical ideals to modern men and women can be confirmed by process of elimination. To be a citizen of the type Rousseau admires is simply not possible any longer: it would require political institutions of a sort that are not found in the world of large, commercially oriented nation states. Nor is it possible for ordinary people to become solitary dreamers of the sort described in the *Reveries*: to be such a person would require an extremely unlikely combination of circumstances and natural genius. This leaves "the natural man living in the state of society," or Emile. Emile, too, represents what for all practical purposes is an unattainable ideal—as Rousseau readily admits. (See his Letter to Philibert Cramer, 13 October 1764 (CG XI:339). See also Judith Shklar, *Men and Citizens: A Study of Rousseau's Social Theory* (Cambridge: Cambridge University Press, 1969), esp. 22–32, and Roger D. Masters, *The Political Philosophy of Rousseau* (Princeton: Princeton University Press, 1968), 3–6). *Emile's* chief value lies in the light it sheds on the human predicament—on what *is* and on what, theoretically, *might* be. But at least one can take some steps in Emile's direction. For example, one can retreat from urban life into rustic simplicity, and one can incorporate at least some of the tutor's methods into one's own child rearing (for example, giving one's child significant freedom and avoiding displays of arbitrary willfulness). *Emile* is a philosophical treatise and not an educational manual: "it is a new system of education the plan of which I present for the study of the wise and not a method for fathers and mothers" (OC III:783). Nevertheless, it is a treatise from which one might derive significant practical use. Even its philosophical exploration of the human condition cannot help but have some practical impact, if only indirectly, by virtue of opening one's eyes and deepening one's perspective.

What place does nature have, and what place *can* it have, in the lives of those who long ago departed the state of nature for artificial civilization? Is there any part of us, apart from our bodies and their impulses, that either is or can be natural? Does the moral realm have any basis in nature—is it possible to partake of natural goodness in social life—or has every acquisition since the departure from the state of nature been but another layer of unnaturalness, alienating us that much more from our natural core?

Broadly speaking, scholarly writings on this question have expressed one of three interpretive tendencies. One tendency is to see in Rousseau's depiction of conscience evidence that nature does indeed play a role in the moral realm. At various places in his work, Rousseau seems to present conscience as a natural phenomenon. More than once he calls it the voice of nature.[6] From this some interpreters have concluded that the departure from the state of nature did not amount to a total alienation from nature. Far from it: civilized man may not be as simply or as perfectly natural as his savage ancestor—unlike the savage, civilized man has unnatural passions and temptations—but he does have a natural core. What's more, that core is larger than the savage's, for the savage lacked conscience: conscience only develops in those in whom reason and sociality have developed. Rousseau makes strong claims for conscience. Conscience, he says, is universal and constant. It is always and everywhere the same, independent of historic epoch and social contingency. Thus nature does indeed extend into the social and moral realm. If we have become alienated from nature, it is because we have ceased to listen to its timid voice, not because this voice is absent or mute.[7]

It is in the "Profession of Faith of the Savoyard Vicar" (in book IV of *Emile*) and in the *Lettres morales* that most of these claims about conscience appear. Not surprisingly, this first interpretive tendency, the tendency to see conscience as evidence that nature extends into the moral realm, is popular among those who read the "Profession of Faith" and the *Lettres morales* as

---

5. The bibliography appears in N. J. H. Dent, *A Rousseau Dictionary* (Cambridge, Mass.: Blackwell Publishers, 1992), 261–74. At *Dialogues* III:213, "the Frenchman" comments that *Emile* "is much read, little understood, and ill-appreciated." One thing at least has changed: it is no longer much read.

6. Rousseau's depiction of conscience is addressed in Chapter 3.

7. Those who subscribe to this interpretation of conscience and nature tend not to formulate it in just these terms. Their emphasis is normally on the particular characteristics of conscience rather than on its natural status. See, for example, N. J. H. Dent, *Rousseau: An Introduction to His Psychological, Social, and Political Theory* (New York: Basil Blackwell, 1988); Maurice Cranston, *The Noble Savage: Jean-Jacques Rousseau, 1754–1762* (Chicago: University of Chicago Press, 1991); and Shklar, *Men and Citizens*.

sincere statements of Rousseau's own views.[8] Not everyone reads them that way, however, and those who do not are apt to express one of the other two interpretive tendencies.

Before moving on to those other interpretations, however, we must take note of a special case. One of the more powerful interpretations of Rousseau's work is the neo-Kantian view. As part of their emphasis on the moral rationalism they find in Rousseau (a rationalism thought to prefigure Kant's), neo-Kantian interpreters have emphasized not only the universality and constancy of conscience but also its rationality, its force, and its comprehensiveness—that is, its ability to serve as a just moral arbiter and behavioral guide. They see in Rousseau's conscience the source of the individual's moral autonomy. Conscience confers dignity on man and allows him to make meaningful use of his freedom. Neo-Kantian interpreters emphasize those places in Rousseau's work where he himself emphasizes the gains conferred by becoming social. In all this the neo-Kantians might rightly be seen as expressing the interpretive tendency described above—except for one thing: while they do indeed emphasize the leading role of conscience in moral life and see conscience as universal, constant, and even autonomous, the neo-Kantians do not recognize conscience as a part or expression of nature. For them, as for Kant, nature refers only to the bodily and the primitive, to the subrational realm of impulse and inclination. Conscience may be universal, but since it requires reason in order to be operative, it is not natural. Nature, in this usage, is that which is *overcome* by reason and conscience. Thus, while the work done by these interpreters can be seen as allied to the interpretive tendency I have described, it certainly cannot be said simply to share it.[9]

The second interpretive tendency stands in stark opposition to the first. A historicist interpretation has arisen according to which Rousseau holds nature to be only minimally important to civilized man. That which is natural in man is thought either to have been far outweighed by the artificial acquisitions of history or to have been reworked or reconstituted by the processes of history,

8. Shklar, for example, takes the *Lettres morales* to be "the clearest and most reliable account of Rousseau's real beliefs" (*Men and Citizens*, 229–30; see also 37–38).

9. For the neo-Kantian interpretation, see Ernst Cassirer, *The Question of Jean-Jacques Rousseau*, trans. Peter Gay (Bloomington: Indiana University Press, 1954), and *Rousseau, Kant, and Goethe*, trans. James Gutmann, Paul Oskar Kristeller, and John Herman Randall Jr. (New York: Harper and Row, 1963); Georges Gurvitch, *L'idée du droit social. Notion et système du droit social. Histoire doctrinal depuis le XVIIe siècle jusqu'à la fin du XIXe siècle* (Paris: Libraire du Receuil Sirey, 1932); and Andrew Levine, *The Politics of Autonomy: A Kantian Reading of Rousseau's Social Contract* (Amherst: University of Massachusetts Press, 1976). This interpretation is also partly shared by Robert Derathé in *Le rationalisme de Jean-Jacques Rousseau* (Paris: Presses Universitaires de France, 1948).

which comes to much the same thing. While in the state of nature man was natural. In leaving that state, he alienated himself from nature. To be sure, nature persists within him, but it persists only in his physical being. Everything moral, everything that has been acquired—including conscience—is a product of history and hence is not natural. What distinguishes this view from the neo-Kantian interpretation is that even conscience and principles of moral and political right are held to be historically and socially determined. Rousseau may call conscience the voice of nature, but what conscience actually says varies over time and across cultures according to prevailing socioeconomic conditions. Nature counts, but History counts more. The most powerful exponent of this interpretation, in my view, is Asher Horowitz. Horowitz faults certain Marxist critics for not recognizing that Rousseau's historicism anticipates their own and thus could be useful to them, and he offers up his own historicist interpretation and appreciation, which he describes as a "Marcusean reading of Rousseau."[10]

The first interpretive tendency might fairly be called ahistoricist. The significance of history is not altogether denied, but nature, largely in the form of conscience, is seen as a vital, unchanging force within civilized man. (The most important effect of history, on this view, was the awakening of ahistorical conscience.) Through conscience, nature provides the standard by which to make moral determinations. The second interpretative tendency, by contrast, is highly historicist. Nature is the realm of necessity and hence has no moral content. Psychically, it is at most a kind of raw material. What we do with that material—how we think, how we live our lives—is decided within the moral realm, the realm of freedom. Seen thus, nature certainly is not, nor does it yield, the standard by which to make moral or political decisions. Rousseau is seen as a step on the road to German Idealism, for which Reason and Freedom, rather than nature, serve as moral and political standards.

Finally, between those who emphasize nature over history and those who emphasize history over nature is a group of scholars who grant serious weight to both and who thus express a third interpretive tendency. Largely on the basis of the *Second Discourse*, these interpreters, like the historicist interpreters,

10. See *Rousseau, Nature, and History*, 4; see also 6–7 and 30–35. For Horowitz's view that conscience is "dependent in its content … on the history of society," see 135–65, and especially 140–42. Others who have offered radically historicist readings of Rousseau are Lionel Gossman, "Time and History in Rousseau," *Studies on Voltaire and the Eighteenth Century* 30 (1964): 311–49; David Cameron, *The Social Thought of Rousseau and Burke* (London: Weidenfeld and Nicolson, 1973); and Stephen Ellenburg, *Rousseau's Political Philosophy: An Interpretation from Within* (Ithaca: Cornell University Press, 1976). These readings do not all speak to the historicity of conscience, but they do speak to the historicity and social-constructedness of human nature in general.

recognize that Rousseau holds a very "low" conception of nature, a conception that excludes nearly everything human and that would therefore seem to be of little or no use to civilized humanity. Unlike the historicist interpreters, however, they recognize from *Emile* and from the autobiographical writings that Rousseau attempts to use nature as a standard for civilized man after all. This view has been most notably articulated by Leo Strauss and others who have followed his lead.[11] These interpreters generally do not agree with the ahistoricists that Rousseau's nature extends into the moral and social realm, but they do argue that Rousseau uses the savage, that is, man in the state of nature, as a kind of formal or psychological standard for civilized humanity. Strauss expresses this view in a simple formula: "Rousseau's answer to the question of the good life consists in the closest approximation to the state of nature which is possible on the level of humanity."[12] History may have removed man from (the state of) nature, but nature, in the form of the savage psyche, can still serve as a model. Thus, both nature and history are accorded real moral significance in an attempt to do justice to the complexity of Rousseau's thought.[13]

My interpretation does not fit any of these descriptions. It departs from each of the three major interpretive tendencies, though it does not depart from each in the same measure. Although I have not set out to write "against" a particular interpreter or school of thought, the interpretation I am offering will read in many respects like a refutation of the analysis offered by Horowitz. I cover much of the same ground and ask many of the same questions but arrive

11. Strauss's interpretation can be found in *Natural Right and History* (Chicago: University of Chicago Press, 1950), 252–94, and "On the Intention of Rousseau," in *Hobbes and Rousseau: A Collection of Critical Essays*, ed. Maurice Cranston and Richard S. Peters (Garden City, N.Y.: Doubleday, 1972). Those who have generally followed Strauss's lead on the question of nature in Rousseau include Allan Bloom, introduction to Rousseau's *Emile, or on Education*, trans. Bloom (New York: Basic Books, 1979), and *Love and Friendship* (New York: Simon and Schuster, 1993); Melzer, *Natural Goodness of Man;* Masters, *Political Philosophy of Rousseau;* and Victor Goldschmidt, *Anthropologie et politique* (Paris: Librairie Philosophique J. Urin, 1974).

12. Strauss, *Natural Right and History*, 282.

13. The three tendencies I have described are different responses to the same question, and as such they share certain premises. Each regards nature and history as separate and distinct realms or principles, and each sees the state of nature as in some sense the primary instance or incarnation of nature. Certain works of Rousseau scholarship do not share these premises and thus do not express any of these three tendencies. Tracy B. Strong's postmodern study, for example, rejects the premise that the state of nature has any defining role in the natural as it is (potentially) knowable to civilized men and women. (See *Jean-Jacques Rousseau: The Politics of the Ordinary* [Thousand Oaks, Calif.: Sage Publications, 1994].) For Strong, the natural life sought by Rousseau entails no return to or replication of any earlier experience. For scholars (such as Strong) who reject either of these premises, the question I have put to Rousseau, the question of whether nature can have a meaningful place in civilized life, is neither problematic nor particularly meaningful.

at dramatically different conclusions. My disagreement with Horowitz and other historicist readers of Rousseau is basic. Whereas they see Rousseau's nature as a long lost starting point, as that which ended or lost its importance when history began, I see it as persisting within civilized human beings—that is, I hold that nature is not limited to the physical realm. Through conscience, it is present in the moral and social realm as well. To be sure, history is enormously important. It can utterly overwhelm nature, in the sense that acquired passions can easily make people deaf to nature's voice. Nor is nature a fully autonomous and comprehensive guide—it is not teleological or prescriptive, as I have already emphasized. But nature *does* persist within us. And it does retain a measure of autonomy: its core is untouched by history and circumstance. Although the variability of law and custom across cultures suggests that nature speaks differently to different peoples, or at least is heard to speak differently, this variability has sharp limits: Rousseau observes that some things are always and everywhere praised or blamed (*LM* 1102–3). This is because nature's innermost principle, expressed in civilized human beings through conscience, is constant. Every human being retains a natural love of harmonious order; such is the meaning of conscience, as we shall see. And this love of order is general enough to inform every corner of human life, if it is allowed to do so. History may have much to do with how that love is expressed, but there are limits to the plasticity of such a love and thus limits to the usurpation of nature by history.

My chief disagreement with the ahistoricist reading of Rousseau lies in the opposite direction. If the historicist interpreters fail to give nature its due, the ahistoricist interpreters grant it too much. The great strength of the ahistoricist interpretation is its recognition that nature does in fact persist in civilized humanity in the form of conscience, that man's departure from the state of nature and his entry into history did not mark the end of nature's meaningful presence in him. But whereas the historicist interpretation overstates the significance of the departure from the state of nature, this interpretation understates it. True, nature did not disappear from man as he wandered out of the garden of original innocence and into history—conscience is indeed the voice of nature in civilized men—but conscience is not the full-throated moral guide that the ahistoricist interpreters (and their neo-Kantian cousins) suggest it is. Conscience is, rather, a general principle, a love of order, whose manifestations are very far ranging but whose guidance is much less direct and articulate than the ahistoricists suggest. In truth, then, it is wrong to say that the ahistoricist interpreters overestimate nature's place in civilized life. Indeed, in an important sense they *under*estimate nature's place. What they overestimate is the clarity with which conscience speaks and the ease with which we might discover its promptings. However, they generally fail to appreciate just how far ranging conscience is. Being a general love of order, conscience can have a bearing on every aspect of life, not just on particular conscious decisions. As nature's agent in the supraphysical realm, conscience is the means by which the soul of civilized man can be made natural. Conscience may not dictate all that one should do in life, but it can inform all that one *is*. And so it turns out to be the source of virtually all that is good and fine—not just morally but also aesthetically and in every other way—in civilized man.

My disagreement with the third interpretive tendency centers less on the relative weight it accords nature and history respectively than on its conception of the content or meaning of nature for civilized humanity. Those who express this interpretive tendency rightly recognize that it is not nature or history alone but rather the interplay between these two forces that stands at the center of Rousseau's thought. These interpreters do acknowledge that nature plays a decisive and broad role in Rousseau's understanding of the good life amid civilization. Yet they tend to limit that role to that of formal standard. Nature is seen as something to emulate from afar rather than something to follow or realize. Nor is nature thought to extend in any substantive way into the moral realm. Conscience and other elements of the civilized natural man's (namely, Emile's) soul are seen as somehow less than truly natural: rather than simply natural, they are "modifications of nature."[14] Only the physical is seen as truly and thoroughly natural. Thus compassion and love, two of Emile's outstanding characteristics and hence, in my view, two hallmarks of civilized naturalness, are said to be "not quite natural but, one might say, according to nature." Only a purely physical sexual desire, of which compassion and love are sublimations, is truly natural according to this view.[15]

The basis of this interpretation is a reading of Rousseau that gives overwhelming precedence, at least with regard to the meaning of nature, to the *Second Discourse*. This work defines nature in the most minimal terms. It is here that Rousseau expresses and even extends the modern tendency to truncate the realm of the natural. Obviously Bloom and the others are aware that Rousseau speaks of nature in another sense, that he presents the civilized Emile and the highly developed hero of the autobiographical writings as "natural men," and that in *Emile* he explicitly articulates "what is natural in the *civil* state" (V:406; emphasis added). But the conception of nature expounded in the *Second*

14. Bloom, *Love and Friendship*, 109.
15. Bloom, introduction to Rousseau's *Emile*, 17.

Discourse is given precedence over those other notions. Civilized naturalness is seen as a secondary naturalness, as a derivative and hence not quite true naturalness. Emile and the solitary dreamer are natural men only in a formal sense: they enjoy something approaching the savage's psychic harmony, but there is nothing truly natural about the *substance* of their souls. I believe, on the contrary, that while civilized naturalness is secondary to savage naturalness in an important sense, civilized naturalness is not merely derivative. True, the naturalness of Emile and the naturalness of the solitary dreamer follow that of the savage in some important respects. The savage *is* the primary incarnation of naturalness, and Strauss is right to characterize the good life in civilization as a kind of replication of the state of nature. But there is also a distinctive, substantive component to post-state-of-nature naturalness—namely, conscience.

Conscience is natural in almost the strongest possible sense: it is an innate principle in the soul whose awakening from latency is automatic and irreversible in civilized man. (Conscience cannot be explained with reference to the savage for the simple reason that the savage had no conscience.) The significance of conscience, a significance that is overlooked or underestimated by all interpretive schools with which I am acquainted, is that it gives a highly particular, substantive meaning to civilized naturalness. Emile and the hero of the autobiographical writings are natural men not only because they replicate certain of the savage's characteristics but also because this replication is produced by conscience, that is, by their innate and far-ranging love of harmonious order. Conscience is no mere faculty but rather a principle informing the development of the entire person. Conscience produces a particular set of substantive characteristics and accounts for the sublimation of brute impulses into elevated desire—which is another way of saying that it is conscience that transforms the stuff of original naturalness (the savage) into civilized naturalness (Emile) or "post-civilized" naturalness (the solitary dreamer). Post-state-of-nature naturalness has a very particular substantive meaning, even if that "substance" is entirely psychological. It is precisely that substance to which the majority of this book is dedicated.

The Plan of This Book

This book begins with the question of ends. What makes the good life good? Wherein lies the goodness of the good life? These questions are addressed in

Chapter 1, where I argue against two popular but mistaken notions. Some have asserted that Rousseau's highest good, the thing for the sake of which other things are determined to be good, is happiness. Others have argued that his definitive good is virtue. I believe, on the contrary, that the definitive good for Rousseau is neither happiness nor virtue but existence, or the maximization of existence, with that term referring here to a quantitative if not quantifiable thing. Further, all three versions of the good life, whatever the differences between them, are shown to have certain features in common. Some of these features constitute a replication of the savage's state of soul, while others go well beyond that original simplicity.

If my interpretation is propelled by a single question, the question of the good life, it is also dominated by a single theme. Central to every part of Rousseau's thinking on the question of the good life is the concept of nature. This is not to say that each version of the good life is somehow to be understood as a natural life. Far from it: although two of the three versions are indeed characterized as natural lives, Rousseau goes so far as to characterize the soul of the citizen as *de*natured. But even if the citizen does not live a natural life, his psychological integrity represents a kind of artificial replication of man's original—which is to say, his natural—condition. Thus, even if only in a formal sense, the citizen meets a standard derived from nature. And if the denatured citizen is conceived with reference to nature, the civilized natural man and the solitary dreamer are much more so. Chapter 2 begins the process of illuminating the role played by nature in all of Rousseau's prescriptive thought.

Readers of the *Second Discourse* know that, for Rousseau, nature refers to origins. The "natural man" was man in his original, brutish state. He was preverbal, premoral, and even presocial. On the *Second Discourse*'s telling, civilization as such is unnatural, as is the development of all but the most primitive capacities. Yet *Emile* depicts the development of what Rousseau nevertheless chooses to call a "natural man living in the state of society," and Rousseau depicts himself in various autobiographical works as yet another kind of natural man. How can this apparent contradiction be resolved? How can the highly civilized Emile, and how can the solitary but exquisitely sensitive being described in the *Dialogues* and the *Reveries of the Solitary Walker*, be described as natural men? Chapter 2 aims to ascertain the criteria of post-state-of-nature naturalness and to illuminate its relation to original, or pure, naturalness.

What is discovered in this chapter is that the primary criterion for naturalness involves the quality of one's self-love. All human beings, according to Rousseau, are creatures of self-love. But there are two basic kinds of self-love, and it is the distinction between the two that marks the difference between natural men and everyone else. What Emile and the solitary dreamer have in common with the original natural man, and what distinguishes all three of those natural men from average civilized men, is that the leading form of self-love in their souls is *amour de soi*. *Amour de soi* is an utterly benign psychic force. The person motivated by *amour de soi* seeks self-preservation and well-being but has no interest in outstripping or hurting others. Indeed, *amour de soi* turns out to be actively benevolent in post-state-of-nature natural men, for it is the source of conscience and compassion. The second kind of self-love is quite different, however. Whereas *amour de soi* is absolute, *amour-propre*, which is the dominant form of self-love in average civilized men, is relative. Those dominated by *amour-propre* compare themselves and their lots with those of others and seek preeminence. Although *amour-propre* is not always and inevitably vicious, it usually is. It usually manifests in a self-seeking that is at least as interested in laying others low as in raising oneself up—indeed, given its relative nature, it often can see no distinction between the two. It was with the birth of *amour-propre* that the species left its original natural state, and it is with this birth that individuals, typically as very young children, depart from their natural innocence today. In most cases, *amour-propre* quickly goes on to become the dominant force—more often than not, a tyrannical force—in the soul. It is not necessary that it do so, however. It is possible for *amour-propre* to be educated in such a way that it forms an alliance with *amour de soi* and so serves the cause of naturalness. When this occurs, the resulting product warrants the title of "natural man." Emile is such a product.[16]

Chapters 3 and 4, which make up the vast majority of this study, address the particulars of post-state-of-nature naturalness, especially Emile's. It is here that my interpretation departs farthest from previous Rousseau scholarship. My purpose in Chapter 3 is threefold: first, to demonstrate that there is indeed a particular substance to civilized naturalness, in other words, that Emile warrants the designation of "natural man" in more than just a formal sense; second, to articulate the outlines of that substance; and third, to illuminate the relation of civilized naturalness to savage naturalness, that is, to illuminate the process whereby civilized naturalness develops out of and upon original naturalness. (The process whereby civilized naturalness evolves out of original naturalness I call sublimation; the director of this process, as it were, is conscience.)

16. The solitary dreamer, Rousseau's other post-state-of-nature natural man, is another story—in a certain sense, a simpler story. Whereas Emile is characterized by an *amour-propre* that is allied with and therefore secondary to *amour de soi*, the solitary dreamer is closer to the original natural man: he simply has very little *amour-propre* to deal with. See "Beyond *Amour-Propre*? Prospects and Possibilities," in Chapter 4.

Ultimately, the third task is the most important, for success there ensures success at the other two. Chapter 3 also includes a comparative discussion. I attempt to underscore Rousseau's distinctiveness by comparing his understanding of nature to the corresponding views of Aristotle and Hobbes and his understanding of sublimation to the positions of Plato and Freud.

Since naturalness is determined first and foremost by the quality of one's self-love, the proper education of self-love is the only means to achieve naturalness amid civilization. Naturalness can only be maintained where *amour-propre* is well governed, that is, where it is allied with *amour de soi*. Accordingly, Chapter 4 undertakes a systematic exploration of *amour-propre*. My first purpose in this chapter is to establish just how consequential *amour-propre* really is. Toward that end I show, first, that *amour-propre*'s appearance is inevitable in every member of society; second, that *amour-propre* is profoundly ambiguous in its moral potential (cited by Rousseau as the source of evil and misery, it is also acknowledged by him to be the source of greatness); and third, that the quality of our *amour-propre* has a decisive influence on our character and behavior.

Next, I undertake to define precisely what *amour-propre* is and how it arises. After surveying a number of mistaken interpretations, I submit my own interpretation, according to which *amour-propre*'s essence has to do chiefly with the chronic need of civilized man to achieve and maintain value in his own eyes. Rousseau lists "good witness of oneself" among man's very few true needs (*Emile* II:81). That need was easily satisfied by the savage, who, lacking self-consciousness, presumably took his own worthiness for granted. In civilized man, however, self-consciousness has enormously complicated the need that was so simple in the savage. The acquisition of self-consciousness has led to the relativization of the need for good witness of oneself and hence to the birth of *amour-propre*. It has done so, and by necessity will continue to do so, in every civilized person. What is not inevitable, however, is the particular character of an individual's *amour-propre* or even its extent—that is, the extent to which it supplants *amour de soi*. *Amour-propre* is sometimes gentle and sometimes cruel; sometimes it takes the form of pride, sometimes vanity. I examine these different forms and their respective sources in order to illuminate the content of civilized naturalness. (I also hope to bring to light—and thereby to make available for our own use—some of the fruits of Rousseau's extraordinary psychological acumen.)

Finally, after this analysis of the nature, birth, and variations of *amour-propre*, I address the possibility of transcending it, a possibility that Rousseau seems to regard as the very highest available to man, even if it is as difficult as it is worthwhile.

This book concludes with an effort at critique. Chapter 5 raises a question that has been lurking in the background all along: How well has Rousseau succeeded at building an understanding of the good life upon a nonteleological conception of nature—indeed, upon a conception of nature whose primary exemplar, the original natural man, is barely human at all? To be sure, Rousseau's conception of nature includes civilized naturalness and the naturalness of the refined solitary; nature does not just refer to the savage state. Demonstrating as much is a major purpose of the earlier chapters. Nevertheless, the original natural state retains a certain priority, and the savage remains in certain decisive respects a model even for the most advanced natural man. Origins are both transcended and not transcended, which accounts for much of the attractiveness but also, as we shall see, some of the more problematic aspects of Rousseau's thought.

1

The Goodness of All Good Lives

Though born free, man is today unfree. Though by nature good, he is today depraved. And though made to be happy, he—we—are not. Such is the well-rehearsed core of Rousseau's philosophical system.[1] What, if anything, can be done?

What we can*not* do is retrace our steps to an earlier, happier time. Such a time did exist. The pure state of nature was a historical reality marked by goodness and happiness. So too was the period immediately succeeding it: the age of tribal society. Indeed, so idyllic was this period that it may fairly be called "the veritable prime of the world" (*SD* 151). Of all this Rousseau is sure.[2] He

---

1. SC I-1:46; *Dialogues* III:211–14, II:130–31, I:23; *Emile* IV:237. For more on Rousseau's claim that his thought was indeed a system, see my Preface, note 1.

2. Regarding Rousseau's belief in the historic reality of the state of nature, see Marc F. Plattner, *Rousseau's State of Nature: An Interpretation of the Discourse on Inequality* (DeKalb: Northern Illinois

is just as sure, however, that the felicity of those epochs disappeared irrevocably with the innocence that had been its protective shield. Human nature has been forever changed. Although it is possible *in thought* to strip away history's distorting acquisitions and reveal man's natural goodness and happiness,[3] no such thing is possible in reality. "Human nature does not go backwards," writes Rousseau, "and one can never return to the times of innocence and equality when one has once left them; that is one of the principles on which [I have] insisted the most" (*Dialogues* III:213). We may no more return to our happy origins than Adam could to Eden.

And yet, as catastrophic as our Fall may seem, we are not altogether without recourse. For one thing, while we cannot recover what was lost, we can at least replicate, if only sometimes and in part, its most valuable features. We can achieve a partial restoration of our original wholeness. We can do so through one of several possible means—through citizenship in a virtuous republic, through a life of solitary contemplation or reverie, or through a life of rustic domesticity. The first of these paths is most famously praised in the *First Discourse* and articulated in the *Social Contract*; the second is described, if not quite explained, in Rousseau's autobiographical writings, most notably in the latter pages of the *Confessions* and in the *Reveries of the Solitary Walker*; and the third appears in part in *Julie, or the New Heloise* and the *Lettres morales* and in full in *Emile*, which Rousseau considered "his greatest and best book" (*Dialogues* I:23).

Partial restoration: one wonders on hearing this prognosis whether one has heard the good news or the bad. In fact one has heard neither. The truly bad news is that what is possible in principle is exceedingly difficult to achieve in practice and is even more difficult to maintain than it is to achieve—and what is possible is only partial in the first place. Rousseau believed very little in the realistic possibility of happiness in the modern world. Although we all seek happiness, that which is actually available to us is a much degraded version of the happiness our ancient ancestors had, and there is not likely to be much of it at that. (One thinks of an old joke: "The food is so bad here," complains one

---

University Press, 1979), and Masters, *Political Philosophy of Rousseau*, 118. Rousseau admits that many of the details of the history he recounts are merely speculative, but he is in earnest about the basic facts of the state of nature. For dissenting views, see Robert Wokler, *Rousseau* (New York: Oxford University Press, 1995), 52–53, and Victor Gourevitch, "Rousseau's Pure State of Nature," *Interpretation* 16, no. 1 (1988): 23–59.

    3. This is the methodological premise of the *Second Discourse*; the premise is explained at *Confessions* VIII:326.

diner. "Yes," answers the other, "and the portions are so small!") What saves us from being utterly comic figures, however, is that neither happiness nor its pursuit is all that makes life worthwhile—which, strange as it may sound to our liberal, Jeffersonian ears, is the good news.

Beyond Happiness, or What Makes the Good Life Good

Like other great moral and political philosophers, Rousseau can be understood in terms of a medical metaphor: he is a spiritual physician who offers a variety of cures and palliatives (some theoretical, some practical) in response to a most extraordinary diagnosis. This much is commonly recognized. What tends to be overlooked or obscured, however, is the complex matter of what it means to be a cure. It is here that the medical metaphor can mislead us. However much physicians may sometimes disagree about appropriate treatments and even about how high to aim (that is, whether to risk survival for the sake of a fuller recovery), they seldom disagree as to what constitutes a complete cure. The standard of health against which one measures the outcome of treatment is ordinarily obvious and universally accepted: successful treatment is defined as the restoration of health; one *recovers*. Just where ordinary medicine is simple, however, spiritual "medicine"—true psychotherapy—is not. Rousseau does not define the good life (in any of its varieties) by the extent of one's recovery of original happiness—nor, for that matter, by the extent of one's attainment of some other kind of happiness. His standard is both more basic and more complex than that. Natural goodness and happiness do play an important role in the formation of that standard. Far from being the last words on the subject, however, they are only the first.

The place of happiness, like so much else in Rousseau's thought, has given rise to competing interpretations whose inaccuracies derive less from mistaken readings than from partial ones. On the one side there are those who regard happiness as the goal of Rousseau's thought, as the ideal for the sake of which good things are good and bad things are bad.[4] These interpreters (let us call them eudaemonists) observe, correctly, that Rousseau bases his most important justifications and criticisms on experiential grounds. Their mistake, though, is in equating Rousseau's experiential standard with happiness.

4. See, for example, Stephen G. Salkever, "Rousseau and the Concept of Happiness," *Politics* 11 (fall 1978): 27–45, and Ronald Grimsley, "Rousseau and the Problem of Happiness," in *Hobbes and Rousseau*, ed. Cranston and Peters, 437–61.

Happiness is indeed one kind of intrinsically good experience. Perhaps it is the best experience; perhaps too it is the one that most shields its possessor from the lure of corruption. But it is manifestly not the only intrinsically good state of soul—not if we understand it in the ordinary sense in which Rousseau himself used the term "happiness" (*bonheur*). There are times, in fact, when one must disregard considerations of happiness altogether and act instead according to the dictates of virtue, even at the direct expense of everything that might seem to be required for happiness.

It is the latter observation that leads to the other common misinterpretation of the place of happiness in Rousseau's thought. According to this view, Rousseau is a proto-Kantian moralist who recognizes the inherent disjunction between the demands of happiness and those of morality and who himself sides with the latter.[5] This interpretation is correct in noting both Rousseau's belief in the inevitable tension between happiness and morality and his demonstrable preference, when a preference is required, for virtue. Where this position errs, though, is in interpreting virtue as an end in itself, as the thing for whose sake all else is judged good or bad. In fact, Rousseau does not see virtue as an end in itself. Instead he loves it because of what it produces in men's souls and because of what it thereby makes *of* men's souls. In this the eudaemonists are right. Pride of place in Rousseau's hierarchy of goods belongs to something experiential. Virtue and freedom and all other human goods *are* good precisely because and insofar as they contribute to something experiential. But what could that something be if not happiness? The answer is "existence," by which Rousseau means the *feeling* of existence.

Existence is not only the ground but also the end of life and its truest measure.[6] The quality of a life—its success—is a function of the amount of its existence; it is a function of the degree to which one feels one's being. Different lives are lived to different degrees. Those who live well live more: they feel life more than others do and thus, using Rousseau's way of speaking, they literally exist more than do those others. That is the very meaning of living well: the goodness of the good life lies precisely in its being a life that is more fully felt. The amount of one's existence, or the degree to which one is alive, has nothing to do with the number of years between birth and death. "To live is not to breathe; it is to act; it is to make use of all our organs, our senses, our faculties, of all the parts of ourselves which give us the sentiment of our

5. This interpretation can be found in Cassirer, *Question,* 70–71, and *Rousseau, Kant, and Goethe,* 56; Gurvitch, *L'idée du droit social,* 260–79; and Levine, *Politics of Autonomy.*

6. Melzer is particularly instructive on this point. See *Natural Goodness of Man,* 38–46, 64–68, 103–5. See also Grimsley, "Rousseau and the Problem of Happiness."

existence. The man who has lived the most is not he who has counted the most years but he who has most felt life" (*Emile* I:42). If life is short for us, Rousseau admonishes, that is "not so much because it lasts a short time as because we have almost none of that short time for savoring it" (*Emile* IV:211).

It is understandable that the centrality of existence in Rousseau's thought has been so often underappreciated, for Rousseau nowhere addresses the matter systematically. He nowhere states the relation between existence and such goods as happiness and virtue, nor does he catalog either the modes of existence or its dimensions. Nor can we infer or deduce a systematic understanding of existence from his writings. The reason for this silence would seem to lie with the rhetorical demands of Rousseau's project. Rousseau's primary goal, or at least his primary practical goal, is to promote a kind of revaluation of civilization's corrupt values. He is a philosopher, but he is also a moralist. And it ill suits the purpose of the moralist to speak with reference to something as strange and abstract as "existence"—not when he can speak evocatively and persuasively of happiness and virtue. Thus, Rousseau is more interested in describing various kinds of experiences and their causes than in explaining the metaphysical substratum of these experiences. Perhaps, too, he avoids such analysis for fear that it would descend into the kind of metaphysics he despises as pedantic and necessarily uncertain. It is not only as a moralist but also as a philosopher that Rousseau eschews arcane terminology.[7] But Rousseau's failure to explain the role of existence does not lessen its vital significance in his thought. It simply means that it is left for his interpreters to reveal this role. How and where, then, can we more fully apprehend the meaning of existence in Rousseau's thought? It turns out that the centrality of existence is nowhere more clearly revealed than in Rousseau's discussions of happiness. The meaning of existence and its preeminent place in Rousseau's hierarchy of goods will become clear only by recharting the same landscape that the eudaemonists and the proto-Kantian interpreters have so differently mapped.

Rousseau's discussions of happiness seem nearly schizophrenic. On the one hand, the vast majority of the causes and conditions that he cites—and thus, too, the vast majority of his maxims—are negative. Remove this, avoid that, delay the other. This is the Stoic Rousseau, the moralist who counsels natural simplicity. Alongside the Stoic, though, is the Romantic—the poet who praises the ecstasies of love, the transports of reverie, and the glories of virtue.

---

7. Rousseau's disdain for traditional metaphysics is evident in numerous remarks. For his most sustained attack, see the third of his *Lettres morales*. See also Cranston, *Noble Savage*, 289.

As different as they are, though, both of these aspects of Rousseau point toward something beyond happiness—toward existence—as the true prize of life.

Rousseau outlines the Stoical side of his understanding of happiness in the early pages of book II of *Emile*. Very much in the spirit of the classical Stoics, he identifies excessive desires as the cause of unhappiness: "[E]very desire supposes privation, and all sensed privations are painful. Our unhappiness consists, therefore, in the disproportion between our desires and our faculties" (*Emile* II:80). Rousseau next asks, "In what, then, consists human wisdom or the road of true happiness?" He answers as follows:

> It is not precisely in diminishing our desires, for if they were beneath our power, a part of our faculties would remain idle, and we would not enjoy our whole being. Neither is it in extending our faculties, for if, proportionate to them, our desires were more extended, we would as a result only become unhappier. But it is in diminishing the excess of the desires over the faculties and putting power and will in perfect equality. It is only then that, with all the powers in action, the soul will nevertheless remain peaceful and that man will be well ordered.

The road of happiness is a road of restriction and circumscription. Since the problem is one of disequilibrium, the solution *in principle* could entail either diminishing the desires or enhancing the faculties. As a practical matter, though, what we need is the former. The excess of desires over faculties is what a psychic economist might call a demand side problem—not too little faculty but too much desire. Hence the overwhelmingly negative thrust of Rousseau's formulas and prescriptions. Whatever expands desire must be controlled. Throughout *Emile* are scattered commentaries and cautions, screeds and stratagems, all arrayed against anything that could cause the emergence of unsatisfiable desire. Everything from fables (II:112–16) to books (III:184) to foresight (II:82) is seen in light of its potential to inspire dangerous desire, especially the fateful desire to be something other than what one actually is (V:445–46, IV:242–43).[8] Such things are not intrinsically bad—indeed, they can be used to wonderful effect—but they are dangerous. Most dangerous of all, though, and therefore most in need of careful and even severe management, is the faculty by means of which these dangers are realized. That faculty is imagination, that great multiplier of desire.

---

8. See also *Bordes* 113–14.

As soon as [man's] potential faculties are put in action, imagination, the most active of all, is awakened and outstrips them. It is imagination which extends for us the measure of the possible, whether for good or bad, and which consequently excites and nourishes the desires by the hope of satisfying them. But the object which at first appeared to be at hand flees more quickly than it can be pursued. When one believes that one has reached it, it transforms and reveals itself in the distance ahead of us. No longer seeing the country we have already crossed, we count it for nothing; what remains to cross ceaselessly grows and extends. Thus one exhausts oneself without getting to the end, and the more one gains on enjoyment, the further happiness gets from us. . . .

The real world has its limits; the imaginary world is infinite. Unable to enlarge the one, let us restrict the other, for it is from the difference between the two alone that are born all the pains which make us truly unhappy. (II:80–81)

Rousseau is neither puritanical nor prosaic. He does not oppose desire and imagination per se, or even great desire and imagination, but rather excessive, unfulfillable desire and whatever promotes it. And he does so for reasons that not even the most calculating hedonist could dismiss without a hearing. His claim, after all, is that for us less really would be more: less desire (or at least less of certain kinds of desire) would bring us less pain and more pleasure— which means more happiness, since the measure of our happiness or unhappiness is a function of the balance between our pleasures and pains. ("The happiest is he who suffers the least pain; the unhappiest is he who feels the least pleasure" [II:80].)

The hedonist, though, could surely be counted on to raise a few questions. Rousseau's prescription as it has so far been revealed calls for us to follow a negative course (*eliminating* excess desire, generally by *restricting* imagination) to a neutral state (that of equilibrium between desires and faculties). Why, though, should this neutral state of affairs be considered happiness? When does something positive get introduced into the equation? Is happiness simply an absence of pain? In fact it is not. Happiness does have a positive content: the sentiment of, which means the *enjoyment* of, existence. It so happens that this enjoyment requires in the first instance less that existence be achieved than that obstacles to it be removed. Excessive desire is bad because the pain of felt privation gets in the way of our enjoyment of existence. Remove that excess and you have opened the way to the sentiment of existence, a feeling that in and of itself gives sweetness to life. "The sentiment of existence, stripped of any other emotion, is in itself a precious sentiment of contentment and of peace which alone would suffice to make this existence dear and sweet to anyone able to spurn all the sensual and earthly impressions which incessantly come to distract us from it and to trouble its sweetness here-below" (*Reveries* V:69). The feeling of existence compensates for whatever life throws at us. "[F]or anyone who feels his existence," Rousseau wrote in his letter to Voltaire on the beneficence of Providence, "it is better to exist than not to exist" (OC IV:1070).[9]

For Rousseau the positive content of all happiness consists in the enjoyment of existence. Existence is the soul and the measure of happiness: different degrees of happiness reflect different degrees to which existence is felt, and different *kinds* of happiness (namely, the citizen's versus the savage's versus the dreamy-contemplative Jean-Jacques's) reflect the different ways in which existence is felt. Different ways? Indeed: existence is never felt and enjoyed except insofar as it is our own. The whole meaning of *amour de soi*, the benign love of self that exists naturally in all sentient life, is love and enjoyment of our own *being*. Thus all happiness, as enjoyment of being, is a manifestation of self-love, and what distinguishes the varieties of happiness from one another are the specific shapes and dimensions that self-love assumes.

In its purest and most exalted variant, happiness is consciously experienced as the exquisitely sweet sentiment of existence. Existence proper is felt as the immediate object of consciousness: one is aware that what one feels is "existence stripped of any other emotion." Such experiences have a decidedly mystical cast, as the boundaries of the self extend or even dissolve, causing one's self to identify with all existence. "I feel ecstasies and inexpressible raptures in blending, so to speak, into the system of beings and in making myself one with the whole of nature" (*Reveries* VII:95). Love of self takes on new dimensions. What is overcome is not *amour de soi* but simply the narrow boundaries of the original *soi*. "Supreme enjoyment," according to Rousseau, "is in contentment with oneself" (OC IV:587).[10] This is all the more true as the self expands. This

---

9. Lest one conclude that "the sweet sentiment of existence" is felt only by those who have achieved the extraordinary (that is, philosophical) detachment described in the passage from the *Reveries* quoted above, it should be noted that Rousseau contends this sentiment is enjoyed by all sorts of ordinary people—"an honest townsman who has passed his life in obscurity and tranquillity, without projects and without ambition; a good artisan, who lives comfortably by his trade; even a peasant" (so long as he is not severely oppressed), and so on (OC IV:1063–64). What is necessary, it would seem, is less a *transcendence* of civilized corruption (à la the Rousseau of the *Reveries*) than *avoidance* of it.

10. See Grimsley, "Rousseau and the Problem of Happiness," for an interesting discussion of the relationship between existence, self-love, and contentment.

highest type of happiness is rare, however. It is not available to most people, if only because the normal circumstances of social life prevent it (though there are other reasons as well [*Reveries* V]).

Other, more ordinary varieties of happiness are no less constituted by the enjoyment of existence than is the happiness of rapturous fusion. What makes them less pure is simply that they are manifestations of a less expansive self-love. There seem to be two general modes in which existence can be enjoyed: in the exercise of one's faculties and in the passive feeling of contentment with oneself. As we have already seen, there is enjoyment—one may feel one's *being* —through *doing*: should some of our faculties remain idle, "we would not enjoy our whole being" (*Emile* II:80). Surely a good portion of the free peasant's and the citizen's happiness derives from the labors that virtually define their respective identities. So too is much of Emile's happiness gained through activity, including the activity of work. Although Rousseau describes him as "the man of nature" (IV:253), Emile is anything but idle. He steers a vigorous course between the agitation of the modern social man and the indolence of the savage.

Presumably the citizen's joy in his patriotic service is different from the peasant's joy in his activity or Emile's in his. It seems probable, though, that the differences between different happinesses are manifest even more markedly in their respective passive elements, that is, in the character of the person's self-contentment. Contentment with self is a direct manifestation of self-love. Different kinds of self-love will therefore produce different kinds of contentment. The self-love of the inhabitant of the state of nature was a simple, nonexpansive and unself-conscious *amour de soi*. Hence his contentment was comparably simple, nonexpansive, and unself-conscious. The *amour de soi* of the Rousseau of the *Reveries* was vastly more expansive and conscious—and so, consequently, was his contentment. The self-love of the citizen, by contrast, is not *amour de soi* but *amour-propre*, the comparative, self-seeking version of self-love that is the source of ambition, honor, pride, and vanity (*SD* 221–22n. o). In the citizen's case *amour-propre* is wholesome because it is extended to the republic at large: the Roman loved Rome first and loved himself only as a Roman, as a fractional part of the larger whole. Hence much of his enjoyment of existence was felt as patriotism and civic pride. And though he wished to distinguish himself individually, his personal ambition was still civic in its substance: he wished to be recognized for excellent service to the nation. The citizen's identity and thus, too, his happiness are essentially connected to the republic. (By contrast, the *amour-propre* of other social men, men who are not true citizens, leads them into vice and relations of personal dependence that so corrupt them as to make true contentment unsustainable.)

As for Emile, he is neither free of *amour-propre* nor a citizen.[11] Nevertheless, like the citizen's, his *amour-propre* is trained and channeled into wholesome and generally eudaemonistic directions, though in his case those directions are pity and romantic love rather than patriotism. Thus he finds a part of his passive enjoyment of existence through his standing relative to others. Unlike the citizen, though (and unlike other social men), Emile is educated to be a "man of nature." "He is a savage made to inhabit cities" (III:205), which means not only that his *amour-propre* is well directed but also that a good part of his self-love remains *amour de soi*. Thus a good part of his happiness consists in the same immediate enjoyment of existence that both the savage and the dreamy-contemplative Rousseau experienced.

Thus far we have seen something of what happiness is. The primacy of existence will not be fully revealed, though, until we take note of what happiness is *not*. Only then will it be fully clear why the eudaemonists are wrong—that is, why happiness, which is constituted by the enjoyment of existence, ought not to be considered Rousseau's highest good and the goal of his thought.

To be sure, happiness is *a* goal of Rousseau's work. Rousseau presents himself in many of his writings as one who hopes through his diagnoses and prescriptions to make humankind happier.[12] In one typical instance, he describes himself as "a man who takes a lively interest in the happiness of others without being in need of them for his own" (*Bordes* 112). This interest is certainly evident in *Emile,* whose maxims, Rousseau claims, "are among those whose truth or falsehood is important to know and which make the happiness or unhappiness of mankind" (I:34). But however much he values it, happiness is not what Rousseau most wishes for us. What he most wishes is not a eudaemonistic state but a moral one: that we be *worthy* of happiness.

Rousseau concludes one of the defenses of his *First Discourse* by stating: "the bitterness of my invectives against the vices I witness arises solely from the pain they cause me, and from my intense desire to see men happier *and especially worthier of being so*" (*Last Reply* 89; emphasis added). Rousseau's primary concern is the moral stature of human beings. That we live virtuously and thereby deserve happiness matters more to him than whether we are happy. Now it is true, as the eudaemonists claim, that Rousseau does not value virtue

---

11. Emile of course does (presumably) become a *kind* of citizen upon completing his education. But the kind of citizen he becomes bears no similarity to what Rousseau normally means by that term, namely, the Roman or Spartan or even the patriotic Genevan. Compare the tutor's description of the dispassionate citizenship appropriate to Emile (V:473–75) with Rousseau's earlier portrait of citizenship in the same work (I:39–40).

12. See, for instance, *FD*, esp. 33, 63–64.

as an end in itself but rather for its experiential yield. This is evident from the way in which he promotes virtue (his case is always based on the claim that virtue brings contentment) and from the character of his condemnation of injustice.[13] (His assault is grounded on the claim that injustice is contrary to nature and therefore produces misery for both perpetrator and victim; if oppression did not also hurt the oppressor it would not be blameworthy.)[14] However, the experience for whose sake Rousseau praises virtue is not what is commonly meant, nor what he commonly means, by "happiness." Happiness is a lasting state of general enjoyment, and as such it depends in part on factors beyond our control (*Reveries* IX:137). The reward for virtue, on the contrary, is something within our own power to achieve: it is what Rousseau variously calls self-respect, self-esteem, satisfaction with oneself, and good witness of oneself.

Self-respect is required for happiness—for true happiness—but it is not identical to it.[15] True happiness necessarily implies a life well lived. One cannot be truly happy without being worthy of it. Worthiness alone, however, does not guarantee happiness. Rectitude has its rewards, but happiness is not always among them. Indeed, the world being what it is, happiness is rarely among them. And least happy of all, it seems, are some of humanity's most outstanding moral specimens: neither Rousseau himself, the best, the most *good*, of men (*Confessions* X:433), nor Cato, "the model of the purest *virtue* that ever was" (*Last Reply* 80), can be said to have been happy. What these two moral exemplars did have, though, and what made their lives eminently rewarding, was the satisfaction that comes of living well. This satisfaction, though morally based, is a psychological reward. To achieve it is to enhance the degree of one's existence—not by extending one's boundaries outwardly (as in reverie or contemplation) but by preventing an existence-diminishing bad conscience and perhaps too by ascending into a realm of greater intensity.[16]

13. Rousseau says of the "sentiment of pleasure at doing good" that "it is through this cultivated sentiment that one arrives at loving oneself and being pleased with oneself" (*LM* 1116). This claim is the centerpiece of the fourth, fifth, and sixth *Lettres morales*. For further discussion of the psychological justifications of virtue, see Salkever, "Rousseau," 32–34.

14. See *Emile* IV:287 and *LM* 1106. For the crux of Rousseau's critique of mastery, see *Emile* II:85 ("[d]ependence on men, since it is without order, engenders all the vices, and by it, master and slave are mutually corrupted") and *SC* I-1:46 ("[o]ne who believes himself the master of others is nonetheless a greater slave than they"). See also *SD* 156, 173–77, 193–203. For a fuller analysis, see Melzer, *Natural Goodness of Man*, 61–63.

15. Does the phrase "true happiness" imply that false happiness exists? It would seem so: Rousseau addresses parts of the *First Discourse*, for example, to "happy slaves" (36).

16. Actually, the satisfaction of goodness and the satisfaction of virtue are two separate things, arising, as they do, from two separate sources. Goodness is a manifestation of *amour de soi*, whereas virtue is a manifestation of *amour-propre*. This difference will be addressed in Chapter 4.

"Good witness of oneself" is one of only three true or natural goods (*Emile* II:81). What makes it so (along with strength and health) is its necessary connection with the sentiment of existence. Existence, as we have already noted, can only be felt insofar as it is felt as one's own, that is, insofar as one enjoys oneself, one's being. And it is only insofar as the self has strength, health, and its own respect that it can be enjoyed. Thus it is for the sake of existence (that is, for the sake of the *enjoyment* of existence) that virtue is good. Virtue brings self-respect, and self-respect is in itself enjoyment of existence. No greater reward is possible: "Supreme enjoyment is in contentment with oneself" (OC IV:587).[17] Living well really *is* the best revenge.

A final question needs to be addressed before leaving the matter of what constitutes the goodness of the good life. If self-respect is a component of true happiness, how wrong are the eudaemonists really? Does it make a difference to say that self-respect rather than happiness ought to be the psychological goal of our actions?

Rousseau's view is that civilized man faces a frequent tension—all too often an insoluble tension—between happiness and morality.[18] For the sake of what is right we must sometimes choose against our happiness. But what that really means is that for the sake of our *self-respect* we must choose against our happiness. But of course what *that* really means is that we are not choosing against our happiness at all, for our happiness will already have been doomed by the circumstances that eventuated in such a choice: once one knows what action is morally required, one can no longer be happy without performing that action. When Julie declines to run off to England with Saint-Preux (in *The New Heloise*), it is because she knows that to choose happiness (romance) over duty (to her father) would be illusory. What she would really be choosing would be the unhappiness of regret. The choice between self-respect and happiness is no choice at all, for one can never possess the latter except by way of the former.

In a certain sense, then, the eudaemonists are right. If self-respect is a requirement of true happiness, one need never choose against happiness. By contributing to or preserving self-respect, the virtuous choice will also be the one that is best from the standpoint of happiness. Nevertheless, the eudaemonist position is misleading to the point of serious distortion, for it implies

17. The experiential yield of virtue, besides being great, is also long-lasting: "the sacrifices made to honesty and justice compensate me every day for what they cost me one time, and for brief privations they give me eternal delights" (*LM* 1103; see also *Confessions* VII:237).
18. See Bloom, *Love and Friendship*, 117–18.

that in Rousseau's view, happiness ought to be the goal of life and the measure of its success, when in fact what really ought to be the goal of life is moral excellence (worthiness of happiness) and what really ought to be the measure of its success is existence. The eudaemonist position understates the moral dimension of the good life and tends to overlook the nature of its goodness.

Happiness, *true* happiness, is an entirely good thing. It can never be had at the expense of any greater good, and what it demands of us is consistent with what the good life as such demands. Consequently, much of what is written in the pages to come applies as much to happiness as to the good life. Even so, despite the overlap, happiness is neither perfectly synonymous with the good life nor its essential content or measure. Rather, the measure of the good life, Rousseau's highest good, is existence, for existence, as we have now seen, is prior to happiness in two senses beyond the obvious logical one. First, it is the very substance, the positive content, of happiness; and second, it can be attained —and can thereby give meaning and quality to life—quite apart from happiness.

Having established the essential criterion of the good life we are now prepared to address its substance. We know now that a high degree of existence is what constitutes the goodness of the good life. But what constitutes its living? *How* can existence be maximized?

The answer is twofold. First, obstacles to the sentiment of existence must be prevented or removed. This is the negative side of the project, the side that culminates in equilibrium between desires and faculties and in psychic unity, or lack of inner conflict. To succeed here is to be free of the painful distraction of unending, unfulfillable desire: one can enjoy existence. But balance and psychic unity—in a word, naturalness—is not enough. What completes the good life is the positive side of the project, to be executed concurrently with the negative. Existence must be increased by the proper development and employment of the faculties; like the development that produces it, this increase is quantitative as well as qualitative. The negative side of the project essentially amounts to regaining (to whatever extent possible) the wholeness that seems to characterize all nonhuman life and that characterized our forebears in the pure state of nature. The positive side, though, accentuates the distinctively human. In this duality is reflected one of Rousseau's characteristic themes: the continuity and discontinuity between man and nature. Rousseau's ideal is the full development of man's distinctive faculties and capacities, but development that accords with original nature—that is, development that proceeds in such a way that psychic unity and the balance between desires and faculties are not too much compromised.

The Two Components of the Good Life

Rousseau's "existence," as we have seen, is the feeling of existence. This feeling requires two things: that we be able to sense it, and that there be something to sense. The more we succeed at fulfilling these requirements, the more we exist—and the better are our lives. Both requirements of the good life can be met to varying degrees; neither is a simple yes or no proposition. Here, though, the similarity between these two requirements ends. The negative task is by its nature a conceptually simpler one, for though it admits of degrees of success, it allows for only so much variety. Success at the negative side of the good life is defined by the approximation of two separate but obviously related ideals: equilibrium between desires and faculties and the lack of inner conflict (or psychic unity). Both of these ideals, however difficult to realize and however much in need of complex strategies, are such that progress toward them can be conceived as progress along a single dimension. The positive task, though—the job of increasing what there is to be felt—can be legitimately performed in countless ways and (it would seem) to an infinite degree. Love, art, friendship, citizenship, virtue, reverie—each of these activities offers its own ways to increase our existence.

As noted above, Rousseau does not address existence extensively or systematically. He nowhere catalogs either the ways to increase existence, the modes of existence, or the dimensions of existence (extent, intensity, and elevation). Nor can we infer or deduce a systematic understanding of existence from his writings. Yet even if he does not thoroughly explicate all the positive possibilities, Rousseau still goes far in developing a fundamentally new conception of the good life on the basis of his unique understanding and elevation of existence. Raising existence to the position of highest good and standard permits him to solve the problem of how to define the good life absent anything like the transcendent, substantive ideals that informed earlier moral traditions. (Existence is itself only a formal standard.) One of the chief conceptual virtues of this approach is that it allows for several varieties of the good life and of happiness while still providing a common standard by which these ideal lives can be defined and by which actual lives can be judged. Another of its virtues is that it sheds light on the ways in which the two components of the good life are related. As we shall see, fulfillment of the negative and positive tasks is interdependent and mutually reinforcing. Desire that is not dissipated can be elevated, and desire that is elevated is in turn the surest defense against dissipation. Thus does Rousseau lay the theoretical groundwork of what we now know as sublimation.[19]

The negative component of living well is essentially the same in all varieties of the good life. Although the lives of the citizen, the solitary dreamer, and Emile are vastly different, each is marked by minimal excess of desire over faculty and a high degree of psychic unity. In this respect, these individuals approximate the condition of man in the pure state of nature, who alone among human beings enjoyed perfect equilibrium and perfect psychic unity. (*Emile* II:80; *SD*, 151) But they only approximate it; they do not equal it. And this in itself proves that the negative component is not all there is to the good life. If it were, the pure state of nature would have been the best epoch, when in fact it was not. The tribal stage was better, even though man's original balance and unity had begun to be eroded. It was better because the losses on the negative side were more than offset by gains on the positive side. Though beset for the first time by obstacles to the enjoyment of his being, man was still better off because his being itself was vastly enlarged through the development of certain capacities. The price exacted by the emergence of embryonic vanity and occasionally vengeful passions was of a lesser magnitude than the pleasures of conjugal and parental love.

And if the epoch of tribal society was better than the pure state of nature, the epoch of civil society is—or rather, could have been—better still. "Although in this state [man] deprives himself of several advantages given him by nature, he gains such great ones, his faculties are exercised and developed, his ideas broadened, his feelings ennobled, and his whole soul elevated to such a point that if the abuses of this new condition did not often degrade him beneath the condition he left, he ought ceaselessly to bless the happy moment that tore him away from it forever, and that changed him from a stupid, limited animal into an intelligent being and a man" (SC I-8:56). This description of what might have been indicates the things that fulfill the positive requirement of the good life. The exercise and development of faculties, the broadening of ideas, the ennoblement of sentiment, and the elevation of soul—each is a blessing because each in some way enlarges our being. The perfect happiness of natural man—his total fulfillment of the negative requirement of the good life—is not Rousseau's ideal. Man can and should be more than "a stupid, limited animal," notwithstanding that animal's negative perfection. Neither is Rousseau a more moderate kind of primitivist: nascent society may have been the best that humanity has known, but it is not the best that it *could* have known or, theoretically at least, that it could know still.

---

19. This point is made by Bloom, though my understanding of Rousseauan sublimation (discussed in Chapter 3) differs considerably from Bloom's. See his introduction to Rousseau's *Emile*, 15–16.

And yet, as the excerpt from the *Social Contract* demonstrates, success on the positive side is also insufficient by itself. Were the enlargement of faculties and ideas to shatter psychic unity or disrupt the balance between desires and faculties, the net result would be a *loss* of existence and a worsening of life (which is why the age of tribal society was in fact better than nearly all of the civil societies that have followed).

For all of Rousseau's accusations against mankind, the most damning is the one he pointedly *refused* to make: "I do not accuse the men of this century of having all the vices; they have only the vices of cowardly souls; they are only rogues and knaves" (*Last Reply* 72). The increasing failure of modern men to satisfy the negative requirement of the good life has taken a severe toll—an ontological toll. "Vile and cowardly even in their vices, they have only *small souls*" (*Emile* IV:335; emphasis added). Despite their enlarged capacities—or rather, *because* of them and the aberrant way in which they have developed—modern men and women have become small. More than unhappy and depraved, they are petty in their desires, their aspirations, their pleasures, and their energies—all because of their dissipation and, especially, their psychic disunity.

Man in the pure state of nature enjoyed the simplest kind of psychic unity, unity of inclination. So, to nearly the same extent, does the member of savage society. The savage "breathes only repose and freedom"—he knows how to enjoy his existence—because he is one with himself, because he "lives within himself" (*SD* 179). As for the citizen, he too is one with himself, but his psychic unity is entirely different from that of the savage. Whereas the savage lives within himself, the citizen defines himself only with regard to others. He "believes himself no longer one but a part of the unity and no longer feels except within the whole. A citizen of Rome was neither Caius nor Lucius; he was a Roman. He even loved the country exclusive of himself" (*Emile* I:40). The citizen has been so denatured, he so completely defines himself as a member of his community, that his selfishness is very nearly synonymous with patriotism. And what does remain in him of natural selfishness is mastered by virtue.[20] The rest of us, though—social men and women who are not citizens in the deepest sense—enjoy neither of these types of unity. We are divided by the conflicting demands of inclination (nature) and duty (society). In modern societies one finds only "double men," says Rousseau, "always appearing to relate everything to others and never relating anything except to themselves alone.... Swept along in contrary routes by nature and by men, forced to

---

20. See Shklar, *Men and Citizens*, 12–19, and Melzer, *Natural Goodness of Man*, 103–4.

divide ourselves between these different impulses, we follow a composite impulse which leads us to neither one goal nor the other. Thus, in conflict and floating during the whole course of our life, we end it without having been good either for ourselves or for others" (*Emile* I:41). This conflict and inconstancy ("floating")—the twin marks of psychic disunity—are the immediate causes of modern man's smallness of soul. "Always in contradiction with himself, always floating between his inclinations and his duties, he will never be either man or citizen.... He will be nothing" (*Emile* I:40).[21] Conversely, those who avoid disunity not only exist more, they also enjoy life. "[R]ender man one," writes Rousseau, "and you will make him as happy as he is capable of being" (*Fragments* 510).

Failure to meet the negative requirements of the good life is the source of nearly all our ills. We would not be lured into injustice, at least not often, if not for the excessive desires that beset us. And we would be able to feel more deeply—to *be* more—were it not for our disunity of soul. But success on the negative side cannot be achieved except in conjunction with success on the positive. The two components of the good life are not only necessary and complementary but mutually dependent.

Civilized man will always be a creature of desire. Great desirousness is the inevitable product of *amour-propre*, which is itself the inevitable product of self-consciousness.[22] The only question is whether these desires will be wholesome and therefore protective of psychic unity or dissipated and therefore

21. What does it mean to "be nothing"? What it clearly does not mean is death, and it is instructive that death—or literal (that is, ontological) nonbeing—is not the greatest evil for Rousseau, despite its being the apparent opposite of Rousseau's greatest good (existence). Nor does "be[ing] nothing" quite seem to refer to what are today called dissociative disorders or any other specific clinical syndrome. Rather, the nothingness of the person who is neither man nor citizen seems to refer to an utter lack of wholeheartedness, to an inability to experience deeply and vividly that which is present to be experienced (everything from sensory stimuli to desire to beauty, love, and especially the inherent sweetness of existence itself). Why should this condition be worse than death? Presumably because it consists in a kind of pain or distress, even if an unacknowledged distress. One who is dead has no unsatisfied needs or desires. One who is alive but who "is nothing," on the contrary, does have unsatisfied needs and desires. As a living being he is a creature of self-love; and self-love, besides being the source of other passions, is also a passion itself—indeed, the most basic passion (*Emile* IV:212–13). The object of this most basic passion is felt existence. It stands to reason, then, that when this passion is denied satisfaction, the result is a condition worse than any other because it is characterized by a deprivation more painful or distressing than any other. He who is neither man nor citizen *lives* a kind of death; he who is literally dead does not. (Indeed, death may not be an evil at all, at least not for those who have lived well. There is considerable reason to believe that Rousseau was in earnest when he spoke of divine justice in the afterlife—as he did not only in his books but also in his personal correspondence.)

22. The utterly decisive and irreversible role of self-consciousness in human development is addressed below in "The Birth of *Amour-Propre*," in Chapter 4.

destructive of psychic unity: "a young man must either love or be debauched" (*Emile* V:470). Dissipation cannot be prevented by strictly negative means. Desire cannot be fenced in. If, however, it is focused on an ideal—if, for example, one is in love—then desire can be kept from dissipating. This is the lesson conveyed by Emile's experience. At first, his foretaste or intimation of love's pleasures, and then, his actual experience of them, make the pleasures of love-less sensuality pale by comparison. And he is further guarded against corrupt temptation by loyalty to his beloved, this loyalty being a source of pleasure in itself. Errant passions are forestalled by the only means possible: noble passions. Emile's positive achievement (love) helps preserve his negative ones (his balance between desire and faculty and his psychic unity).

The reverse also holds true. Emile's early negative education, the education that long delays the emergence of *amour-propre* and thereby strengthens his psychic unity and balance, serves the positive component. Emile would not be capable of great love or virtue had he not been kept from things that would have awakened excessive or unhealthy desires, especially the desire to be something other than what he is (hence Rousseau's caution during Emile's early education regarding books, fables, foresight, and imagination). The constraint of his energies within fairly narrow bounds creates the psychic pressure that is required for the elevation of his passions and tastes. This is the basis of sublimation: Emile's tutor transforms the low (undifferentiated sexual desire) into the high (intense romantic love) by preventing the early and easy satisfaction of desire and by teaching Emile what is at first a salutary lie but becomes, through being taught, a wonderful truth—namely, that the name of his desire is in fact love and that its object is a worthy beloved. Emile's education "concentrates the wishes of a great soul within the narrow limit of the possible" (IV:253) and thereby prepares them to be lured upward until their object, à la Diotima's ladder of love, is "imperishable beauty" (V:446).[23]

Sexual sublimation is the paradigm of the necessary relationship between the two components of the good life. Neither the balance between desires and faculties nor psychic unity can be maintained unless desire is elevated, and this elevation cannot be achieved unless high degrees of balance and unity have been preserved in the first place. In fact, sexual sublimation is more than the paradigm. It is at the core of the entire project of social man's healthy development. For not only romantic love but also compassion and community spirit, the fundament of any decent society, are powered, at least in part, by sublimated sexuality.

23. See Plato, *Symposium*, 211.

We have now made a start at understanding Rousseau's thinking on the problem of the good life. Yet we have made only a start, for our discoveries thus far—regarding existence as the highest good, regarding the meaning of happiness, and regarding the common (two-part) shape of all versions of the good life—have been largely formal. How can existence be enlarged? With what content ought the two components of the good life be filled, and by what standard(s) should our pursuit of this content be guided and judged? The answers to these questions will appear as we shift focus from existence as such (which, for all its significance, is given only cursory treatment by Rousseau) to nature (a thing only slightly less abstract but one that occupies Rousseau mightily). We now need, and are ready, to inquire into this all-important matter.

2

Nature and Human Nature, Part I
What Is Natural?

Our philosophers never fail to display the word *nature* pompously at the beginning of all their writings. But open the book and you will see the metaphysical jargon they have decorated with this fine name.

—Rousseau, *Dialogues*

Rousseau ... constantly speaks of "nature" as though it were a simple, almost self-evident notion, but as soon as his reader tries to understand its precise function in the many and varied contexts in which it is used, he may be unable to arrive at a clear and consistent comprehension of its meaning.

—Ronald Grimsley, "Rousseau and His Reader"

Rousseau's effective elevation of "existence" to the position of summum bonum constituted a revolutionary departure from older traditions of thought. Certainly Rousseau was not the first to suggest that there are degrees of reality or that the good life is somehow bound up with a high degree of existence or aliveness. Platonism, for example, asserts that the "higher" things, the *ideas*, are not just superior to but are also more real than the concrete particulars of the material realm and that life is well lived to the extent that it accords with or participates in the perfection of these most real things. Likewise Christianity conceives of salvation in essentially ontological terms. Its promise, more than relief or even happiness, is *life*: the saved are reunited with a God who is

The Rousseau quotation can be found at III:239n; Grimsley's words are from "Rousseau and His Reader: The Technique of Persuasion in *Emile*," in *Rousseau After 200 Years: Proceedings of the Cambridge Bicentennial Colloquium*, ed. R. A. Leigh (New York: Cambridge University Press, 1982), 225.

the ground, the source, the suchness of being.[1] Nor was the "sentiment of existence" original with Rousseau. Numerous predecessors and contemporaries had already written of its inherent goodness.[2] What Rousseau did, though, was to ascribe to existence a power and autonomy—and end-in-itself status—that it had not hitherto been accorded.[3]

Prior to Rousseau, the maximization of existence was understood only with reference to something beyond itself. It was seen as a good, but not a self-sufficient good. Hence it was not to be pursued as an end in itself. This is probably most clearly evident in the case of Christianity, according to which eternal and exalted existence is the gift of God and comes only to those who seek it through him. Existence is impossible—indeed, inconceivable—without God. God is the essential referent. The good life, the life of maximized existence, is the godly life. However difficult it may be to achieve this life, and however much the duality of our nature limits our ability to govern ourselves well, the most fundamental moral questions have been settled by his revelation. For classical philosophy, at least in its Socratic versions, the task of determining what is good is not as simple or as sure as it is for Christianity. Reason must work, and work through fallible human agency, where revelation reveals. Neither Plato's nor Aristotle's teachings are dogmatic. Yet there exists in classical philosophy, as in Christianity, an essential referent without which the idea of enhanced existence has no meaning. Where the Christian looks to God, the classics look to nature. Human beings are understood to be part of the natural whole and, as such, to have a specific, constant nature of their own. The good for man is sought by examining this nature and trying to deduce from it how

---

1. "Be thou faithful unto death, and I will give thee a crown of life" (Revelation 2:10). The promise of life also appears in the Hebrew Bible: "Choose life—if you and your offspring would live—by loving the Lord your God, heeding His commands, and holding fast to Him. For thereby you shall have life" (Deuteronomy 30:19).

2. Among those who preceded or paralleled Rousseau in writing of the sentiment of existence as an inherently good thing were Diderot, Saint-Lambert, Senac de Meilhan, the abbé de Lignac, d'Aguesseau, and John Norris, an English disciple of Malebranche. The basic idea, if not the term itself, also appears in Montaigne's essay "Of Experience." For a survey of the views of these figures (except for Montaigne) and their relations to the philosophy of Rousseau (as well as those of Descartes and Malebranche), see Georges Poulet, "Le sentiment de l'existence et le repos," in *Reappraisals of Rousseau*, ed. Simon Harvey et al. (Manchester: Manchester University Press, 1980), 37–45.

3. Melzer puts it well: "Rousseau is certainly not the first to have claimed that there is a natural sweetness to mere life but he seems to be the first to have made that sweetness the final end of life and the root of all happiness. Most of the thinkers who spoke of 'the sentiment of existence,' for example, also described it as pleasant, but they did not attribute to it such completeness and self-sufficiency. They did not go on to conclude, as Rousseau does, that man possesses the ground of his happiness and being within himself" (*Natural Goodness of Man*, 41).

humans ought to live—what ends they ought to pursue and how they ought to pursue them. The good life is the life lived in accordance with nature.[4]

What, then, of Rousseau? We have already seen that for him the good life is synonymous with a high degree of existence. We have seen, further, that in each of its variants the good life has two components: the negative component, which consists in the avoidance or removal of obstacles (such as rampant desires and inner conflicts) that prevent one from enjoying one's existence, and the positive, which consists in the literal extension of one's existence through the development of faculties and capacities. But how are these formal goals to be achieved? Is there no essential referent, no *substantive* source of guidance, defining and pointing the way to the good life? In fact there is, though not to the extent that there is either for Christianity or for classical philosophy. *Rousseau's conception of what is good for human beings is informed by his understanding of nature.* Psychologically, morally and politically, nature is Rousseau's touchstone. In this he bears at least a superficial resemblance to such classical philosophers as Aristotle. The resemblance is not much more than superficial, however. For, as we shall see, Rousseau's particular understanding of nature is such that the guidance it provides is necessarily less substantive and less specific than the guidance provided by the nature (the *physis*) of the classics.

For the classics, nature comprehended the whole of the human realm, including the proper ends of human life. For Rousseau, by contrast, nature refers not to ends but to origins, and to unrecoverable origins at that. The pure state of nature refers to a real, historic—or rather, prehistoric—period of time. Only those parts of man extant during this earliest period can be considered natural in the strict or pure sense. The faculties and characteristics that were not present in the pure state of nature but that, rather, were acquired over the many centuries that have elapsed since the close of that epoch are not natural. Among these acquired and therefore unnatural phenomena are nearly all the distinctive marks of humanity, including reason, language, sociality, self-consciousness, love, shame, envy, pride, vanity, and virtue. The wholly natural man, the inhabitant of the pure state of nature, was a veritable brute: the pure state of nature was a "state of animality" (*SD* 219n. 1). Nature has nearly nothing in common with the distinctively human and would therefore seem to have little to tell man about how he ought to live.[5]

---

4. None of this is to say that the enterprise of classical philosophy is either practically or conceptually simple (see note 7 to the Preface). But however difficult to follow or even apprehend, nature is at least the purported standard of classical moral and political philosophy. See, for example, Aristotle, *Nicomachean Ethics* 1098a8–17. See also Plato, *Gorgias* 499e6–500a3, and *Republic* 369c10–372b8 and 451c–466d.

Yet in spite of its apparent inadequacy nature *does* give guidance. His conception of nature is as central to Rousseau's understanding of the human good
as the classics' was to theirs. The good life, the life of enlarged existence, is for
Rousseau, as it was for Aristotle, a life lived in accordance with nature. Or,
rather, it is for Rousseau, as it was *not* for Aristotle, a life lived in accordance
with nature. For whereas accordance with nature was for Aristotle something
that could be conceived in objective terms (such as exercising certain virtues),
what it means for Rousseau is the recovery or re-creation of certain subjective
conditions that prevailed in the pure state of nature (namely, psychic unity
and the consequent enjoyment of existence). Strauss, who correctly identifies
the apparent uselessness of Rousseau's nature as a moral or political guide,
observes with equal correctness that nature performs a key function after all:
"Rousseau's answer to the question of the good life takes on this form: the good
life consists in the closest possible approximation to the state of nature which
is possible on the level of humanity."[6] The question, of course, is what exactly
does this mean? If most of what we are is by definition unnatural, what could
it mean to live in accordance with nature? And what reason is there to think
that an attempt to make our predominantly unnatural selves accord with our
brute origins would be worthwhile—that it would be desirable and successful
or even coherent?

But before we examine Rousseau's conception of naturalness in human life,
we need to address a preliminary matter of decisive importance. Rousseau is
famous as a discoverer of History. He shook the pillars of older modes of philosophical inquiry by contending that human nature itself had been changed
over time by various vicissitudes.[7] Some interpreters have gone so far as to

---

5. This observation is central to both the second and the third interpretive tendencies described
in the Introduction.

6. *Natural Right and History*, 282. I would add to this, however—and herein lies my departure
from Strauss and the interpretive tendency he originated—that the naturalness of the good life as
lived by Emile (and Jean-Jacques) is characterized by more than just an approximation of the state
of nature. One of the major purposes of the present study is to demonstrate that post-state-of-nature
naturalness has a defining, substantive content that was unknown in the state of nature. See Chapters 3 and 4. For Strauss's view regarding the apparent insufficiency of (Rousseau's) nature as a source
of human guidance, see "The Three Waves of Modernity," in *An Introduction to Political Philosophy*,
ed. Hilail Gildin (Detroit: Wayne State University Press, 1989), 90.

7. Rousseau was not the only discoverer of History, nor even the first. Vico made his own discovery, earlier in the eighteenth century, and his criticism of figures like Hobbes and Pufendorf on
the grounds they mistakenly assumed men of the past to have been the same as men of the present
prefigures Rousseau's own criticism of these same people. (See Giambattista Vico, *The New Science
of Giambattista Vico (Scienza nuova)*, trans. T. G. Bergin and M. H. Fisch [Ithaca: Cornell University
Press, 1948], section 314.) But if he was not the first, Rousseau nevertheless is the most important

suggest that for Rousseau there is no longer any such thing as human nature.[8] They believe that for Rousseau "human nature" refers to a set of characteristics that are accidental in origin, and that it can again be re-formed by the right social institutions. But such a radically historicist reading of Rousseau is not only wrong, it renders his political and educational programs incoherent. Those programs, whether the massive projects of the *Social Contract* and *Emile* or the more modest ones that appear in the *Lettres morales* and the *Letter to d'Alembert*, are based on the premise that there *are* limits to the plasticity of human nature, both in practice and in theory, and that the human condition can be understood and ameliorated only if these limits—or, to put it positively, only if the universal givens of human nature—are respected.

The Fixedness of Man's "Present Nature"

Rousseau was indeed a kind of evolutionist, though perhaps transformist would be a better term.[9] The *Second Discourse*, written a full century prior to Darwin, recounts the history of the human species from its brute origins to its present state (*SD* 103–4). It tells the *history of human nature*.[10] Although some of the details of this history are admittedly conjectural, its basic themes and premises are not.[11] Human beings have changed radically over the ages: "Like the statue of Glaucus, which time, sea and storms had so disfigured that it looked less like a god than a wild beast, the human soul, altered in the bosom

---

discoverer of History, if only for the massive impact of the *Second Discourse*. (I know of no evidence to suggest that Rousseau was acquainted with Vico's work, which was to remain relatively obscure until the nineteenth century.)

8. This is the historicist interpretation described in the Introduction.

9. Rousseau did not subscribe to anything like Darwin's evolutionism. Rousseau believed in the permanence of both species and the dividing lines between species. The evolution he recounts in the *Second Discourse* is a sequence of changes by which primitive man became civilized man. There is no suggestion that primitive man descended from any nonhuman ancestor. (See Jean Starobinski, *Jean-Jacques Rousseau: Transparency and Obstruction*, trans. Arthur Goldhammer [Chicago: University of Chicago Press, 1988], 326–28.) For this reason, the word "transformism" is probably a better term for Rousseau's view than "evolutionism."

10. It is because Rousseau purports to outline the development of human nature itself, rather than just human events, that I have chosen to refer to his theory as transformist rather than historical. His account does include what might properly be called history (which is why the word "history" will appear in what follows), but the history he tells is part of the even larger story of man's transformation.

11. See note 2 to Chapter 1.

of society by a thousand continually renewed causes, by the acquisition of a mass of knowledge and errors, by changes that occurred in the constitution of bodies, and by the continual impact of the passions, has, so to speak, changed its appearance to the point of being nearly unrecognizable" (_SD_ 91).

The substance of this change and its causes and consequences will be addressed later, at least insofar as they relate to the education of Emile. For now let us simply establish two facts: first, that whatever the importance he ascribes to history, Rousseau believes that there still is such a thing as human nature, meaning a universal and fairly fixed set of needs, capacities and characteristics; and, second, that in Rousseau's view the elements of man's original nature continue to exist in his present makeup—that they have been neither erased nor supplanted, but rather overlaid and thereby transformed by historical acquisitions.

The second of these claims is the easier one to establish, though its precise meaning is exceedingly complex and will no doubt remain a live issue for Rousseau interpreters. It will suffice to take note of a few passages from the _Second Discourse_. In the first, which immediately precedes the comparison to Glaucus, Rousseau poses the philosophical challenge that faces him in a way that demonstrates his belief in the continued existence of at least some of man's original elements: "how will man manage to see himself as nature formed him, through all the changes that the sequence of time and things must have produced in his original constitution, and to separate what he gets from his own stock from what circumstances and his progress have added to or changed in his primitive state?" (91). A little later he comments that "it is no light undertaking to separate what is original from what is artificial in the present nature of man" (92–93). The clear implication is that at least some of the elements of original human nature, of natural human nature, persist in civilized man.

That elements of our original nature remain within us does not quite mean, though, that we remain good to that extent. For what was good about natural man was a result not of particular good qualities but of the order of the whole of his being. Thus the unfortunate development of the species has entailed the corruption of what had originally been good qualities as well as the addition of new, bad ones. Calling humans to listen to their history, Rousseau announces: "It is, so to speak, the life of your species that I am going to describe to you according to the qualities you received, _which your education and habits have been able to corrupt but have not been able to destroy_" (104; emphasis added). The paramount example of this phenomenon is undoubtedly self-love. Natural in origin, it was good in natural man and could be good in a properly educated civilized man. In the typical civilized man, however, benign *amour de soi* has mutated into fractious pride and vanity.

But if human nature has changed to the point where the good has turned bad, does it even make sense to speak of a present human nature? Is there anything more to what Rousseau calls "the present nature of man" than just the principle of change?

Some interpreters of Rousseau have argued that if human nature has changed, then it is changeable, and that if it is changeable it really does not exist. According to these individuals, man has no nature, only a history. Or at most, if one insists on holding onto the term "human nature," one could say that although such a thing exists, it consists of nothing more than malleability, nothing more than the single decisive characteristic that Rousseau calls perfectibility.[12] Perfectibility, the capacity that has made history possible, is thought to imply infinite plasticity.

The first indication that this is an inaccurate characterization of Rousseau's view (and of the implications of his view) arises from the very belief we just observed: that the elements of original human nature persist in modern man. The persistence of these original elements suggests limits to the plasticity of human nature. No matter how much the statue of Glaucus had changed, its basic shape and the bulk of the matter of which it was made remained the same. But there is more reason than just this to conclude that Rousseau finds it meaningful to speak of a present, fixed nature of man, even if that present nature is a composite of original (natural) and acquired (artificial) elements.

A careful reading of the *Second Discourse* reveals that in Rousseau's view, the evolution of humanity has not been without a certain logic, a logic so rigorous, in fact, that one may fairly conclude that only three outcomes were possible for the human species: (1) remaining in its original state, (2) advancing to and then remaining at the stage of savage or tribal society, or (3) evolving in the particular way that it did. This logic has not been an especially happy one, as Rousseau's nostalgia for tribal society and his pessimism toward the future attest. Nor has it been a redemptive or Rational one, as it would later be seen to be by Hegel. Yet however ambiguous the results, there is a logic, a logic that ultimately accounts for the universality and fixedness of man's "present nature." The process of evolution as Rousseau depicts it is best understood as a chain of inevitable awakenings. What was not inevitable was how far the

---

12. See Horowitz, for example, who argues that "[h]uman nature ... is ... not something fixed or static; nor does it appear whole, either at the origin of the historical process or as an abstract end transcending it. Human nature is, rather, constituted in historical activity" (*Rousseau, Nature, and History*, 81).

process would proceed—that is, which of the three possibilities would be the endpoint. What was inevitable, though, was that the outcome would be one of those presented above: the realm of possibilities was limited to three stations along the same track.

Man might have remained in the pure state of nature forever. Midway through the *Second Discourse* Rousseau claims to have shown "that *perfectibility*, social virtues, and the other faculties that natural man had received in potentiality could never develop by themselves [and] that in order to develop they needed the chance combination of several foreign causes which might never have arisen and without which he would have remained eternally in his primitive condition" (140; emphasis in original). It required "different accidents" to initiate the process of history.

The second possibility was for humanity to remain perpetually at the stage of savage society, which was not only "the happiest" but also the "most durable epoch": "The more one thinks about it, the more one finds that this state was the least subject to revolutions, the best for man, and that he must have come out of it only by some fatal accident" (151). Once humanity "progressed" beyond this stage, however, the historic die had been cast. The remaining stages of human evolution or history were made inevitable by the discovery of metallurgy and agriculture—the "great revolution" that "ruined the human race" by creating property and the specialization of labor and, thereby, great mutual dependence and social inequality (152–55).[13]

"By leaving the state of nature, we force our fellows to leave it, too" (*Emile* III:193). "Leaving the state of nature" here refers to the departure from savage society.[14] Once the first individuals stepped out of the state of nature by staking and enforcing claims to property, others were compelled by the requirements of self-preservation to follow suit, lest they find themselves propertyless in a propertied world. With the advent of property came intensive specialization of labor and the accompanying revolution in consciousness—namely, the accelerated development of foresight, calculation, and the manifold features of moral and social psychology.[15] Ultimately, though, the reason that human

13. For a succinct explanation of why the "invention" of metallurgy and agriculture made the remaining (and ruinous) stages of evolution inevitable, see Masters, *Political Philosophy of Rousseau,* 175–97.

14. Although distinct from the *pure* state of nature, savage society nevertheless belongs to the state of nature because it is prepolitical, with "each man ... being sole judge and avenger of the offenses he had received" (*SD* 150).

15. Previously, the only specialization was the sex-based division of labor that had come about with the advent of nascent society. (See *SD* 147.) Under that arrangement, individuals had ceased to be self-sufficient, but each family *was* self-sufficient.

consciousness and human nature *had to* develop as they did once the state of nature was left behind is that the faculties and characteristics that would later be actualized in human beings were natural potentials from the first, requiring in order to be awakened only that some very general conditions obtain.

The acquisition of new characteristics over the millennia consisted largely in the awakening of naturally latent capacities. Consider the following passage from *Emile*, in which Rousseau contrasts man's original simplicity with his present condition. "In the beginning," he says, nature gives man "with immediacy only the desires necessary to his preservation and the faculties sufficient to satisfy them. It put all the others, as it were, *in reserve in the depths of his soul*, to be developed there when needed" (II:80; emphasis added). Rousseau gives us to understand that he considers the infant born into civilization to be as similar in its constitution to the infant born in the state of nature as a domesticated animal is to its wild counterpart. The "civilized" infant might be less hardy by virtue of the domestication of his species, but all the capacities and tendencies of his soul—all his psychic potentials—replicate those present in the savage infant.[16] That human beings of all epochs have been born with the same psychic potentials is also suggested by the striking parallels between the order in which Emile's capacities appear over the course of twenty years and the order in which these same capacities appeared in the human species at large over "multitudes of centuries."[17]

One of the striking themes in all of Rousseau's major works, all the more striking for its apparent tension with his vindication of nature, is how easily man seems to succumb to the lures and satisfactions of what is corrupt. We find in the *Second Discourse* that "the rich ... *had scarcely known* the pleasure of domination when they soon disdained all others" (157; emphasis added). We learn from Rousseau's discourse on babies' tears in *Emile* that even at this early stage of life, before one has even had the opportunity to depart from

16. Rousseau believes in the permanence of species. It is unclear what he could mean if not that all humans, of whatever historic epoch, have essentially the same nature. One should be careful, however, not to underestimate the change entailed in domestication. It is instructive that, in connection with his suggestion that the orangutan may be human, Rousseau implies that the only way to know for sure would be to examine the progeny of the sexual union of a human being with an orangutan (*SD* 208–9n. j). If Rousseau believed that primitive man was constitutionally *identical* to civilized man, he could have and presumably would have suggested a much less offensive test: namely, that an orangutan be raised as a civilized human being to see whether it would actually become one. Thus, if all of civilized man's capacities and tendencies were present in the savage, as I have suggested, the awakening of those capacities and tendencies would seem to require the passing of generations.

17. See Masters, *Political Philosophy of Rousseau*, 172, for a suggestive comparison of Emile's (ontogenetic) development with the species' (phylogenetic) development.

nature, the corrupt taste for domination is easily aroused: "The first tears of children are prayers. If one is not careful, they soon become orders" (I:66). Although Rousseau denies the existence of "a natural spirit of domination" and insists that the taste for domination, like all evils, is a product of human agency (in this case, the product of the parents' or nurses' excessive solicitousness), he admits nearly in the same breath that "it does not require long experience to sense how pleasant it is to act with the hands of others and to need only to stir one's tongue to make the universe move" (I:68). It is not clear why the pleasures of domination should be at all enticing, let alone so powerfully and quickly addicting, unless there is either a latent taste for them by nature or, if not a latent taste, at least a latent capacity for that taste.

Throughout *Emile* we observe just how fragile are the products of even the best possible, the most natural, education. The book is replete with dire warnings to avoid this or that lest the entire project collapse utterly, and we perceive that the reason for this is that Emile has by nature the potential—the all-too-easily actualized potential—for the same evils that have already been actualized in most people. Indeed, as we shall see in greater detail in Chapters 3 and 4, what distinguishes the successfully educated Emile from his less fortunate counterparts is not that he has different psychic structures than they have, but rather that in Emile's case the more ambiguous or dangerous psychic capacities are educated in such a way as to preserve his well-being. He, like them, develops *amour-propre*. He even develops vanity. Or, to put it a little more precisely, one could say these things are awakened in him as they are in everyone else. On the subject of vanity, emulation, and glory, Rousseau has this to say to those who would have his advice: "These dangerous passions will, I am told, be born sooner or later in spite of us. I do not deny it. Everything has its time and its place. I only say that one ought not to assist their birth" and thereby, presumably, strengthen them (*Emile* IV:226). Whether examining Rousseau's account of man as he is, as he was, or as he might be, we find that the same basic features are assumed to be present. Natural man, savage, citizen, bourgeois, Emile—each has the same deep structures, the same native constitution. What separates one from another is "only" whether and how these same faculties and capacities have developed.

Finally, if the acquisition of new characteristics were not a matter of actualizing natural potentials, it seems doubtful that Rousseau would have referred to the capacity for such acquisition as "perfectibility" (*perfectibilité*). "Perfectibility" makes sense only if there was already something present to be perfected—to be awakened or activated and then developed. Here, though, it would be well to remember one of Rousseau's basic tenets. To say that various faculties and capacities were awakened from latency does not mean that they are natural in the pure sense. Only that which *actually* existed in the pure state of nature is natural in that sense.

The purpose of this cursory examination of Rousseau's evolutionism or transformism has been only to establish that Rousseau does believe in such a thing as human nature. I have tried to confirm that what he calls man's "present nature" is just that—a nature, meaning a set of universal and fixed needs, faculties, and tendencies. But this present nature is quite clearly a composite of (purely) natural and unnatural elements. Not even the most inevitable of human acquisitions is natural, for none of them is *completely* inevitable: the species could have remained either in the pure state of nature or at the stage of tribal society. The fact that humanity could have remained at an earlier stage makes it possible to insist on the unnaturalness of the road actually taken. The fact that there was only one possible road to take if in fact one was to be taken, though, accounts for the universality and fixedness of man's "present nature." It allows Rousseau to say of the great educational undertaking of *Emile* that "wherever men are born, what I propose can be done with them" (P:35).

As different as they are from their natural ancestors, civilized human beings share the same nature with one another. They are made of the same clay. But human nature is not destiny. Though it defines needs and possibilities, it does not determine character—else there would be no major differences among human types, whereas in fact there are enormous differences among those who share the same present nature. The virtuous Spartan had the same nature as the corrupt Parisian (*FD* 37). Clay, in the end, is only clay. What really counts is how it is molded.[18]

Charting the Human Landscape

Two Chasms—One Bridgeable, the Other Not

Nature plays different roles in Rousseau's various conceptions of the good life. But there is one respect in which nature serves as a positive model for all the variants. What we have been calling the negative component of the good life

---

18. To conclude that thus far the species had only three evolutionary possibilities is not to preclude additional possibilities in the future. Speaking of our limited knowledge of the soul, Rousseau

is nothing other than the approximation "on the level of humanity" of natural man's psychic unity and balance. Each of Rousseau's conceptions of the good life, whatever its other features, borrows that much from life in the state of nature. Even the denatured citizen partakes of this natural quality. His "denaturalization" refers to the means to this natural end, not the supplanting of the end itself. Denaturalization refers to the fact that the citizen is educated to be virtuous (rather than good) and to conceive of himself first and foremost as a citizen rather than as a man. He is taught to derive his sentiment of existence and his sense of self from his (unnatural) participation in a collective. The process of denaturalization, in fact, is precisely what enables him to approximate natural man's unity and balance. It establishes what amount to functional substitutes for natural things. Law, for example, is made to have the psychological force of natural necessity (*Emile* II:85). The result is a human being who, through unnatural means, achieves a natural or at least a nature-mimetic quality of soul. In this the citizen is far more in accord with nature than is his inwardly conflicted bourgeois counterpart, in whom nature is contradicted, not served, by the unnatural.

The fundamental polarity in Rousseau's prescriptive thought is therefore not the one between nature and society, which has so often been seen as such. Rather, it is the one between accordance with nature and contradiction with nature. Deeper than the chasm between natural man and citizen is the one that finds both of these men together on one side and the conflicted, excessively desirous person—the typical social man—on the other. For it is the latter polarity, not the former, that translates into the all-important opposition from a moral and psychological standpoint: the conflict between being well-souled, or living a good life, and not living well.

At this point, though, it would be helpful to make a terminological refinement. Quite obviously there are enormous differences between the natural man and the citizen, whatever their (negative) similarities. There is a reason, after all, that the distinction between the two has been so widely recognized. Readers of *Emile* are told emphatically from the earliest pages that no one can be both man and citizen and that the difference between the two is a matter of being educated according to nature versus being "denaturalized," which is Rousseau's own word (*dénaturer*) (I:39–40). Let us therefore apply the label

---

raises the following question: "How do we know that it doesn't have an infinity of other faculties which, to be developed, are awaiting only an appropriate organization or the return of freedom?" (*LM* 1097). Whether he raises this question in earnest or merely in order to underscore the limits of our understanding is impossible to know.

"natural" only to those whom Rousseau himself calls (or implicitly describes as) natural—that is, to the denizen of the state of nature, Emile, and the socially marginal Jean-Jacques of the *Dialogues* and *Reveries*.[19] And let us say of those who bear some resemblance to one of these three exemplars that they are, to the extent of this likeness, close to nature. (Here are included, for example, members of savage societies, free peasants, and those who lead more cultivated but retiring lives.)[20] As for the denatured citizen, though, rather than call him natural (he is not) or say that he lives in accordance with nature (a phrase that perhaps overstates the relationship), let us say that he lives—or that his soul is—in a kind of *correspondence* with nature. The citizen's soul is well ordered and as such, though not natural, corresponds to the order that existed, by nature, in primitive man's soul.[21]

In light of this new terminological distinction, let us modify what was said above and say instead that the crucial chasm in Rousseau's human landscape is between those who live in a way that is consistent with nature, or who maintain a positive relation with nature (whether it be a relation of identity, accordance, or correspondence), and those who do not but who, rather, live in contradiction with nature by virtue of their lack of psychic and moral integrity.[22] Confirmation that this is indeed the case, that this gulf is deeper by far than the one between nature and society, is found in the fact that the latter

19. Jean-Jacques as a man of nature also appears in the *Confessions*, though it is not until the latter parts of the book that he even partially succeeds at adopting a way of life that accords with the naturalness he has managed to preserve throughout the course of his checkered life. For two different interpretations of the *Confessions* as the story of a return to nature, see Christopher Kelly, *Rousseau's Exemplary Life: The Confessions as Political Philosophy* (Ithaca: Cornell University Press, 1987), and Ann Hartle, *The Modern Self in Rousseau's Confessions: A Reply to St. Augustine* (Notre Dame: University of Notre Dame Press, 1983).

20. Examples of the latter are the residents of Clarens in *Julie* and perhaps Madame de Warens at Annecy and Chambéry. An indication of the meaning and requirements of such a life is found in the *Lettres morales*, which can be read as an instruction manual for those who wish to achieve a closeness, if not a return, to nature.

21. As Patrick Riley writes, the general will, which is the leading principle in the citizen's soul, "echoes an orderly nature." See *The General Will Before Rousseau: The Transformation of the Divine into the Civic* (Princeton: Princeton University Press, 1986), 258. (Some scholars have gone so far as to suggest that, for Rousseau, citizenship is compatible with or even expressive of nature—a view that I do not share. Strong, for example, writes of Emile: "that which makes him human [read: natural] requires that he be a citizen." See *Politics of the Ordinary*, 138; see also 22–23, 65, 76. My reasons for rejecting this view are expressed throughout this book.)

22. The semantic distinctions used to designate the different relations to nature are inevitably arbitrary, but they are necessary. The following table illustrates some of the relations between the key terms used in this chapter, including terms that will be introduced in the sections yet to come. The capitalized words represent the five human types that constitute the range of basic possibilities in Rousseau's work; the five are defined by the relations to nature that they embody.

pair of contraries are not irreconcilable. That is to say, whereas a compromise between consistency with nature (psychic unity and balance) and contradiction with nature (the moral and psychic ills of the divided man) necessarily produces a corrupt result, as must any compromise between health and sickness or between probity and corruption, a reconciliation between nature and society can produce a good result, preserving the integrity of each element. One finds in Rousseau's work several instances of such successful reconciliation. Among these are the Golden Age of nascent society described in the *Second Discourse* and the idyllic life at Clarens in *Julie*, as well as passages in both *Emile* and the *Dialogues* in which Rousseau gives voice to his wish, as a natural man, for "the sweetness of true society."[23] One might even include as an example of a nature-society reconciliation Rousseau's contemporary Genevans, whose civic life seems to have been considerably more tempered by naturalness than was, say, that of the Spartans.

The reconcilability of nature and society does not contradict Rousseau's insistence upon the incompatibility of nature and citizenship. Apart from their single basic similarity (their shared psychic integrity, their positive relationship with nature), natural man and citizen are indeed cut from wholly different cloth: "one must choose between making a man or a citizen, for one cannot make both at the same time" (*Emile* I:39). Nature and citizenship are roads that do not meet. Nature and *society*, however, are not such utter contraries. The inhabitant of the pure state of nature was indeed asocial. So, too, though perhaps not so completely, is the "Solitary Walker" of the *Reveries*. But these are only two of Rousseau's three ideal natural types.[24] The third, the mature Emile,

---

Consistency with nature:
   —Correspondence with nature: the VIRTUOUS CITIZEN
   —Naturalness, or three "m[e]n of nature":
     —The INHABITANT OF THE PURE STATE OF NATURE, also known as the original natural man or the savage
     —EMILE, a "natural man living in the state of society" (III:205)
     —The JEAN-JACQUES of the *Reveries*, *Dialogues*, and latter parts of the *Confessions*
Contradiction with nature:
     —Those who lack psychic unity and balance: the TYPICAL SOCIAL MAN, the bourgeois, and those who are ambitious for vanity's sake

23. The natural man's love of "the sweetness of true society" is described at *Dialogues* III:225. Another statement of natural man's (Jean-Jacques's) sociability appears at II:165, where friendship is listed among Jean-Jacques's four requirements for happiness. See also II:118, where we are told that "absolute solitude is a state that is sad and contrary to nature."

24. As the preceding note indicates, the Jean-Jacques of the *Dialogues* is more sociable than the Jean-Jacques of the *Reveries*. Not that he has much of a social life, but he does miss one, whereas the Jean-Jacques of the *Reveries* has more happily reconciled himself to his solitude.

is social. "[A]lthough I want to form the man of nature, the object is not, for all that, to make him a savage and to relegate him to the depths of the woods" (IV:255). Hardly. Lover, friend, and benefactor, Emile is Rousseau's paradigmatic example of the reconcilability of nature and society. He is a wholesomely social man whose sociability is an integral part of his naturalness.

By considering two of its more important divisions and their relative depths we have made a start in mapping Rousseau's landscape of human possibilities. But if we wish to achieve a more comprehensive and even systematic understanding, we shall have to approach the terrain from a different perspective. The human terrain must be charted in human terms—that is, in terms of ideal human types (which are already abstract enough) rather than in the terms of disembodied philosophical principles.

Five Human Types, Three Natural Men, One Civilized Savage

Rousseau's corpus presents a cast of characters whose richness is matched only by Plato's and Nietzsche's in the annals of philosophical literature. Myriad personalities populate his works, exhibiting a panoramic range of dispositions and widely varying degrees of moral health. Yet for all its variety and respect for individuality, Rousseau's human landscape is defined by five basic types: first, the divided, corrupt social man, exemplified most commonly by the bourgeois but most perfectly (according to Rousseau) by the vain, malicious philosophes who conspired against Jean-Jacques;[25] second, the virtuous citizen of the ancient, austere polis; third, the inhabitant of the pure state of nature; fourth, the Jean-Jacques of the *Reveries* and selected other autobiographical depictions; and fifth, Emile.[26] These figures represent the fundamental alternatives

---

Many readers have failed to respect the distinction between sociability and citizenship. Thus they have read *Emile* as an attempt to reconcile nature and citizenship, not just nature and society. (See, for example, John Charvet, "Individual Identity and Social Consciousness in Rousseau's Philosophy," in *Hobbes and Rousseau*, ed. Cranston and Peters, 462–83. Strong makes a similar interpretation. See note 21 to this chapter.) True, Emile in the end will take part in a political community. But his soul is that of the civilized natural man and as such is worlds away from the soul of the true citizen. There is every reason to believe that Rousseau is in earnest when he insists upon the necessity to choose between raising a man and raising a citizen.

25. Christopher Kelly and Roger D. Masters observe that the conspirators are seen by Rousseau as "the victims of the most extreme departure from nature just as much as they are the vicious perpetrators of a crime against an innocent man." See their introduction to Rousseau's *Dialogues*, xxv.

26. The order in which I have listed these five types reflects only the order in which I treat them in the following discussion. It does not reflect any sort of rank order, except that the first is the lowest by any moral standard.

that are or have been available to humanity. They represent the set of basic responses to the question of how to live, for together they constitute the full range of basic responses to the most decisive substantive question facing men and women in Rousseau's view: namely, the question of one's relation to nature—whether, and if so, how, one lives in a manner consistent with nature. Consequently these exemplars serve as poles of moral and psychological orientation. Real men and women can be best understood and their lives most equitably judged according to their similarity to one or another of the five ideal types.

Of the five types, only the first, the social man who lacks both moral and psychological integrity, lives in contradiction with nature in the deepest sense. He alone (though, alas, "he" is the majority of humanity) does not live a good life. Divided in his soul between the conflicting demands of nature and society, he is neither natural nor wholesomely denatured, neither good nor virtuous, but instead vain, restless, and unhappy—and consequently short on "existence." Each of the remaining four types, by contrast, does represent a life consistent with nature's harmonious essence. Each is marked by a relatively high degree of psychic unity and balance. What distinguishes these four from one another are the different ways in which their consistency with nature is achieved and manifest.

The citizen, as we have already seen, achieves his consistency with nature through the paradoxical means of denaturalization. The centerpiece of his denaturalizing education is the transformation of his natural self-love into patriotism, which in its wholesome form is nothing other than extended and virtuous but unnatural *amour-propre*. (All *amour-propre* is unnatural in the pure sense, but what makes the citizen's unnatural even in a less strict sense is the extreme extent to which it supplants his natural individualism.) He is consistent with nature in the sense that he manifests an inner order and an outer benevolence (toward his fellow citizens if not to outsiders) that replicate on the human level the harmonious order of nature. Thus can Rousseau, the apostle of nature, admire the citizen, in whom nature seems to have been so decisively overcome.[27] But the citizen's replication of nature is after all a rather abstract and artificial one. It begins and ends with the merely formal fact of

---

27. The citizen does retain certain other natural characteristics, however, such as strong erotic and familial attachments. Indeed, his patriotism, the defining characteristic of his denaturalization, develops as an extension of familial love (*Emile* V:362–63). For more on the naturalness of the denaturalized citizen, see Joel Schwartz, *The Sexual Politics of Jean-Jacques Rousseau* (Chicago: University of Chicago Press, 1984), 47–61.

order. The *substance* of this order—his self-understanding and view of the world—has its basis in an artificial collective and so is itself artificial. It is for this reason that, however consistent it may be for him to admire the virtuous citizen as a human possibility, Rousseau never describes the citizen as natural. That label is reserved for others—for three others, to be exact.

Each of the three remaining exemplars—the savage, Jean-Jacques, and Emile—is explicitly described as a natural man.[28] The savage, or the inhabitant of the pure state of nature, is natural in the pure sense. With him there is no need to speak of accordance with nature or with some basic principle of nature. He is—or rather, was—simply natural, for his endowments, motivations, and behavioral repertoire owed nothing to history or his own doing. All was as it had originally been. He was a natural man because he was exactly as nature had made him. He was natural in the same pure sense that a tree or even a rock is natural. Certainly his freedom and perfectibility distinguished him from the rest of nature, from the tree and the rock, even conferring on him a unique dimension of spirituality.[29] But his possession of these attributes did not compromise his naturalness. Although they ultimately proved to be the gateway out of the state of nature, freedom and perfectibility were not— and are not—unnatural. However ambiguous their potential effects, freedom and perfectibility are themselves parts of nature just as surely as man's physical attributes, for they, as much as the latter, were present in the first man. They antedated history. And whatever else "nature" means in Rousseau's work, its primary meaning is origins.[30]

What else does "nature" mean in Rousseau's work? The question arises as we turn to our remaining two exemplars. For not only the savage but also Jean-Jacques and Emile are labeled "m[e]n of nature." How can this be so? As far distant as they are from the savage—and from one another, for that matter— how can these two figures, one a man of extraordinary imagination, the other sociable, and both richly endowed with sense and sensibility, be natural men? "There is a great difference between the natural man living in the state of nature and the natural man living in the state of society" (*Emile* III:205). That is apparent. What is not apparent, though, is why Jean-Jacques and Emile should be considered natural at all, *in any sense*. And why them but not the

---

28. See, for example, *SD* 95, *Emile* III:205, IV:255, and *Dialogues* II:107, 114, 158.

29. See *SD* 113–15.

30. Rousseau's equation of what he calls "nature" in the *Second Discourse* or what he calls "what is natural in the savage state" in *Emile* (V:406) with origins is apparent throughout both works. See especially the preface to the *Second Discourse*, in which "natural man" and "original man" are used interchangeably.

citizen (who does live in a certain accordance with nature)? Presumably Jean-Jacques and Emile share some crucial trait or traits with the savage. Rousseau's application of the same label to each of these three types tells us that he sees a defining commonality among the three "men of nature," a shared core that not only distinguishes them from the corrupt social man but also unites them in opposition to the well-souled citizen and constitutes their naturalness. An adequate understanding of Rousseau's nature will depend on our discerning this common core.

The common ground between the savage, Jean-Jacques, and Emile will not be found in their respective activities or inclinations, nor among their specific cognitive or emotional capacities. The most superficial examination reveals that great differences abound between them at these levels. For example, the savage is indolent, and so is Jean-Jacques, at least by his own account; but Emile is active and has a taste for the pleasures of mastery (of things, not men).[31] One finds similar disparities with regard to their respective capacities as thinkers: the savage is no more a *res cogitans* than are the beasts, who themselves possess a kind of brute prudence, whereas Emile and Jean-Jacques are quite capable reasoners, to say the least. Indeed, they are both scientists of sorts, the former in the service of his immediate interests, the latter for aesthetic pleasure (*Emile* III:167–72; *Confessions* XII:537; *Reveries* V:64–65). If we look at that most distinctively human mental capacity, imagination, we observe that the savage lacks it altogether, as does the young Emile. On the other hand, Jean-Jacques possesses extraordinary imaginative ability, and the mature Emile veritably lives off of the fruits of imagination, for imagination is a vital ingredient in the romantic love (and therefore a prerequisite for the conjugal love) that gives his life so much of its meaning. As for the passions, the same degree of difference seems to obtain. The savage is asocial and premoral, which means that all of his desires are exclusively physical, whereas both Jean-Jacques and Emile partake of a moral dimension in their passions and desires: they are respecters of persons as persons, which is to say that the judgments and feelings of others are included among the objects of their desires. However, if the realm of everyday passions does not encompass the common ground of the three natural men, it does at least point to it. For the common core, the common naturalness, uniting the three is located at the source of the passions, which is self-love.

---

31. "All men are naturally lazy" (*Dialogues* II:144). Yet Emile enjoys the mastery that comes from practical science and learning a trade.

The corrupt social man is motivated predominantly by an unwholesome *amour-propre*; the citizen, by an *amour-propre* that is wholesome, which is to say, virtuous. In neither of these cases does much *amour de soi* survive society's education. In the three so-called men of nature, by contrast, *amour de soi* does survive. And it is this, the survival of man's original self-love, that signifies naturalness amid the innumerable artifices and acquired faculties of civilization.

In the savage, *amour de soi* goes altogether untouched, for there is nothing— there is no society—to taint or transform it. With Jean-Jacques the story is more complicated. His is indeed a story of survival. He does develop *amour-propre*—at an early age—but for reasons unique to his own genius he is able to maintain his natural goodness, his *amour de soi*, and eventually to shuck or transcend (for the most part) the heart-constricting tentacles of *amour-propre*. He seems always to have felt, and to have felt the value of, his—man's—natural goodness. And, miraculously, he is able to put his outstanding intellect and imagination in the service of nature: first by discovering and articulating the principle of natural goodness, then in living according to the precepts he draws from it, and finally by telling the tale. The details of his story—how he manages to maintain his benign self-love and thereby remain a natural man in spite of *amour-propre* and other, even more conspicuously unnatural characteristics—is too large a subject to be taken up here, and in any event it has been thoughtfully addressed by others.[32]

Our concern, rather, is how Emile is able to maintain *his* naturalness—and for that matter, whether it is consistent and meaningful for Rousseau to call him natural at all. For if Jean-Jacques's naturalness is a complicated affair, Emile's is even more so. Although he is not the exceptional man that Jean-Jacques is—or perhaps *because* Emile is not exceptional by birth—it is even more difficult to understand his naturalness than Jean-Jacques's. Sociable and active, he has fewer apparent affinities with the savage than does the solitary, indolent *promeneur*. To the question, Why is Jean-Jacques able to maintain his naturalness, his *amour de soi*, in the face of society and his own *amour-propre*?, we may answer: Because he has an extraordinary genius. How, though, does Emile, with his ordinary endowments, maintain *his* naturalness, his *amour de soi*, in the face of society and his own *amour-propre*? A complete answer to this question requires an explanation of what it means to be a "natural man living in the state of society," an explanation that will occupy the remainder of this book.

32. See especially Kelly, *Rousseau's Exemplary Life*; Hartle, *The Modern Self*; and Schwartz, *Sexual Politics*, 98–102.

But before we move on to the question of Emile's naturalness we still need to determine the more general and basic meaning of naturalness in human life. Why does Rousseau consider the survival of *amour de soi* sufficient grounds for being a "man of nature" even when that man has a host of acquired characteristics? Why does that one natural trait outweigh all the unnatural ones? To be sure, *amour de soi* alone does not make a man natural in the pure sense; only the inhabitant of the pure state of nature qualifies for that distinction. But it *is* enough to merit the designation of naturalness in a looser sense. Before examining the particulars of Emile's naturalness, we must determine as best we can why Rousseau would choose to confer the label of naturalness upon anything less than the purely natural origins of the species—why, that is, he allows for such a thing as "the natural man living in the state of society" or for any such creature as "a savage made to inhabit cities" (*Emile* III:205).

Rousseau's assignment of the "man of nature" label to those in whom *amour de soi* has survived, to those who are not dominated by *amour-propre*, is, in the first place, a reflection of the supreme importance he attaches to the question of self-love.[33] That question is one of "which" or "what kind," not "whether." Every human being, from the most evil to the most benevolent, is fundamentally shaped and motivated by one kind of self-love or another. Every desire and passion derives from it. "The source of our passions, the origin and the principle of all the others, the only one born with man and which never leaves him so long as he lives is love of self [*amour de soi*]—a primitive, innate passion, which is anterior to every other, and of which all others are in a sense only modifications" (*Emile* IV:212–13). Every feeling—and therefore every other part of the psychic economy—comes from this same wellspring. Even compassion and public-spiritedness have their sources in self-love: the former is a natural outgrowth of *amour de soi*, the latter is an expression of well- and civically educated *amour-propre* (*Emile* IV:235n, *Dialogues* II:158; *Emile* IV:252).[34]

Originally, all self-love was *amour de soi*. That is why Rousseau refers to it (in the passage quoted above) as the origin and principle of all our other passions. But if *amour de soi* is the wellspring, history (including our own personal history, which after all reflects the history of the species) has opened a great distance between ourselves and that source, subjecting the rivers of passion to

---

33. The term "self-love" is used here to represent the generic category that includes both *amour de soi* and *amour-propre*. To avoid confusion, and because there is no adequate English equivalent of *amour-propre*, these terms will always be rendered in French.

34. The respective roles of *amour de soi* and *amour-propre* in producing compassion and public-spiritedness are addressed in Chapters 3 and 4.

tortuous geography and mixing into them the waters of foreign tributaries. The source of the passions "is natural, it is true. But countless alien streams have swollen it. It is a great river which constantly grows and in which one could hardly find a few drops of its first waters" (*Emile* IV:212). That is to say, self-love is the source of all the passions, but self-love is no longer what it was in the state of nature. It is no longer only one thing. Nor is it even the same thing in all civilized human beings. In most it has become an admixture of *amour de soi* and *amour-propre*, with the latter in the dominant—indeed, in a tyrannical —position (*Dialogues* II:144, 154). It is they to whom Rousseau is referring in the quoted lines. It is they in whom impure alien streams (*amour-propre* in its base, egoistic form) have overwhelmed original, natural self-love. But even the self-love of post-state-of-nature natural men, of those from whom *amour-propre* is absent or in whom its rule is sharply limited, has undergone great modification. The *amour de soi* of Jean-Jacques and Emile is not the same as their natural predecessor's. It has been changed—not polluted by alien streams but deepened and enriched by the acquisition of new faculties and sensibilities.

No question is more important for humanity than the question of self-love. Whether and to what extent one is motivated by *amour de soi* or *amour-propre* and how *amour-propre* is educated—these are the factors that determine how one experiences one's existence and how one conducts oneself. Self-love shapes our passive experience of the world because it determines our conception of our interests, and it is interest, personal or otherwise, that governs our attention. Self-love shapes our activity because it is "the source of our passions [and] the origin and principle of all the others," and it is the passions that motivate human activity.[35] Self-love determines who and what we are, for it is the fountainhead of all our sentiments, and for Rousseau it is sentiment that constitutes the substance of our identity. As the source and principle of all sentiment, self-love is *the* decisive ingredient in the psychic economy and, consequently, the thing most consequential for the moral and political realms.

Given this momentous significance, we should not be surprised that Rousseau accords to self-love such singular philosophical status—that he makes it the sole consideration in determining whether one deserves to be designated a "man of nature." Despite their numerous unnatural acquisitions, both Emile and Jean-Jacques are called natural because they join the savage in

---

35. "Each age has its own springs that make it move, but man is always the same. At ten he is led by cakes, at twenty by a mistress, at thirty by the pleasures, at forty by ambition, at fifty by avarice" (*Emile* V:431). Emile, too, is led by passions. The goal of his education is to shape him to be led by wholesome and sublime passions. See "*Amour-Propre's* Influence on Character and Behavior," in Chapter 4, for a more detailed exposition of self-love's influence on character and behavior.

being motivated (predominantly) by *amour de soi* rather than *amour-propre*. Their possession of this one natural characteristic—even though it is present in a rather attenuated form—outweighs all their accumulated unnaturalness. Of course that one natural characteristic, *amour de soi*, is not really one at all. It is manifold in its productions and effects, analogous in its influence on the individual to the influence, as seen by a later observer, of a people's social condition on its everyday life: it "creates opinions, gives birth to feelings, suggests customs, and modifies whatever it does not create."[36]

For all their obvious differences, their shared freedom from *amour-propre*'s dominion makes the three men of nature alike in the most decisive respects. Each "lives [predominantly] within himself" (*SD* 179), enslaved neither to opinion nor to agitated, unfulfillable desire and able, therefore, to enjoy as much of the sweetness of existence as his capacities and the world around him permit. Those who live under the dominion of *amour-propre,* by contrast—or rather, those who live under its *tyrannical* dominion (a qualification that exempts the denatured but virtuous citizen)—lack precisely these two freedoms. They are slaves both to opinion and to excessive, inherently unfulfillable desire. Therein lies the immediate source of their unnaturalness, therein lies what keeps them from being natural even in the loose, or civil, sense. The general or more remote cause of their departure from nature is *amour-propre*. But the immediate source of unnaturalness is enslavement to opinion and rampant desire, for this dual enslavement is what actually separates them from nature. It does this in two respects: it distorts their perception of the world, causing them to mistake appearance for reality and prejudice for truth; and it disrupts their psychic equilibrium, the balance between faculties and desires, by subjecting them to desires whose objects are as innumerable as they are illusory. It places them in Plato's cave and, what's more, sets them chasing after the shadows.

This contrast with their unfree cousins helps clarify just what is natural about Jean-Jacques and Emile and why Rousseau accords each the designation "man of nature" solely for their being governed by *amour de soi* rather than *amour-propre*. They are natural because and precisely to the extent that they resist enslavement to opinion and desire. As *amour-propre* is the general cause of unnaturalness among the corrupt, *amour de soi* is the general guardian of naturalness among the natural. As enslavement to opinion and desire is the immediate source of the former's unnaturalness, freedom from the tyranny of opinion and desire is the fence immediately protecting the naturalness of the

---

36. That later observer, Alexis de Tocqueville, was himself a serious student of Rousseau. De Tocqueville, *Democracy in America*, trans. George Lawrence, ed. J. P. Mayer (Garden City, N.Y.: Anchor Books, 1969), 9.

latter.[37] Through this dual freedom, *amour de soi* preserves naturalness just where *amour-propre* destroys it. Rather than distort perception, *amour de soi* preserves clear sight of reality, permitting an unbiased even if incomplete apprehension of nature; and rather than disrupt psychic equilibrium, *amour de soi* preserves the relative equality of faculties and desires, the primary human instance of the harmony that is nature's hallmark and the very substance of its goodness. Neither Jean-Jacques nor Emile is a cave dweller, and as for their natural predecessor, while he may at times have taken refuge in a cave, he was never shackled there and so was never long kept from the light of the sun.

"What Is Natural in the Savage State" and "What Is Natural in the Civil State"

Rousseau's principle of natural goodness is usually interpreted, correctly, as a statement about man. It is also, however, a statement about nature. Beyond establishing the naturalness of goodness (its statement about man), it also establishes the goodness of the natural: everything natural is good. "Everything is good as it leaves the hands of the Author of things; everything degenerates in the hands of man" (*Emile* I:37). But what does goodness mean when applied to the universe of nonmoral things, to that portion of "everything" that is not made up of civilized human beings (civilized humans being the only morally endowed pieces of creation)? In fact, it means the same thing in that context as it does when applied to man, for even when ascribed to man, goodness is not a moral concept (virtue, not goodness, is the moral concept, for goodness is negative and refers to inclination rather than will). Goodness can be ascribed to nothing *but* the universe of nonmoral things, and what it means, simply, is harmonious order.[38] The original natural man, the inhabitant

37. In Emile, this freedom is the result of the successful development of virtue; he achieves what Rousseau elsewhere calls "moral freedom, which alone makes man truly the master of himself" (SC I-vii:56). See *Emile* V:442–46: "Up to now you were only apparently free. You had only the precarious freedom of a slave to whom nothing has been commanded. Now be really free. Learn to become your own master" (445). In Jean-Jacques, however, there is little virtue and hence just as little moral freedom. His freedom from opinion and desire is a matter not of self-mastery but of the immunity that comes with an absence of *amour-propre*. His freedom is an extended natural freedom rather than moral freedom.

38. That the natural goodness of man is not a moral attribute has been widely recognized in recent scholarship. (For Rousseau's basic description of natural man's goodness, see SD 128–31.) Less widely noted, however, is that the meaning of this goodness is order. For an illuminating discussion of the meaning of nature's goodness, see John T. Scott, "The Theodicy of the *Second Discourse*: The

of the state of nature, was good both for himself and for others. He was well ordered both as a whole in himself and as a part of the larger whole. His faculties were equal to his desires, and he did not interfere with the greater natural order surrounding him, including the internal order of his fellows. As a well-ordered being he was able to enjoy the sweetness of existence and had no reason to keep others from the same.

But it is not only the original natural man who is good, or ordered. That description fits everything and everyone that is natural, including "the natural man living in the state of society." To the extent that he is natural, the natural man living in society must have preserved or re-created the goodness, the order, of his vastly simpler forebear. He too is well ordered, both in himself and as part of the larger whole. Clearly, though, the naturalness—the harmoniousness—of the civilized natural man differs considerably from that of the original natural man, if only because there is so much *more* in him to be harmonized. The harmony of the original natural man came secure and ready-made from "the hands of the Author of things," whereas that of the civilized natural man is threatened at every turn by new acquisitions and confrontations. In the education of a civilized natural man, there is so much to be balanced, so much to be delayed, so much to be shielded from. Even under the friendliest imaginable circumstances, the task of maintaining naturalness is difficult beyond any realistic hope of complete success, for the real dangers—and the source of the less-than-friendly circumstances that prevail in the world—lie within: the chief threats to naturalness arise from the inherently ambiguous potentials embedded in the mental and emotional faculties that are (and must be) present in any civilized adult.

The difficulty of maintaining naturalness is perhaps most effectively conveyed by a passage in the *Dialogues* in which Rousseau performs a utopian exercise (I:9–13). "Picture an ideal world similar to ours, yet altogether different." What is it that makes this world ideal; how is it "altogether different" from ours? The difference, it turns out, is not primarily one of social circumstances. Rather, people in the ideal world are able to maintain their naturalness—they remain good—only because nature acts upon them more powerfully than it does upon us, in the real world.

> Nature is the same there as on our earth, but its economy is more easily felt, its order more marked, its aspect more admirable. Forms are

'Pure State of Nature' and Rousseau's Political Thought," *American Political Science Review* 86 (September 1992): 696–711.

more elegant, colors more vivid, odors sweeter, all objects more interesting. All nature is so beautiful there that its contemplation, inflam-
ing souls with love for such a touching tableau, inspires in them both
the desire to contribute to this beautiful system and the fear of troubling its harmony; and from this comes an exquisite sensitivity which
gives those endowed with it immediate enjoyment unknown to hearts
that the same contemplations have not aroused....

The inhabitants of the ideal world I am talking about have the good
fortune to be maintained by nature, to which they are more attached,
in that happy perspective in which nature placed us all, and because of
this alone their soul forever maintains its original character. (I:9)

It seems that for men and women to be natural would require even more than
a perfect alignment of circumstances. Nature itself would have to change, at
least in the degree to which it reveals its order to humanity. Only then, with
its edifying harmony more pronounced than it is in our world, would people
succeed in keeping to what Rousseau elsewhere calls "the road of nature"
(which, incidentally, he also calls "the road of happiness") (*Emile* V:443).

Aside from this implicit point about the difficulty of maintaining one's natural goodness, the passage raises another issue of even more pressing relevance
to this stage of our inquiry. The inhabitants of the ideal world, says Rousseau,
maintain their "original character"—or rather, "their *soul* maintains its original character." What this means—at least in part, as he goes on to explain—
is that these utopian beings are creatures of *amour de soi* rather than *amour-
propre* and that they therefore have all the wholesome characteristics that follow from that good form of self-love. But the breadth of the phrase "original
character" suggests that we should pursue the matter further and ask whether
there is anything else, anything besides *amour de soi*, that might be included
among the features of the "original character" that are maintained. To put it
more crisply, what is the relation between original naturalness and naturalness
amid civilization? Does the latter have any further connection, any more intimate connection, with the former than their shared goodness or, which is
the same thing, the survival of *amour de soi* and the attendant freedom from
opinion and desire? In fact, there is a critical substantive relation between the
two kinds of naturalness, a relation that entails more than just a shared set of
characteristics.

"One must not confound what is natural in the savage state with what is
natural in the civil state," Rousseau cautions (Emile V:406). But neither must
one overstate the difference. Not only does civilized naturalness share the

goodness, the harmoniousness, of savage naturalness, civilized naturalness is *informed* by its savage predecessor—not completely, to be sure (conscience, a key element of civilized naturalness, was not present in savage naturalness), but in considerable part. And the reason for this is that all the positive characteristics of the original man are present as well in modern man. The inhabitant of the state of nature was a very limited being. We who are civilized possess an enormous additional quantity of characteristics, but these additions are just that, and they overlay rather than supplant the features that the original man possessed. We are all born into the state of nature—"L'homme *est* né libre" (Man was/*is* born free) (SC I-1:46)—even if we begin to depart from it almost immediately. One might say that "the natural man living in the state of society" has within himself, like a homunculus, "the natural man living in the state of nature." The harmony (the goodness) that characterizes the civilized natural man must therefore necessarily be a harmony between and among the original and the acquired. The goal of a natural education is to bring one's acquired characteristics into a concordant relationship with the original ones. It is by virtue of this concordance that those acquired characteristics, which by definition are unnatural in the pure sense, become natural nevertheless, in the civil sense.

The concordance between the acquired and the original is a matter of the former fitting itself to the latter, not the other way around. The acquired must be made continuous with, or at least not subversive of, the original. The original is nature in the pure sense, which is to say nature in its *primary* sense, not only historically but also conceptually. Emile could not have been imagined had the original natural man not been discovered. (It is not for nothing that Rousseau calls Emile "a savage made to inhabit cities" [III:205].) Naturalness in the civil state would be a meaningless concept without reference to naturalness in the savage state. If Rousseau seems to alternate casually between the two usages of "nature," that is because they are so intricately related, and because Emile's civilized naturalness can neither be conveyed nor comprehended without reference to nature in its pure sense.

It is instructive that, in a massive book about the education of a natural man, Rousseau never speaks in terms of actualizing or realizing nature. Instead, his vocabulary is one of cooperation or teamwork, as when he describes his task as Emile's tutor: "We work in *collaboration* with nature, and while it forms the physical man, we try to form the moral man" (IV:314; emphasis added). This statement of educational principle testifies to the relationship between the two meanings of "nature" in his work. The nature that is explicitly spoken of here is the "nature" of the *Second Discourse*. This is nature in the pure sense, understood as the realm of origins—the nature that does not encompass man's moral being. And yet it is only with reference to *this* nature—it is only by "collaborating" with it—that we can determine or even conceive of nature in its other, civil, sense. What makes Emile a natural man is that his formation by his tutor as a moral man accords with his formation by nature as a physical man. His acquired characteristics extend and deepen his "original dispositions" (I:39). This, and only this, is what it means to be "natural in the civil state."

The first stages of our inquiry into the meaning of nature in Rousseau's work have consisted largely in recognizing and drawing distinctions: between that which is consistent with nature and that which is not; between those who are "men of nature" and those who are not; between man and citizen; between *amour de soi* and *amour-propre*; between "the natural man living in the state of nature," or "what is natural in the savage state," on the one hand, and "the natural man living in the state of society," or "what is natural in the civil state," on the other. But a full grasp of the outlines of Rousseau's understanding requires that we recognize a certain *unity*, a unity that is revealed in the intimate relationship between civilized naturalness and its savage forebear, and a unity that justifies the ascription of the label "natural" to both the savage and Emile. Although it is true that what is natural in one epoch may not have been so in an earlier one, the basic principles of naturalness are constant. Nature's two aspects (of which Rousseau's two usages are expressions) are aspects of a single, coherent whole.

In *Emile*, Rousseau several times points out the distinction between the two kinds of naturalness. But in the one passage in which he formally sets out to define "nature," he makes no such distinction. There are no multiple meanings. Instead, there is a single, philosophically coherent definition that implicitly allows for a multiplicity of versions (one each for a multiplicity of epochs) and that also, again implicitly, illustrates the relationship between the two kinds of naturalness:

> We are born with the use of our senses, and from our birth we are affected in various ways by the objects surrounding us. As soon as we have, so to speak, consciousness of our sensations, we are disposed to seek or avoid the objects which produce them, at first according to whether they are pleasant or unpleasant to us, then according to the conformity or lack of it that we find between us and these objects, and finally according to the judgments we make about them on the basis of the idea of happiness or of perfection given us by reason. These

dispositions are extended and strengthened as we become more capable of using our senses and more enlightened; but constrained by our habits, they are more or less corrupted by our opinions. Before this corruption they are what I call in us *nature*. (I:39; emphasis in original)

What is nature in man? It is his "original dispositions" (*dispositions primitives*), a phrase Rousseau employs in the very next line to describe what he has just defined. But what "original" means, as the quoted passage indicates, is more than just what was present at birth, and more even than what was present in the adult in the state of nature. The dispositions that Rousseau here calls "nature" are at least in part the products of reason. Our judgment, our senses, our enlightenment can contribute to and be a part of nature.[39] But these acquired faculties can contribute to naturalness only to the extent that they extend and strengthen, rather than corrupt, the native dispositions. And this—the requirement that these faculties collaborate with what is native—is a straightforward expression of the relation between what is natural in the civil state and what is natural in the savage state. Whatever in us that is not purely natural but that strengthens or extends what *is* purely natural, is, by virtue of this amplification, natural in the civil sense. And whoever lives according to dispositions that are extended and strengthened versions of the savage's dispositions is, to that extent, a natural man or woman living in the state of society.

We began our inquiry into Rousseau's "nature" by taking note of a paradox. Nature serves as a standard and goal in Rousseau's moral thought even though, at least in its primary sense, it does not encompass the moral realm. Rousseau seems to seek human guidance from a nonhuman source. That paradox has now been resolved, and if a certain tension still remains, that is perhaps less a reflection of Rousseau's philosophizing than of the subject of his philosophy. Nature's first meaning is indeed incapable of providing human guidance, but nature has a fuller meaning that does provide guidance even while taking its bearings from the nonhuman first meaning. But this guidance is neither easy to attain nor easy to follow. It is not a simple thing to extend and strengthen one's natural dispositions or even to know how to try to do so. Once one has left the state of nature for the civil state, nature ceases to speak very clearly— or, which is much the same thing in its effect, one ceases to hear its voice very distinctly. And so we are told, for example, to "[d]istrust instinct as soon as you

39. See also *Dialogues* III:214: The "man of nature ... behaves uniquely according to his inclinations *and his reason*." (emphasis added)

no longer limit yourself to it. It is good as long as it acts by itself; it is suspect from the moment it operates within man-made institutions. It must not be destroyed, but it must be regulated, and that is perhaps more difficult than annihilating it" (*Emile* IV:333–34). Indeed, things have reached such a pass that the preservation of naturalness amid civilization requires extensive and, if we may judge from Jean-Jacques's performance as Emile's tutor, ingenious artifice. "One must use a great deal of art to prevent social man from being totally artificial" (IV:317).

It is one thing to recognize that what is natural in the civil state is so because of its relation to what is natural in the savage state—that it takes its bearings from the lodestar of pure nature. It is quite another thing to recognize and keep sight of that lodestar amid the crowded firmament that society places before our eyes. How Rousseau does this—how he purports to deduce what is natural for us from what was natural for our nonhuman forebears—is the subject we must turn to next.

3

Nature and Human Nature, Part II
Emile, or the Naturalization of Second Nature

Whatever promotes or preserves *amour de soi*—whatever strengthens or extends it, whether directly (through the harmonious cultivation of higher faculties) or indirectly (through the limitation of *amour-propre*)—is natural in the civil state. Such is the formula that underlies *Emile* and every other exposition of civilized naturalness that appears in Rousseau's work.[1] To establish this was one of the chief purposes of the preceding chapter. But what *does* promote or preserve *amour de soi*? Or, to put the question in those terms of Rousseau that we just encountered, what would extend and strengthen our "original dispositions"? What is wanted is the substance with which to fill out the formula.

1. Civilized naturalness is treated most thoroughly in *Emile*, but it is also treated in the *Lettres morales*, in the idyllic portions of *Julie*, and (with some obvious qualifications) in the depiction of Rousseau's "ideal world" in the *Dialogues* (I:9–12).

That substance is available to us in the person of Emile. Rousseau's bildungsroman is many things—educational treatise, philosophical proof of natural goodness, political commentary, romance—but everything else that it is, is subsidiary to its being Rousseau's answer to the question of how to promote and preserve *amour de soi* in a civilized man. (That it has been seen by some as a loosely organized compendium of stories and observations surely stems from a failure to appreciate the unifying centrality of this theme.)[2] Little if anything about *Emile* is superfluous from this point of view—least of all its novelistic structure.

The novelistic form best suits the great emphasis Rousseau places on moral-psychological development as opposed to right decision making in his moral thought. Man is a creature of passion, and his passions, as we have already seen, are ultimately informed by the quality of his self-love: not only the objects of the passions but, more important, their strength vis-à-vis his will is determined by the extent to which *amour de soi* has mutated into *amour-propre* and by the specific character of that *amour-propre*. And this, the question of self-love, is predominantly a developmental matter, a matter ordinarily settled in the years of childhood and youth. Without right development there is little hope of either good or virtuous behavior later in life. *With* right development, by contrast, there is every possibility that the end product, be he man or citizen, will behave well. Hence the bildungsroman *Emile* rather than a more conventional ethical treatise. (Even where he counsels people in whom he does not presuppose a very happy development, Rousseau still aims his reformatory efforts at developing the heart rather than at convincing the mind. The goal in such cases, as evident in the *Lettres morales*, for example, is to nurture the overwhelmed but natural, and therefore not quite atrophied, gentle and sociable passions—that is, to accomplish in the present at least some of the moral-psychological development that should have occurred before.)

Indeed, the novelistic form not only emphasizes development, it allows for a step-by-step *depiction* of development, and such a depiction is the only way the meaning of civilized naturalness can be accurately conveyed. As we saw in the preceding chapter, there is no conceiving of civilized naturalness without reference to original or savage naturalness. Besides approximating the savage's psychic unity and balance, the natural man in the state of society also retains

---

2. The failure to appreciate the coherence of *Emile* is a particular instance of the larger failure to appreciate the coherence of Rousseau's thought in general. For a survey of interpretations that explicitly claim that Rousseau's thought is self-contradictory or otherwise incoherent (and there are many more interpretations in which the claim is made implicitly), see Gay, introduction to *The Question of Jean-Jacques Rousseau*, 3–17.

within himself the savage's positive characteristics. The savage remains, as it were, within his more complex successor, much as—or rather, *exactly* as— the child and youth remain within the man. Civilized naturalness (which is sociable) grows upon, if not out of, savage naturalness (which is not sociable). Any real understanding of civilized naturalness must therefore be developmental in its approach. Thus, a proper account of Rousseau's conception of what is natural in the civil state needs to be told as a story. Hence, again, the bildungsroman *Emile* rather than a more conventional, static account. The novelistic form was not absolutely required, of course, but the only other alternative would have been something like the kind of developmental psychology texts that have appeared from within the modern academy. Such an alternative would have been less worthy of Rousseau's literary artistry and less successful than *Emile* at conveying what is surely the most extraordinary and compelling teaching of the book: namely, the irreducible sublimity of the civilized savage's soul. (With this last point we have identified another purpose served by the novelistic form.)

The novelistic form, then, permits Rousseau to give a full account of "the natural man in the state of society." *Emile*'s narrative reflects the primacy of developmental considerations in Rousseau's moral thought and articulates how civilized naturalness evolves out of its savage forerunner, while the book's poetry conveys what it is that is good about this human possibility in the first place. In performing these functions, the novelistic form highlights the distinctive character of Rousseau's understanding of nature—its peculiar blend of "high" and "low," or "moral" and "physical"—which distinguishes it from both ancient and modern perspectives even while evincing affinities to both.

Between Aristotle and Hobbes, Between Plato and Freud: A Word on Rousseau's Distinctiveness

Thus far in this inquiry we have not been much concerned with Rousseau's place in intellectual history. Our focus has been more narrow, with the aim of isolating, through a kind of resolutive analysis, the core meaning of nature insofar as the concept applies to human beings. Now, however, as we prepare to work our way back out from the core—as we prepare to articulate the substance of civilized naturalness by exploring how it develops out of or upon savage naturalness—it would be useful to look at Rousseau against the backdrop of the philosophical traditions with which he contended and which would later contend with him. Approaching such questions as whether and in what sense various "higher" capacities are natural and in what sense they are related to "lower" ones (these "lower" capacities constituting the sum of naturalness in its primary sense), we are inevitably reminded of the changeful history of the concept of nature, and in particular the great rupture between ancient and modern understandings. Where does Rousseau stand amid the major currents of this history?

As many have observed and as we shall presently see, Rousseau's understanding of nature and the human good in some ways stands between the leading classical and (early) modern understandings. Standing between them does not make it a mere hybrid, however. To the contrary, Rousseau propounds a startlingly original understanding of the natural. Although he does have certain pronounced affinities with the ancients, and though his understanding of nature in its pure sense is decidedly modern, his visions both of (natural) human possibilities and of the means to actualize them are quite distinctive. And yet there is no better way to illustrate that originality than to look at his thought against the background of those other positions. Because he was so steeped in the work of ancient and modern philosophers, because he did share a great deal of their respective impulses and assumptions (not to mention their vocabulary), and because today's readers are tempted to read into Rousseau the thought of later thinkers, the surest way to approach Rousseau on his own terms is by way of those positions (even including one view that was formulated long after his death) with which his thought shares some similarities but from which it is ultimately and decisively distinct.

Students of political philosophy have devoted much attention to the intellectual revolution of the sixteenth and seventeenth centuries, a revolution that began (ostensibly) with a narrowly scientific methodological discovery but that soon transformed not only our way of looking at certain things but our way of seeing everything, including man. The astounding success of the newly discovered scientific method at unlocking the secrets of nonhuman nature (or what Rousseau would later call the "physical" realm) gave rise to the hope— and the hope to a tendency—to see all problems as amenable to the explanatory and hence also to the ameliorative power of the new natural science. What this tendency inevitably entailed (and herein lies the philosophical revolution) was nothing less than the reinterpretation of the world. If problems were going to be solved by the methods of physical science, they would need to be reduced to physical terms, that is, to matter in motion. And so they were. Modernity would witness the launching of ambitious enterprises whose aim was to achieve in the social and political realms what Copernicus, Galileo, and Newton had achieved or were achieving in the nonhuman realm. (The most comprehensive and influential of these efforts was doubtless Hobbes's.) Society would join nature in being scientifically understood and, by grace of this, would be subject for the first time to effective, rational management. The mastery of nature would include the mastery of human nature. The Great Instauration would be complete.[3]

To be sure, not everyone was won over to materialism or protomaterialism. Spirituality, or freedom of the will, continued to be passionately maintained as a serious philosophical doctrine, and not just among the ecclesiastical ancien régime. Yet in one important respect, the scientific revolution of early modernity did produce a nearly universal change in the intellectual landscape: "nature" was newly conceived, by nearly all philosophical parties, as a world of mathematized objects that could in principle always be explained by the deterministic laws of the physical sciences. Nothing in nature, according to this new view, is impenetrable to the dissecting eye of modern science. Whatever will not yield its secrets to natural (writ: physical) science—whatever is not reducible in principle to matter in motion—is simply not a part of nature.

Materialists and corporealists, of course, did not concede that any supranatural realm existed—at least not in any sense that would be meaningful to man. For them nature included everything; nothing exists in this world whose behavior is not in principle explainable by the deterministic laws of natural science. But even those who did not accept materialism accepted the new mechanistic conception of nature. That which eludes the explanatory power of mechanistic science—namely, human and/or divine will—was seen as existing apart from nature. Thus, while the two camps disagreed about the reality of nonmechanistic phenomena, they did not disagree about the meaning of "nature." Nor, one might add, did they disagree about nature's supposed silence on moral matters. Understood as the realm of objective necessity, nature can tell us much about how things are but nothing about what they, or we, ought to be; that kind of knowledge (or belief) would have to come from some other source. The terms of the debate were remarkably widely accepted by the time Rousseau's century dawned. What was at issue was "only" the scope of the natural realm, not its defining characteristics.[4]

3. The phrase, coined by Francis Bacon, refers to the method by which man might use science to gain mastery over nature. (See his preface to *Magna Instauratio*.) Whether or not Bacon envisioned scientific mastery of *human* nature, others certainly did; and in so doing they effectively expanded the compass of the ideal propounded by Bacon.

4. The terms of this debate have not been successfully challenged in subsequent generations:

This redefinition of nature marked a momentous break with the dominant philosophical tradition of the preceding centuries. To be sure, there had been strands of thought both in classical antiquity and in the Christian Middle Ages that can fairly be seen as having anticipated or in some way prepared the ground for the modern conception of nature. Greek thought especially had seen tremendous variety on all important questions. And for all the ecclesiastically enforced orthodoxy of the Middle Ages, there was still significant diversity among late medieval thinkers on questions as fundamental as the nature and scope of divine will.[5] Nevertheless, during the many centuries preceding the scientific revolution, one understanding of nature, and man's relation to nature, *was* dominant, and that view was something very different from what Galileo, Bacon, and Descartes successfully promulgated as a superior replacement.

This old way of understanding nature, like so much else in the prevailing philosophical thought of the late Middle Ages, derived from an outlook that might best be described as Christianized Aristotelianism. Nature, according to this view, both includes human beings and is teleological. Because of this combination, nature was seen as a legitimate (apart from Scripture, the *only* legitimate) source of moral guidance. Far from mastery, what was desired was a life lived in accordance with nature, with "accordance" understood as the realization of the universal, natural human potential for one or another form of a life of logos.[6] Certainly one did not question the naturalness of the highest human capacities. Under the modern regime, the higher capacities would be either reduced to yet-to-be understood manifestations of matter and motion or interpreted as nonnatural phenomena. Prior to the modern reconceptualization, though, reason and freedom were considered natural not only because they are innate capacities but also, and especially, because they are the instruments most necessary for the realization of the natural human potential. For Aristotle and his followers, we might say, the higher capacities were natural precisely because they *are* higher.

What was at issue in the seventeenth century has continued to be at issue, and what was no longer at issue—the nature of nature, so to speak—has largely remained thus. (It remains to be seen whether today's postmodernists or champions of premodern traditions will succeed in overturning this most characteristic feature of modern thought.) For a brief but incisive summary of the matter, see Leon Kass, *The Hungry Soul: Eating and the Perfecting of Our Nature* (New York: Free Press, 1994), 3–9.

    5. The rift between nominalism and scholasticism is perhaps the preeminent example of theological pluralism.

    6. "Logos," whether understood in its classical sense (as reason) or its Christian sense (as the Word), was expressive of a natural moral order.

Where, on this philosophical battleground, is Rousseau? We seem to find him on both sides of the divide. Rousseau in part accepts and even radicalizes the modern truncation of nature while nevertheless maintaining the naturalness of what he understands to be the highest human capacities. He both extends and repudiates the modern tendency. He extends it by denying the naturalness of anything that did not exist in the pure state of nature. Man in the pure state of nature—for which we may substitute, "man by nature"—is prerational and premoral. Nature has been pared down to exclude everything that most of us recognize as distinctively human. Yet Rousseau also repudiates this very tendency to truncate nature by presenting the superlatively human Emile and Jean-Jacques as exemplars of naturalness. In this he seems to be holding with the premoderns' more inclusive and less mechanistic conception of nature. He is able to move in these two directions simultaneously because he holds a conception of nature that embraces two parts: what is natural in the savage state and what is natural in the civil state. And he is able to do this successfully because, as we shall see, the two parts fit together coherently. Indeed, the genius of Rousseau's view lies precisely in its integration of these two parts—or, to put it another way, in its articulation of how the high evolves out of the low without being reducible to it.

A geometric analogy might be the best means of representing Rousseau's apparent midway position between the Aristotelian and early modern (Baconian, Cartesian, Hobbesian) conceptions of nature.[7] Aristotelian nature can be aptly represented as a pyramid or an equilateral triangle whose peak stands for the higher human faculties, the proper use of man's higher faculties being nature's highest expression (see the diagram).[8] The modern conception of nature, accordingly, would be most accurately pictured as a truncated pyramid, or trapezoid. What for Aristotle was the peak of nature was now denied natural status; spirituality, if its existence was conceded at all, was removed to the *super*natural realm. Keeping with this scheme, we might represent Rousseau's more complicated conception of nature as a trapezoid that is even more squat or truncated than that of the early moderns but upon which rests a triangle drawn in broken lines, a triangle that, combined with the trapezoid, constitutes a pyramid after all. The solid lines encompass that which is natural in the

---

7. The geometric analogy that follows is intended as a heuristic tool, not an exact representation: "if I momentarily borrow the vocabulary of geometry in order to express myself in fewer words, I am nevertheless not unaware that geometric precision does not exist in moral quantities" (SC III:1–80).

8. Nature's highest production is the well-formed human being: "man is the best of the animals when completed." Aristotle, *Politics* 1253a31.

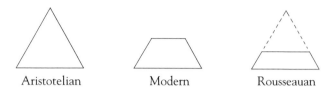

savage state; the broken lines, that which is natural in the civil state. That the latter should be represented by broken lines is appropriate for at least two reasons. First, that which is natural in the civil state was historically, and is developmentally, secondary to original nature. But even more than that, what is natural in the civil state is logically secondary as well: in order for the higher human capacities to meet the criteria of naturalness in any sense, they must preserve the harmony of nature in its primary sense; and for this to be the case, the developmental direction of these higher faculties must in effect be continuous with, or projected from, that which is natural in the savage state.

However simplistically, the geometric analogy illustrates the affinities between Rousseau's idea of nature and those of the Aristotelians and the early moderns. It illustrates Rousseau's acceptance of both a modern, truncated view of nature (which he designates as that which is natural in the savage state, or in the pure sense) and a more "vertically" inclusive view (which he designates as that which is natural in the civil state). We must be careful, however, not to invest the geometric analogy with more meaning than it can bear. It expresses *affinities* between Rousseau's view and the others, not absolute likenesses. In adopting as his conception of what is natural in the savage or primary sense a very limited, truncated realm of human (perhaps one even ought to say, animal) capacities, Rousseau is indeed close to his modern predecessors and contemporaries; and where he differs from them in this it is because he goes even further than they, is even more modern than those moderns, as it were. But when he extends the designation "natural" to what he recognizes as the higher expressions of humanity—when he reappropriates the rest of the pyramid for nature—he is not as close to the Aristotelians as one might have first suspected or as the analogy might seem to suggest.

Although Rousseau does in effect repudiate the moderns' exclusion of the higher capacities from the realm of nature, and in so doing does indeed evince an affinity to the older, Aristotelian view, the particular capacities that Rousseau considers man's naturally highest—his notion of what constitutes the peak of the pyramid—is not the same as what constitutes the peak of the Aristotelian pyramid. In short, whereas nature's peak is for Aristotle a life of reason, a life characterized at its very highest by the practice of philosophy, nature's peak for Rousseau is the enlarged feeling of existence that is achieved by the development of advanced cognitive and emotional capacities in a way that extends and deepens *amour de soi*. What for Aristotle is defined as an intellectual attainment is for Rousseau a sentimental one. What is sublime for Rousseau—and the sublime *is* natural, as we shall see—are certain kinds of feelings, feelings of love: love of the good, love of virtue, love of beauty—love of anything or anyone that embodies these things.

I introduced comparisons with Aristotle and the early moderns in order to position us to appreciate the distinctiveness of Rousseau's view concerning the naturalness of what I have been calling the higher human capacities. Yet part of what is distinctive about Rousseau's view is the very meaning and nature of "the high." Thus we have reached the boundary beyond which these comparisons lose their illustrative power. Hobbes, for all the severity of his rejection of Aristotle, at least shared with him the conviction that the exercise of reason at its highest, which is to say philosophy, is the most elevated and rewarding of all activities. (Those "voluptuous men" who neglect philosophy, wrote Hobbes, do so "only because they know not how great a pleasure it is to the mind of man to be ravished in the vigorous and perpetual embraces of the most beauteous world.")[9] The quarrel between ancients and early moderns concerned the *status* of the high—Is it natural? Is it reducible to physical properties or activities?—more than its content. And so Rousseau's reconceptualization of the sublime ultimately places him apart from, rather than between, Aristotle and the early moderns.

Fortunately, though, just as comparisons with Aristotle and Hobbes cease to be useful, another set of comparisons suggests itself, promising to be even more illuminating. As we prepare to consider the question of sublimity, and with it the phenomenon known today as sublimation, we might recall the two figures—again one ancient and one modern—who offer the most comprehensive (secular) accounts of the soul's elevation to the sublime. Plato and Freud present us with an even more perfect dichotomy than Aristotle and his modern critics—one which, as a backdrop, throws Rousseau's distinctiveness into even sharper relief.

Plato and Freud offer competing accounts of how an individual can ascend from base desirousness to a more elevated state. Each tells of an upward channeling of psychic energy, a channeling that simultaneously reduces gross

9. Sir William Molesworth, ed., *Epistle to the Reader*, vol. 1 of *The English Works of Thomas Hobbes*, 11 vols. (London, 1839–45).

indulgence of the appetites and produces the finer things of life. Each holds, further, that this channeling cannot be taken for granted, at least not very much of it; some sort of education is needed to ensure that the process occurs. But Plato and Freud contradict one another almost perfectly with regard to the precise nature of this channeling. Indeed, what they offer are nearly diametrically opposed accounts of how, on what basis, and with what effect human desire—and with desire, behavior—can be elevated. Or, to put it another way, what we have are opposing accounts, one teleological and the other materialistic, of the very phenomenon that Rousseau explains as the emergence of nature's higher aspect (that which is natural in the civil state) from its lower, animal aspect.

Rousseau's psychology does not match up as neatly with either Plato's or Freud's as those two do with one another. Rousseau does not recognize a tripartition of the soul, for example. In fact, he nowhere explicitly lays out a comprehensive theory of moral and psychological development, at least not systematically. But Rousseau does join Plato and Freud in providing an account of the elevation of desire from low to high. And while the substance of the high is neither Platonic nor Freudian nor exactly in between, the character of the elevation, the process by which the soul ascends toward sublimity, can be understood—indeed, can best be understood—with reference to the two more famous teachings.

Let us look first at Plato. Emerging from several dialogues—most especially the *Republic,* the *Symposium,* and the *Phaedrus*—is a comprehensive and largely consistent account of the process of spiritual elevation. According to this account, the lower desires (such as wanton lusts for sex and power) come from ignorance. They are the result of a misapprehension of what one really wants, in that they stem from a misunderstanding of what alone would truly make one happy. (As for moderate and lawful bodily appetites, they too derive much of their power from ignorance, though they do have a legitimacy that their immoderate counterparts lack.) Socrates' foremost educational task in the *Republic* is to convince Glaucon that what the young man takes to be thymotic or political desires (desires for honor and glory) are in fact longings of a higher variety. It is the Good that he, and indeed that each of us, wants.[10] The Good is not only the highest thing but also the most real—which means that desire for the Good, however idealistic it may sound, is in a fundamental sense the most realistic of desires. To the extent that one's eros is directed toward objects lower than the Good—or lower than the form Beauty, which is, so to

10. *Republic* 505d–e.

speak, the face of the Good as it appears to those who behold it—one will remain unsatisfied.[11] Both social peace and individual fulfillment require an elevation of desire, and the higher the better.

As baseness is a result of ignorance, elevation proceeds as a consequence of learning. Through lengthy and difficult education—an education possible in its fullest measure for only a few—one's desires are made to progress upward, rung by rung, from more limited and less real objects to greater and more real ones. This ascent requires both discipline and intellectual apprehension. Discipline is required in order to keep the yet-to-be elevated energy of desire from being spent in the pursuit of lower objects. The soul has only so much energy, and the direction of this energy, this eros, toward any one object necessarily reduces the amount available for others: "[W]e surely know," says Socrates in the *Republic*, "that when someone's desires incline strongly to some one thing, they are therefore weaker with respect to the rest, like a stream that has been channeled off in that other direction."[12] The agent of this discipline is *thymos*, the soul's spirited part. Above *thymos*—directing its work of negativity even while beholding the superiority of higher objects and so laying hold of the next rungs on the "ladder of love"—is the soul's reasoning part.[13] Reason is thus the hero of the story. Reason both governs appetitive behavior (through its agent, *thymos*) and performs the positive work of intellectual apprehension. The latter task proceeds as a series of ascending recognitions. Reason recognizes, first, that a particular body is beautiful; next, that bodily beauty as such is more worthy of love than any particular body; then, that the beauty of souls is greater than bodily beauty; and then that the beauty of knowledge is greater still, until finally one has become a true philosopher, loving wisdom and Beauty as such.[14] It is unclear whether the objects met on the lower rungs lose all their attraction as one climbs the ladder,[15] but what is clear is that the main force of one's desire gets directed at the objects encountered on the highest rung one has attained, for these higher objects are more attractive not only innately but also because they are truer instances of the very quality that was attractive in the lower objects.

---

11. The status of Beauty varies among the dialogues. In the *Symposium*—specifically, in Socrates' recounting of Diotima's discourse—Beauty and the Good are treated as nearly synonymous. In the *Republic*, by contrast, Beauty is not so elevated.

12. *Republic* 485d.

13. The "ladder of love," or "scala amoris," is, I believe, an apt description of the universe of erotic possibilities described by Diotima. It should be remembered, however, that the phrase is an invention of scholars; it is to them, not Plato, that the necessary quotation marks refer.

14. *Symposium* 210a–212b.

15. Gerasimos Santas notes that this has been a bone of much interpretive contention. See *Plato and Freud: Two Theories of Love* (New York: Basil Blackwell, 1988), 42, 56n. 45.

What Plato describes as desire's ascent, Freud calls sublimation (*sublimieren*). "Sublimation" has more than one meaning even within the realm of moral psychology. In its broadest sense it denotes the phenomenon of upward channeling without any presupposition that the lower is either the truer or the more natural state of desire.[16] Employed in that sense, it would be a fair label for the process described by Plato. But this is not the sense of the word as it is used by Freud or, for that matter, by those such as Nietzsche who preceded him in using the term.[17] For Freud, sublimation means converting desire that is originally and (therefore) naturally low—meaning, for him, lawless and lustful—into higher feelings—specifically, into love of such things as beautiful objects and abstract ideas. Used in this narrower sense, sublimation is not an accurate label for the process that Plato describes. (When Freud nevertheless does seem to apply the term in its narrow sense to Plato's account, it is because, following the lead of some less than careful colleagues, he misreads Plato as proto-Freudian.)[18]

Far from following Plato, Freud reverses him in perhaps the most fundamental respect. Platonic sublimation is the upward channeling of what by nature ought to be high; it is a process wherein education leads to a going-up to nature, to a more real and hence more satisfying level of desire. For Freud, by contrast, sublimation is a necessary and expedient but less than happy escape *from* nature; it is necessary because what is natural would kill us, or at least most of us, but it is ultimately sad because this kind of deflection of desire's true aims can yield at best only secondary, substitutive satisfaction.[19]

---

16. This meaning is sometimes overlooked. See entry 5.a. under "sublimation" in the *Oxford English Dictionary*, 2d ed., vol. 17 (Oxford: Clarendon Press, 1989).

17. For elaboration on the history of the word and concept, see Walter Kaufmann, *Nietzsche: Philosopher, Psychologist, Antichrist*, 4th ed. (Princeton: Princeton University Press, 1974), 211–56.

18. The colleagues were Nachmansohn and Pfister. (See Santas, *Plato and Freud*, 154–57, for a brief account of Freud's reading of Plato.) That Freud is wrong in his reading of Plato is my view, not Santas's.

19. Freud offers this assessment in *Civilization and Its Discontents*: "[A] technique for fending off suffering is the employment of the displacements of libido which our mental apparatus permits of and through which its function gains so much in flexibility. The task here is that of shifting the instinctual aims in such a way that they cannot come up against frustration from the external world. In this, sublimation of the instincts lends its assistance. One gains the most if one can sufficiently heighten the yield of pleasure from the sources of psychical and intellectual work. When that is so, fate can do little against one. A satisfaction of this kind, such as an artist's joy in creating, in giving his phantasies body, or a scientist's in solving problems or discovering truths, has a special quality which we shall certainly one day be able to characterize in meta-psychological terms. At present we can only say figuratively that such satisfactions seem 'finer and higher.' But their intensity is mild as compared with that derived from the sating of crude and primary instinctual impulses; it does not convulse our physical being" (James Strachey, trans. and ed. [New York: W. W. Norton, 1961], 28).

Sublimation is the program of the reality principle, a principle born of the resigned recognition that pleasure is not our lot.

Another major difference between the two psychologies, related to the first difference, should also be noted. Just as Freud's tripartition of the soul corresponds to Plato's (ego to reason, superego to spiritedness, id to the appetites), so does Freud's account of the mechanism of sublimation parallel Plato's. Where for Plato sublimation is a project directed by reason and employing spiritedness, for Freud it is directed by the ego and engages the assistance of the superego. Yet whereas for Plato all three parts of the soul are natural and, presumably, innate, for Freud neither the ego nor the superego is natural or innate. The ego develops only in response to the frustration of the id's desires, while the superego is altogether a cultural product. Neither of sublimation's active parties is innate or natural, which underscores, if any underscoring is needed, how weak the connection is between satisfaction and the sublime—and how weak, therefore, the resemblance is between Freud and Rousseau.

For Freud, who is the true exemplar of modern science as it considers the soul, sublimation, however glorious, is still a distant second best: it may be the best practicable psychic regime, but it falls far short of the undoctored pleasures of instinctual satisfaction. For Rousseau, by contrast, sublimity, as experienced for example in the contemplation of moral beauty, inspires "involuntary transports," "noble delirium," "holy enthusiasm," and "those sublime strayings which elevate us into the empyrean next to God himself" (*LM* 1101)—hardly the grim stuff of the reality principle.

Thus, Rousseau is closer to Plato than to Freud, and not only in the fact of their shared poetic philosophizing. Though not a Platonist, Rousseau gives an account of sublimation whose essence, as we shall presently see, has significant affinities to Plato's work. While Rousseau's notion of what constitutes sublimity is distinctive and resists comparison with either Plato or Freud, and although he presents no corresponding tripartition of the soul, Rousseau provides an account in which sublimation is in a real sense natural and, consequently, a great gain for the individual in whom it takes place. For Rousseau, there is no question of secondary, substitutive satisfaction: nothing is as deeply gratifying, as eudaemonistically rewarding, as experiencing the sublime. And as for the psychic agents of sublimation, they, as we shall also see, though not

---

Freud altered his theory of sublimation somewhat over the years, but the elements I have cited—including his insistence on the comparative mildness of sublimated satisfactions—were common to all versions. For a brief review of his thinking on this matter, see Santas, *Plato and Freud*, chap. 6, esp. 139–44.

active in the original natural man, are nevertheless natural. In these respects Rousseau's account leans toward Plato's and away from Freud's. Ultimately, though, Rousseau's account veers away from Plato's as well. Two divergences are especially significant: (1) Rousseau defines the sublime in sentimental rather than ontological terms, and (2) Rousseau locates not just the energy but also something of the basic pattern of sublimity on the lowest, most primal rung of the ladder: although the high is not reducible to the low, it is informed by it. The state of nature never ceases to be a source of standards for judging even the most advanced human beings. Origins persist—not only positively but also normatively.

Thus, in the end the Platonic and Freudian accounts are useful to an understanding of Rousseau less as opposing poles of a continuum than as positions by which to gauge the full measure of Rousseau's distinctiveness.

Sublimation in Rousseau: Conscience as Alchemist

Although the term itself never appears in Rousseau's works, sublimation has been increasingly recognized as key to his understanding of healthy human development. Whether the precise nature of the process has been as well understood, however, is somewhat more doubtful. Even the best interpretations have tended to miss one or another of the features that together comprise the peculiar character of Rousseauan sublimation.

No one has shed more light on the significance of sublimation in Rousseau's thought than Allan Bloom. Nevertheless, Bloom's interpretation requires some correction. When Bloom writes that "[s]ublimation as the source of the soul's higher expressions ... was introduced to the world by Rousseau," he is using "sublimation" in its narrower and more usual sense. According to Bloom, Rousseau's discovery of sublimation provided him with the means to escape the reductive implications of the modern understanding of nature:

> Rousseau's attempt to comprehend the richness of man's soul within the context of modern scientific reductionism led him to an interpretation which is still our way of looking at things although we have lost clarity about its intention and meaning. Rousseau knew that there are sublime things; he had inner experience of them. He also knew that there is no place for the sublime in the modern scientific explanation of man. Therefore, the sublime had to be made out of the nonsublime;

this is sublimation. It is a raising of the lower to the higher.... [The] last two books of Emile then undertake in a detailed way the highly problematic task of showing how the higher might be derived from the lower without being reduced to it, while at the same time giving us some sense of what Rousseau means by the sublime or noble.[20]

This interpretation is worth special notice because it rightly and uniquely understands sublimation to be the key to Rousseau's vision of everything that is fine or excellent in man. It rightly locates the source of love and of virtue, the source of compassion and nobility, in the elevation of what begins as undifferentiated sexual desire. Ultimately, though, this interpretation goes astray in an important respect.

Bloom is correct in maintaining that Rousseau believed in the existence of sublime things and that he did so based on his own inner experience. Bloom is also correct in noting that Rousseau found "the modern scientific explanation of man" unable to account or even make room for the sublime. But Bloom errs in interpreting the nature of Rousseau's predicament and solution. Rousseau does indeed propound sublimation as the means by which one achieves spiritual heights: higher attachments arise directly from the transformation, the elevation, of mere bodily appetite. But the sublimation Rousseau describes is not sublimation in the narrow sense. Instead, it is sublimation in the broad sense, sublimation in the sense that includes the kind of elevation of desire that Socrates seeks to promote in Glaucon. Sublimation in the narrow sense refers to "the sublime [being] made out of the nonsublime"; this view sees nothing naturally sublime in man, and so sublimation is not natural. The upward transformation of desire as Rousseau describes it, though, *is* natural. It is so because it is accomplished through the agency of the one psychic element that is both innate (in other words, natural in a very strict sense) and sublime: conscience.[21]

Conscience, as we shall presently see, is the source of all that is sublime in human beings. And conscience is fully a part of our natural, our *innate* or original, endowment. Bloom's error, then, is to assume that Rousseau fully accepted the modern scientific understanding of man. In fact, Rousseau did *not* "attempt to comprehend the richness of man's soul within the context of modern scientific reductionism." Rousseau did subscribe to much in the modern view. Indeed, as we have repeatedly noted, in important respects he went

20. Bloom, introduction to Rousseau's *Emile*, 15–16.
21. Although, being innate, conscience is natural in a very strict sense, it cannot be considered natural in the strictest, or pure, sense, since it was not active in the pure state of nature.

even further in reducing nature than his predecessors had (by subtracting reason and sociability from the catalog of man's original natural characteristics, for example). But his insistence upon the naturalness, *the primary naturalness*, of conscience—his insistence that a sublime inner force exists in every human heart—removes him from the camp of modern reductionists. Rousseau "knew that there is no place for the sublime in the modern scientific explanation of man." Indeed. But since he did not fully subscribe to that explanation in the first place, he did not need to postulate the derivation of the sublime from strictly nonsublime sources.

The essence of Rousseau's view is that, strengthened by a natural education, the one thing that is sublime from the start (namely, conscience) transforms animal sexual energy into such elevated phenomena as compassion, romantic love, conjugal love, friendship, taste, sensibility, and virtue.[22]

Before turning to the particulars of sublimation, to the questions of what is sublime and how sublimation occurs, it is necessary to clarify what sublimation accomplishes, that is, what the problem is to which sublimation stands as the solution. Sublimation does not explain the appearance of higher mental *faculties*. As we saw in the previous chapter, the higher faculties, whether cognitive or emotional, are awakened from natural latency by a certain confluence of circumstances. What are customarily called the "acquired" faculties are in fact not so much acquired as stimulated into development, like seeds that are watered.[23] What sublimation refers to is nothing so morally neutral. Rather, it explains the wholesome, which is to say either good or virtuous, development of sentiment.

As part of a natural education such as Emile's, sublimation explains how man's higher capacities, those that in the pure sense are unnatural, can be made

22. In this, sublimation bears an interesting resemblance to another kind of alchemy depicted in *Emile*, namely, its account of the origins of the sense of rightful possession (or what is called "a sort of property" in the *Second Discourse* [146]), an account that Rousseau borrows from Locke's account of the origins of property in the state of nature (*Emile* II:98–99; Locke, *Second Treatise of Government*, chap. 5). Just as the sense of rightful possession is created by mixing what is by nature one's own (that is, one's labor) with what belongs to no one (the common), so sublimation occurs through the mixing of what is by nature sublime (namely, conscience) with what is not sublime. In both cases the active element (labor, conscience) so enriches the acted-upon elements (raw materials of the earth, raw materials of the psyche) that they, the latter, become kin to the former: what had been unowned becomes rightful private possession and what had been submoral becomes sublime—the transformation occurring in both cases by virtue of the near-infinite addition of value by the active element. (A major difference between Rousseau's account and Locke's is that, for Rousseau, labor only establishes a sense of rightful possession, whereas Locke suggests that labor establishes full property rights. For Rousseau the establishment of full property rights requires consent. Rousseau's debt to Locke's account of the origins of property is also evident in the *Second Discourse*, 154.)

23. See "The Fixedness of Man's 'Present Nature'" in Chapter 2 above.

natural after all. That is, it explains how his higher capacities can be made to extend and/or deepen *amour de soi* and to shape *amour-propre* in such a way as to make it the source of loving rather than irascible social passions.[24] Sublimation is the mechanism whereby morally neutral sexual energy becomes morally laudable love. It is the mechanism whereby higher sentiment is produced. And as it is sentiment that shapes the rest of man, the sublimation of sexuality ensures, as much as anything can, the proper development and employment of all man's faculties and capacities, sentimental and nonsentimental alike. Thus sublimation is centrally responsible for the development of "the natural man living in the state of society."

Sublimation did not occur in the state of nature, for conscience speaks only to those in whom reason has developed (*Emile* I:67; *Beaumont* 935–36). Sublimation therefore explains much of the difference between the different kinds of natural men. But the difference that it most explains is not the one between Emile and the original natural man but the one between Emile and his unnatural counterparts in civilization. *Sublimation makes for the whole difference between civilized goodness and corruption.* It is the means to the naturalization of second nature.

Let us now look at Rousseauan sublimation proper, beginning with an examination of conscience, the key to the whole enterprise. The reason conscience can do so much for Rousseau is that it *is* so much. A careful reading reveals that conscience, *la conscience*—this is a word he does use—plays an even larger and more decisive role in Rousseau's understanding of a well-developed person than reason does in Plato's.[25] On its face, Rousseauan conscience seems not so different from a certain conventional understanding of conscience. Conscience has long been understood as a moral sense, an inner source of moral judgment that expresses approval and disapproval through a variety of feeling states. Conscience on this view is thought to be universal, at least in its more general output. (While people, and peoples, differ in many specific moral judgments, everyone except the psychopath knows, for example, that murder and theft are wrong.) And so it is for Rousseau. Conscience for him is an innate,

24. In fact, sublimation is not unique to a natural education. It occurs as part of a denaturalizing, civic education as well, and it accomplishes much the same thing in the citizen as in the natural man, albeit within a different context: citizens, too, are devoted to their families. In them, too, sexuality has acquired a moral dimension.

25. The French *la conscience* has two meanings, rendered in English as conscience and consciousness, respectively. Fortunately, Rousseau's use of the term is clear enough to know which meaning he intends in each instance. There need be no doubt that what I have understood to be Rousseau's treatments of conscience are indeed just that.

universal source of moral guidance and judgment. Basing his view to a significant degree on his own experience, Rousseau concludes that conscience is an
active and articulate, even if somewhat timid, force. It prescribes general rules
of conduct and even provides individuals with detailed guidance before they
act; and it repays them accordingly—that is, justly—with either contentment
or distress, afterward and for a long time to come.[26]

That Rousseau's best known discourse on conscience comes from the mouth
of a character, the Savoyard Vicar, whose basic philosophical views seem to
differ in some respects from Rousseau's own does not count against the present
interpretation.[27] For while the Vicar's Profession is the most famous of
Rousseau's discussions of conscience, it is not his only one. And those other
disquisitions—most notably the *Lettres morales* but also numerous passages in
several other works, including *Emile*—do not differ fundamentally from the
Vicar's account on any of the points that we have so far noted. Wherever they
appear, in whoever's mouth they are placed and to whomever they are
addressed, Rousseau's discussions of conscience consistently portray it as a
universal, active, inner force for good.

26. Few interpreters would dispute the accuracy of this description. What has been disputed,
however, is the universality of conscience's principle(s) over time—a challenge that goes, if not to
the accuracy, certainly to the significance of this description. Horowitz, for example, sees Rousseau
as rejecting the "ahistoricity" of conscience. Rousseau's nature, Horowitz maintains, does express
itself through conscience, but the promptings of conscience are as much the product of history as of
nature; nature does not express or manifest itself except through a medium that has been fundamentally shaped by history. (See *Rousseau, Nature, and History*, 42–46, and Strong, *Politics of the
Ordinary*, 127.)

This interpretation of Rousseau, needless to say, is very much at odds with the one propounded
here. Whereas Horowitz elevates history to the prime place in Rousseau's philosophical anthropology, my reading of Rousseau finds history to be a force that interacts with but does not fundamentally determine the substance of nature. History, in my view, can work in consonance with nature by
awakening its hitherto dormant aspects; and it can work at cross purposes with nature, by overlaying
nature's always benign manifestations with corruption and distortion. But nature, in the interpretation advanced here, is in its essence untouched and untouchable by history. Thus conscience,
nature's voice, is in *its* essence independent of history. The voice may vary in richness and volume
according to the varying levels of moral and intellectual development among people, but the basic
principle underlying conscience's messages is always the same, as we shall see in the coming pages.
(That the volume of this voice can vary—that conscience can be and in fact generally *is* drowned
out by the din of corrupt civilization—is the reason for conscience not being the sufficient, full-
throated moral guide that some interpreters have taken it to be. See "Rousseau, Nature, and History"
in my Introduction to this book.)

27. Some interpreters—Pierre-Maurice Masson and Maurice Cranston, for example—regard the
Vicar's profession as Rousseau's own. (See Masson, *La religion de J.-J. Rousseau*, 3 vols. [Paris: Plon,
1916], and Cranston, *Noble Savage* 197n, 321, 348: "the 'Profession of Faith' was very much a profession of his own faith.") Indeed, Rousseau gives us ample reason to think that a good part of the
Vicar's Profession does represent his own outlook. See *Reveries* III:34–35.

Thus we read, for example—and each of these passages appears someplace other than the Vicar's Profession—that "[t]here is . . . at the bottom of all souls an innate principle of justice and moral virtue anterior to all national prejudices and to all the maxims of education. . . . [I]t is to this principle that I give the name of conscience" (*LM* 1108);[28] that "this first sketch is not drawn by the hand of man but is graven in our hearts by the Author of all justice" (*Emile* II:100n); and finally, "A rule prior to opinion exists for the whole human species. It is to the inflexible direction of this rule that all the others ought to be related. . . . This rule is the inner sentiment" (*Emile* V:382).

Conscience lay dormant in the original natural man; it requires a certain degree of reason or enlightenment in order to be awakened (*Emile* I:67; *Beaumont* 935–36). Once awakened, though, it can never be completely stifled: "The most corrupt souls wouldn't be able to lose this first inclination entirely: the thief who robs passersby nevertheless covers the nakedness of the poor." Such, at least, is the position taken in the *Lettres morales* (1107). The line taken in the *Dialogues*, written during a prolonged period of personal distress that seems to have included an element of paranoia, is somewhat more bleak, though not utterly so:

> Those innate feelings that nature has engraved in all hearts to console man in his misery and encourage him to virtue can easily, by means of art, intrigues, and sophisms, become stifled in individuals; but soon reborn in the generations that follow, they will always bring man back to his primitive dispositions, just as the seed of a grafted tree always reproduces the wild stock. . . . The voice of conscience can no more be stifled in the human heart than that of reason can be stifled in the understanding; and moral insensitivity is as unnatural as madness. (III:242)[29]

Even if conscience is extinguishable in individuals, says the Rousseau of the *Dialogues*, it will always be part of human beings' innate endowment.

The consolation of conscience to which Rousseau refers is no mean thing.

28. I take "moral virtue" in this instance as a reference to both goodness and virtue. Although the distinction between goodness and virtue is real and important, Rousseau sometimes uses "virtue" in a more general everyday sense, especially in works whose intended audience is comprised of the general reading public rather than philosophers. (See note 66 to this chapter for another example of this usage.) The same line appears with only minor alteration in the Vicar's Profession (IV:290).

29. In the *Second Discourse*, Rousseau makes a similar claim on behalf of natural pity. "[T]he most depraved morals," he says, "still have difficulty in destroying [it]" (131). Natural pity, as we shall see, is a part of conscience.

A good conscience is one of only three real needs: "Take away strength, health, and good witness of oneself, all the goods of this life are in opinion; take away the pains of the body and the remorse of conscience, all our ills are imaginary" (*Emile* II:81). Accordingly, the pleasures of a good conscience out-last and far outweigh the foregone pleasures that might have been purchased in violation of conscience: "the sacrifices made to honesty and justice compensate me every day for what they cost me one time, and [in return] for brief privations give me eternal delights" (*LM* 1103). Indeed, so great are the pleasures of conscience, and so persistent is the pain of remorse, that the whole of Rousseau's moralism reduces to a single prescription: following the promptings of the inner voice, he writes, "is my whole philosophy and, I believe, the whole art of being happy that is practicable for man" (*LM* 1104–5).[30] Rousseau's is a position which, if true, surely satisfies Glaucon's famous demand: goodness (or justice, to use Glaucon's term) leads to happiness and so is its own, incomparably great, reward.[31] Obviously, though, this great truth remains hidden from the vast majority of civilized men and women, for whom the siren songs of interest and passion seem to promise happiness while the delight in goodness seems a hopelessly threadbare myth: "Consider that to delight in doing good is the reward for having done good, and that one does not obtain it before having merited it. Nothing is more kind than virtue but it does not show itself thus except to those who possess it" (*LM* 1117).[32]

As all of these quoted remarks indicate, Rousseau sees in conscience much the same thing that Jews, Christians, and others have seen in it, especially since the Protestant Reformation. There is nothing unique in his postulating an innate moral sense. But he sees in this moral sense much more than others do. Conscience to him is all that it is for them and then some. And in that, in the range of its functions and in its developmental significance, Rousseau's conception is indeed unique. Or so I intend to demonstrate.

Let us consider the following psalmodic passage from the fifth of the *Lettres morales*. "Conscience, conscience," sings Rousseau,

---

30. See also *LM* 1107, where, speaking of the torment of remorse, Rousseau says that if we but "obey nature we will know with what sweetness it approves what it has commanded and what charm one finds in tasting the inner peace of a soul content with itself."

31. Glaucon's challenge to Socrates appears at *Republic* 361a–d.

32. This is surely one reason for Rousseau's insistence that conscience requires the support of religious faith—specifically, the belief in divine justice in the afterlife. (See, for example, *Emile* IV:312–15.) It is not clear, however, that this requirement applies to Emile, in whom nature's strong presence diminishes the power of corrupt temptation.

divine instinct, immortal and celestial voice, certain guide of a being that is ignorant and limited but intelligent and free, infallible judge of good and bad, sublime emanation of eternal substance who renders man like unto the Gods; it is you alone who makes the excellence of my nature.

Without you I sense nothing in myself which elevates me above the beasts except for the sad privilege of wandering from error to error with the help of an understanding without rule and a reason without principle. (LM 1111)[33]

Rousseau is justly famous for the passion of his rhetoric. Few writers within any discipline can match the emotional expressiveness of his prose. But the passion of his rhetoric should not be taken to mean that he is exaggerating, that he does not quite mean everything he says—least of all when he makes categorical, philosophical statements such as the ones quoted above.[34] We may therefore take Rousseau at his word in the preceding excerpt, a passage that reveals something of the full meaning and significance of conscience in his thought.

Several elements of that paean are worth notice, beginning with the sustained reference to divinity. The chief effect of stressing conscience's status as "divine instinct" or "emanation of eternal substance" is to underscore its perfection and its power. (A similar effect is achieved in other places by presenting conscience as the "voice of nature.")[35] Conscience is more than reliable; it is "infallible," not just in conveying a set of rules but also in its role as counselor and judge, telling us on a case-by-case basis how to apply the rules of good conduct. But the central claim of the passage, and the one that is most relevant to the interpretation I am trying to advance, is the ontological claim: conscience and conscience alone elevates our "ignorant and limited" being to a level

33. Parts of this passage are repeated almost verbatim by the Savoyard Vicar (*Emile* IV:290). The most notable difference is that the Vicar speaks of only one God.

34. Even when a sweeping claim seems to be contradicted within the same work—such as in the *First Discourse*, where high praise for a certain few philosophers and scientists appears alongside a bitter, blanket denunciation of the arts and sciences—that is not because Rousseau has overstated his case. Rather, the contradiction arises from the layered presence of separate arguments that, while obviously in some conflict with one another, nevertheless are internally consistent and ultimately reconcilable. (With regard to the example of the *First Discourse*, see Strauss, "On the Intention of Rousseau," and Masters, *Political Philosophy of Rousseau*, 205–13.) Although there is almost always more to Rousseau's philosophical claims than meets the eye, what does meet the eye is sincerely presented as truth; it may be taken at face value as long as one does not ignore what lies behind and beyond its face.

35. See, for example, *Emile* IV:267, 286–87 and the fifth of the *Lettres morales*.

above that of the beasts. Freedom and perfectibility set human beings apart from the animals.(*SD*, 114–15) But it is conscience that makes of this separateness a true superiority. Conscience is itself sublime. And, being such, it is the sole source of whatever excellence we have, which takes us at last to the heart of the matter.

In calling conscience the sole maker of "the excellence of my nature" (*LM* 1111), Rousseau is making an extraordinary claim. He is crediting conscience not only with telling us what justice demands in this or that situation—not an inconsiderable task in itself—but also with being the source of everything else that is distinctive and excellent in human nature. If conscience is the sole source of human excellence, then it must ultimately be responsible for every manifestation of this excellence. Rousseau's claim can be taken to mean no less. We must therefore attribute to conscience all of the capacities and inclinations that express or manifest this excellence. If friendship or romantic love or conjugal and parental love evince "the excellence of [our] nature"—and clearly they do for Rousseau—then they owe their existence to conscience.[36] If a fine aesthetic sensibility, one that finds joy in the truly beautiful, is a part of "the excellence of [human] nature"—and, again, it certainly is for Rousseau —then it too owes its existence to conscience.[37] If the disinterested love of truth is a mark of excellence—and we are justified in concluding that Rousseau sees it as such, for he adduces his own love of truth in support of his claim to personal excellence—then it too would not exist but for conscience.[38] Rousseau's estimation of modern humanity may be dim, but his assessment of human *possibility* is a veritable rainbow in its variety of excellences. One need only consider the multiplicity of fine qualities in Emile or in the somewhat less consistent but more brilliant Jean-Jacques. Conscience alone is the

36. That Rousseau deems these loving relations expressions of the excellence of human nature is manifestly clear from the celebratory treatment he gives them in *Emile*, in *Julie*, and even—most tellingly—in the *Second Discourse*, where familial love is said to inspire "the sweetest sentiments known to men" (146–47).

37. A fine aesthetic sensibility is to be found in both of Rousseau's exemplars of natural excellence, Emile and Jean-Jacques, and so may safely be said to be an expression of the excellence of human nature. Indeed, some have suggested that for Rousseau, it is beauty that gives value to love. See, for example, Joseph Cropsey, *Political Philosophy and the Issues of Politics* (Chicago: University of Chicago Press, 1977), 328–29.

38. See almost any part of the *Dialogues*, a work of self-justification to which the claim of a disinterested love of truth is central. Here is one example: "In all other books, I first recognized the passion that had dictated them and the personal goal the author had in mind. Only J-J [Jean-Jacques] seemed to seek the truth with rectitude and simplicity of heart" (I:53). Note, too, that Rousseau had chosen as his personal motto the words of Juvenal: "vitam impendere vero" (to devote one's life to the truth).

source of all this excellence, the source of all this sublimity. It is the sun behind the rainbow.

How does conscience accomplish all this? Rousseau nowhere specifies the precise mechanism whereby conscience engineers or otherwise guides the development of these excellent qualities. Nor can we infer the details from his writings. Indeed, not even the inculcation of virtue nor the love of virtue, the most obvious of conscience's developmental accomplishments, is fully explained. Rousseau eschews metapsychological speculation, just as, and probably for the same reasons that, he avoids metaphysical speculation.[39] And yet this lacuna is perhaps less significant than it may seem, for Rousseau does provide a full account of the order and the general principles of wholesome moral development. And the remaining mystery, the mystery of how, specifically, conscience causes the development of higher sentiment—the mystery of the mechanics of sublimation—is neither greater than nor very different from the mysteries surrounding all manner of cognitive and physiological development. After years of studying our various mental and physical capacities, we still only know—science only knows—at best *that, when,* and in a certain, limited sense, *how* they develop. (The "how" of which we have some knowledge concerns only the genetic encoding and transmission of instructions, not the original writing of the instructions.) Of formal and final causes, science, as such, knows nothing. Science does not understand how it is that our various capacities are made to appear, how it is that the capacities to speak or to reason or to appreciate music or art—or even the capacities simply to walk or run—all absent in the infant, later appear.[40] So it is understandable that Rousseau does not tell us with regard to moral and sentimental development what science still does not know with regard to cognitive and physiological development.

In any event, to inquire after the mechanism whereby conscience accounts for human excellence, to ask how conscience does what it does, is to ask the wrong question of Rousseau. Conscience as such does not *do* anything. It is neither a faculty nor a part of the soul per se. It is not an actor. Rather, to use a category that Rousseau introduces in the *Second Discourse,* conscience is a *principle of soul.*

39. Rousseau widely advertised his view that man's efforts at metaphysical speculation had so far proved useless and unreliable. See, for instance, the third of the *Lettres morales.* See also Cranston, *Noble Savage,* 289.

40. One sometimes concludes, incorrectly, that because science has come to understand the phenomenology of a certain thing's development it has grasped the original or final *causes* of the development. It might be useful to note that the widespread dissemination of knowledge about human genetics and reproduction has taken little or no toll on the popular sense of the mystery and miracle of life—and perhaps has even enhanced it.

In the *Second Discourse*, Rousseau seeks to explain with scientific economy the workings of the soul of man in the pure state of nature. He wants to reduce the many disparate desires of natural man to the fewest possible motivational categories and finds that a pair of categories will suffice: "I believe I perceive in [the soul] two principles anterior to reason, of which one interests us ardently in our well-being and our self-preservation, and the other inspires in us a natural repugnance to see any sensitive being perish or suffer" (95). Such are the two principles that suffice to explain the comparatively limited inclinations of the original natural man. These two principles do not adequately illuminate the vastly deeper and more complex soul of the civilized natural man, however. To explain Emile's soul, Rousseau needs deeper and more complex principles. In place of the savage's simple, unself-conscious self-love, Rousseau needs a deeper and self-conscious self-love, one that comprehends sociable impulses and needs: he needs an admixture of enriched *amour de soi* and well-regulated *amour-propre*. And in place of the savage's unarticulated repugnance to see others suffer, Rousseau needs a larger principle that includes that repugnance but goes well beyond it—a principle that can account for true moral and sentimental excellence. It is this principle that he calls conscience. Conscience, then, is to Emile and to Jean-Jacques what the repugnance to see his fellows suffer was to the savage. It is a principle of soul, a minimal scientific explanation of many psychic phenomena.[41]

A further similarity exists between the savage's and Emile's respective pairs of principles of soul. In each case the second principle ultimately proves to be an aspect or consequence of the first—an aspect or consequence, that is, of benign self-love. In the final analysis, it is the savage's *amour de soi* that makes him feel repugnance at seeing another suffer and that makes him refrain from needlessly injuring others. And it is *amour de soi* that ultimately accounts for conscience as well. The following lines from the *Lettre à Beaumont* make this point quite clearly while also confirming, or at least suggesting, that conscience is indeed the successor to the savage's repugnance to see others suffer. This passage also articulates with great succinctness the *content* of this principle of soul called conscience.

> Amour de soi is not a simple passion, but has two principles, namely, the intelligent being and the sensitive being, whose well-being is not

---

41. For a useful discussion of the scientific sense of a "principle of soul," see Masters, *Political Philosophy of Rousseau*, 143–46. Masters, however, addresses only pity, the principle of soul so identified in the *Second Discourse*; he does not interpret conscience as a principle of soul.

the same. The appetite of the senses tends to that of the body and the love of order to that of the soul. *This second love, when developed and made active, is called conscience;* but conscience is only developed and only acts from enlightenment. It is only by acquiring enlightenment that man succeeds in knowing order; and it is only when he knows it that his conscience leads him to love it. (936; emphasis added)[42]

What is conscience? It is "the love of order ... when developed and made active." "Love" in this instance clearly does not refer to a passion; rather, like the "love" in "love of self," the word refers here to something more basic than and anterior to the passions. It is the *source* of passions and sentiments. It is a principle of soul.[43]

Rousseau considers conscience to be an aspect of *amour de soi* because it tends to the well-being of a part, the highest part, of the self: the soul. Surely, never has something designated as self-love been further removed from selfishness. Yet calling conscience an aspect of self-love is perfectly in keeping with Rousseau's understanding of *amour de soi* as something good.[44] *Amour de soi*, we recall, is nothing other than the enjoyment (and the wish for the continuation) of existence as it is experienced through the vessel of the self.[45] The

42. This translation was done by John Hope Mason and appears in *The Indispensable Rousseau*, ed. Mason (New York: Quartet Books, 1979), 233.

43. If conscience is the source of passions and sentiments, why is it not cited as a principle of soul in the *Second Discourse?* After all, this work describes the whole of humanity's development, including the stage in which conscience has appeared, and not just the state of nature, in which conscience was latent. Moreover, the *Second Discourse* does mention free will, which also was not active in the original state. My answer to this objection is that, although conscience is indeed a principle of soul for post-state-of-nature natural men, conscience has not, alas, been a major source of *actual* experience and behavior. (The world has not seen many Emiles or Jean-Jacques.) Given the corruption that has accompanied the development of the species, the love of order has had little impact on us—it has had little explanatory power—and so has no necessary place in a work whose intention is to explain why we are the way we are and not what we might or ought to be. It is also quite possible that, at the time he wrote the *Second Discourse*, Rousseau had not yet discovered the centrality of the love of order in civilized naturalness—or even the very possibility of civilized naturalness, which, after all, also is not mentioned in the *Second Discourse*. (We do not doubt that Rousseau believed in the theoretical possibility of an Emile just because no such thing is mentioned in the *Second Discourse*.) Indeed, the absence from the *Discourse* of any reference to civilized naturalness, whatever the reason for it, would seem to be sufficient reason for the absence of any reference to the love of order.

44. Rousseau consistently maintains not only that *amour de soi* is good but also that it is the source of goodness toward others: "Love of men derived from love of self [*amour de soi*] is the principle of human justice" (*Emile* IV:235n).

45. See "Beyond Happiness ..." in Chapter 1 above.

deeper and more developed the self, the closer *amour de soi* comes to approximating a love of nature or a love of existence itself. What does it mean to say
that the self becomes deeper and more developed? In Chapter 1, we encountered part of the answer: it is possible for one to experience much of nature or
much of existence as part of one's self, for one's felt identity can be vastly
expanded—as, for example, Jean-Jacques's is in the fifth of his *Reveries*. We
now meet with another part of the answer: a large part of the deepening and
development of the self consists in the development of conscience. As "love of
order," conscience is also love of nature or love of existence as such. For the
order that is referred to, the object of the love that is conscience, is the harmony of the cosmos, the harmony that Rousseau discerns in every part and
aspect of existence save those that have been fouled by the hand of man. The
savage, lacking an activated conscience, enjoyed existence only insofar as his
brute senses permitted. Emile or Jean-Jacques, by contrast, enjoy existence
more fully because, with activated consciences, they are able to enjoy, they are
able to love, what reason reveals to them of nature's essential quality, its won-
drous order.[46]

Rousseau nowhere defines the "order" which he identifies as the object of
(the love that he calls) conscience; he does not state explicitly either that it
lies in a formal principle of coexistence or that it has any substantive content.
But he does give significant indications of what the concept means for him,
even if these indications only arise from particular examples of order. Most of
these examples are drawn either from music or, even more, from botany.
Examples from the latter context are examined in Chapter 4. For now it must
suffice to say that the order Rousseau has in mind is such that one might
describe it as a delicate harmony, and not, say, as uniform and repressive. The
order that it is natural to love is the order that Rousseau finds, for example, in
eighteenth-century Italian music (at least the part of it he admires) or in the
complex structures of plants, not the order found in what Rousseau considered
the heavy-handed and tortured harmonies that characterized most French
music in his lifetime, and certainly not the order that would later serve as an
organizing principle of political totalitarianism.[47] The best way to apprehend

46. The inhabitants of Rousseau's "ideal world" in the *Dialogues* are similarly rewarded. Their
ability to appreciate nature's order allows them to enjoy its beauty and "inspires in them both the
desire to contribute to this beautiful system and the fear of troubling its harmony," a desire and fear
that in turn bring them an "exquisite sensitivity" and "enjoyment" unknown to those who are less
able to appreciate nature's order (I:9).
47. Sparta yes, fascism no. Rousseau could admire Sparta because, though not natural, it restored
to its citizens something comparable to the psychic unity—the inner harmony—that characterized
the savage and because it replaced lost natural freedom with civil freedom. Facism, on the other

the character of the "order" Rousseau has in mind, however, is simply to attend throughout our inquiry to his reading of the universe of things that are not man-made, for Rousseau sees everything in that universe as expressive of this order. Of course, Rousseau does believe that human beings can replicate or participate in this order (such as by listening to good music or by botanizing). But they can do so only by aligning themselves with the principle governing the universe of things not man-made: "Whatever is good and in accordance with order is so by the nature of things, independently of human conventions" (SC II-6:65).[48]

To be sure, Rousseau at times seems to refer to conscience as something more limited than a principle of soul. Indeed, in *most* cases he uses the word in a narrower, more conventional sense in which "conscience" signifies a faculty, an intrapsychic actor, a doer of deeds. Earlier in this chapter I gave several examples of such usage in *Emile* and the *Lettres morales*. In those instances Rousseau used the word "conscience" to denote an inner moral sense, a presence that speaks to us and rewards and punishes us. But when he uses the word in that narrower, more conventional sense, he is in fact speaking of a particular expression or effect of conscience as principle of soul. His primary definition of conscience is the broader one: conscience as principle of soul supersedes conscience as psychic actor (or conscience as moral faculty) because it subsumes it. It could only be conscience in its broader sense that Rousseau has in mind when he credits it as the maker of all human excellence, for the moral faculty as such cannot possibly be supposed to have informed the development of every higher sentiment.

As a principle of soul, conscience has multiple manifestations and so admits of several somewhat different but ultimately consistent characterizations. Thus we find Rousseau describing it variously as an "inner feeling" (*Dialogues* III:242), as the voice of nature (*Emile* IV:286), as the "inner voice which judges me" (*LM* 1104), and as an "innate principle of justice and moral virtue anterior to all national prejudices and to all the maxims of education" (*LM* 1108; see also *Emile* IV:289). None of these descriptions is inconsistent with

---

hand, by denying both kinds of freedom, stifles both the inclinations and the wills of its subjects and thereby constricts the degree to which they exist, or so I believe Rousseau would say. Whether he could make a principled, philosophical distinction between the order that it is natural to love and the kinds of (or pretenses to) order that he found objectionable is not immediately apparent.

48. It is instructive that Rousseau speaks merely of being in accordance with order, and not of being in accordance with *good* order. The clear implication is that the order found in nature is good as such: to speak of "good order" would be redundant. For more examples of this usage, see *Emile* II:85, 88, and IV:213, 235.

the notion of conscience as a principle of soul whose primary content is a love of order. Perhaps the most illuminating of Rousseau's descriptions, though, is one he places in the mouth of the Savoyard Vicar. Conscience "is to the soul what instinct is to the body" (*Emile* IV:286). What is useful about this particular formulation, even more than the way it emphasizes that conscience is an aspect of self-love, is that it helps make clear just what it means to say that conscience is a principle of soul. Rousseau compares conscience not to the many instincts of the body but to "instinct," in the singular.[49] Used thus, "instinct" refers to the general principle that underlies the body's many particular instincts; it refers to the generality behind the particulars. Likening conscience to the body's instinct therefore achieves a comparable effect: it captures the defining characteristic of conscience as a principle of soul—namely, that it is unitary but manifold in its effects, that it is a general principle (a love of order) that manifests itself in multifarious ways.

Rousseau never calls conscience a principle of soul. In fact, he does not bother to reduce Emile's soul to any set of principles. His method in *Emile* consists far more of constructing than deconstructing, of elaborating rather than boiling down to basic principles. It is only in the *Second Discourse*, whose method is far more conventionally scientific, that he is concerned with identifying principles of soul. Nevertheless, I have argued that conscience should be considered a principle of soul. I maintain that, if Rousseau had used the *Second Discourse*'s scientific methodology on Emile, he would have identified the love of order—that is, conscience—as a principle of the civilized natural man's soul. (I would also maintain that, had he used this method in his autobiographical works, he would have identified the love of order as a basic principle of his own soul.) I also believe that, while it may have suited Rousseau not to bother identifying principles of soul in *Emile*, our understanding of that work and of his thinking about nature generally is enhanced when we identify these principles ourselves.[50]

There are two basic reasons for considering conscience a principle of soul. First, as we have now seen, the love of order is found at the bottom of nearly all of Emile's characteristics, including all of his moral, aesthetic, and spiritual excellences. In discovering the manifold effects of conscience, we perceive that goodness, virtue, good taste, love of beauty, and appreciation of nature's harmony are all manifestations of the same principle. (We shall have more to

49. See *LM* 1111 for a similar description.
50. Although it is not explicitly identified as a principle of soul, the love of order is mentioned as a basic source of (good) behavior in *Emile*—and in such a way as to *imply* that it is indeed a principle of soul, second in motivational power only to the love of self (of which it is a part). See IV:314.

say about the relations between these manifestations of the love of order, that is, between moral and aesthetic excellence, later in this chapter.) Conscience, in other words, explains a lot. It proves to be the common source of Emile's most outstanding characteristics and so affords us some insight into the meaning of nature. Second, the effects of conscience cannot be attributed to any other single cause—which is to say that conscience is not reducible to any more basic phenomenon.

To be sure, conscience depends upon a variety of faculties in order to have its effects. At a minimum it depends on the ability to perceive the relations between things, and in many of its manifestations it depends specifically on the ability to identify with other people. Without that ability, neither true pity nor any of the social virtues that Rousseau sees as deriving from pity—generosity, clemency, benevolence, and so on— can exist (SD 131–32). Yet none of the faculties on which conscience depends can in itself, or even in combination with others, account for the manifold effects of conscience. The ability to identify with others, for instance, is only a capacity. It cannot explain why one should *want* to identify with others. And it certainly cannot explain any of the aesthetic and spiritual, as opposed to the narrowly moral, effects of conscience. Simply put, a full understanding of Emile's or Jean-Jacques's soul is not possible without respecting the decisive role of the irreducible love of order. Everything natural is orderly, or harmonious. Every natural man, whether savage, civilized, or "post-civilized" (as we might call Jean-Jacques), partakes of this order: every natural man enjoys psychic order and is harmoniously disposed toward the world around him. Emile and Jean-Jacques, however, not only *are* orderly, they *love* order as well, and they are altogether shaped by this love.

Its breadth and generality as a principle of soul make conscience something larger than a moral sense. In its primary sense (that is, as a principle of soul), conscience is a *source* of the moral sense, and a source of other sensibilities as well, including aesthetic and what one might call philosophical and scientific sensibilities. Yet it is not for nothing that Rousseau chooses the morally freighted "conscience" as the name for this newly discovered, apparently supramoral principle-of-soul. For while conscience is indeed something prior to the moral sense, it is nevertheless an essentially moral thing after all. The love of order is itself a moral principle. Indeed, the love of order constitutes the innermost meaning of goodness, virtue, and justice. To be good is to have maintained natural psychic unity and balance, which is to say, natural order; to be virtuous is to have aligned one's will with the general will, which is to say, with the order dictated by reason; and justice might well be defined as living in a way that is consistent with either natural or rational (that is, civil) order, depending on whether one is a man or a citizen.[51] Consequently, every true expression of this love of order—every effect of conscience, even those that have to do with taste or aesthetic sensibility or devotion to truth—is at root a moral phenomenon. Let us examine in more detail some of the many ways in which this love of order manifests itself in Emile.

The first product of conscience is pity. Ordinarily for Rousseau, "pity" denotes the sentiment of commiseration: one shares another's suffering and, now suffering oneself, wishes for the other's suffering to end. This sentiment, being a product or manifestation of conscience, appears only after one has acquired some degree of self-consciousness, some awareness of one's relations to others. Emile learns to feel pity only when his nascent and as yet unconscious sexual passion leads him to appreciate his connectedness to others of his kind (IV:220–27). Prior to that point he is simply incapable of pity. The young Emile is surely good and even admirable. As he comes to his fifteenth year, "Emile is laborious, temperate, patient, firm, and full of courage" (III:208). He has good judgment, which is untouched by prejudice or concern for the opinion of others. He has learned how to die—or rather has never forgotten. "In a word, of virtue Emile has all that relates to himself." But until he gains knowledge of his relations with others, he has no capacity for pity and therefore none of the social virtues. It takes knowledge of one's social relations, which itself presupposes an ability to imagine or feel oneself in the plight of suffering others, to awaken the natural capacity for pity.

> Social attachments develop in us only with our knowledge. Pity, although natural to man's heart, would remain forever inactive without imagination to set it in motion. How do we let ourselves be moved to pity? By transporting ourselves outside ourselves; by identifying with the suffering being. We suffer only to the extent that we judge him to suffer; it is not in ourselves but in him that we suffer. Think how much acquired knowledge this transport presupposes! How could I imagine evils of which I have no idea? How could I suffer when I see another suffer, if I do not even know that he suffers, if I do not know what he and I have in common? (*Languages* IX:261)[52]

---

51. See *SD* 119, where Rousseau cites "love of order in general" as a source of "maxims of justice and reason." Love of order in fact is one of two such sources. The other is "the known will of [the] creator," a pairing that underscores Rousseau's belief in the perfection of conscience understood as the love of order.

52. See *Emile* IV:221–27 for more on pity's dependence on imagination.

Just as it lies dormant in the young child, so pity lay dormant in the young childhood of the race. At most, man in the pure state of nature felt a kind of instinctive repugnance at seeing the suffering of his fellow sensitive beings, a repugnance that, unlike full-blown pity, did not require imagination or reflection. In this man was like other animals, such as the horse that takes care not to trample a living body. Now it is true that in some places Rousseau seems to indicate that pity *was* in fact present in the original natural man. But when he does so, he quite clearly is not speaking of pity as the sentiment of commiseration.[53] Exactly as he does with "conscience," Rousseau employs a word that ordinarily denotes a specific psychic phenomenon—and that he himself frequently employs in just such a way—to represent a principle of soul. When he speaks of pity in the pure state of nature, he is speaking of pity not as a full-blown sentiment but either as an instinctual repugnance or a principle of soul—exactly as he says he is (*SD* 95, 130).[54]

Rousseau's dual usage of "pity" ended between the publication of the *Second Discourse* and the writing of *Emile*. In the *Second Discourse*, "pity" is alternately a principle of soul and the sentiment of commiseration. In *Emile*, "pity" is no longer a principle of soul; it is only a sentiment. What seems to have occurred is less a change in Rousseau's thought or methodology than a change in the philosophical demands he faced. In the *Second Discourse* he needed to explain the goodness of a being who felt no love or sympathy for anyone else. For that,

53. The sentiment of pity is conspicuously absent from Rousseau's portraits of primitive naturalness: it is found neither in man in the pure state of nature (*SD* 137) nor in the preadolescent Emile (III:208).

54. It should be noted that, with respect to pity, Rousseau gives a different account of the state of nature, or what he calls "the first times," in the *Essay on the Origin of Languages*. There Rousseau holds that men were tender with their loved ones but hostile toward those they did not know; he does not mention the presence of pity even as a principle of soul (such as repugnance at the sight of suffering) (IX). I have given precedence to the *Second Discourse* because Rousseau himself treats it as authoritative on those issues on which it seems to depart from the *Essay* and because it is not at all clear that by "the first times," Rousseau means to refer *exclusively* to the very first period of human life. His first note to Chapter 9 of the *Essay* suggests that he means to include in "the first times" not only the pure state of nature but also later stages of the state of nature, stages in which hostility and other ills were present, even according to the account given in the *Second Discourse*. Regarding its account of what pity actually is, and what cognitive mechanisms it presupposes, the teaching of the *Essay* is entirely consistent with Rousseau's other works.

For his recognition and elucidation of the distinction between pity as a sentiment and pity as a principle of soul, I am indebted to Roger Masters (see note 41 to this chapter). For an alternate means of reconciling Rousseau's two uses of "pity," which she interprets as references to pity in its "immanent and active forms," see Mira Morgenstern, *Rousseau and the Politics of Ambiguity: Self, Culture, and Society* (University Park: Pennsylvania State University Press, 1996), 56–63. Morgenstern also reviews interpretations that see Rousseau's dual use as simply contradictory or incoherent (namely, the interpretations of Starobinski and Charvet).

it was enough to posit a principle of soul that manifested itself in a combination of indifference to others and instinctual repugnance at seeing them suffer, a combination that was as benevolent in its effect as the full-blown sentiment of pity would have been—hence the choice of "pity" to represent that principle-of-soul. ("Conscience" appears but once in the *Second Discourse*, in the dedicatory epistle to the Republic of Geneva, where it clearly denotes the faculty of moral judgment, not a principle of soul [85].) With regard to Emile, by contrast, the very same modern-scientific approach, the very same kind of attempt to reduce the workings of the soul to as few basic principles as possible, requires the positing of a larger principle of soul. The highly complicated soul of the civilized natural man cannot be explained by the same principle used to explain the relatively simple soul of the savage. An explanation of the civilized natural man requires a principle of soul that manifests itself in phenomena whose effects go far beyond those of pity; it requires a principle of soul whose effects are multifarious and multidimensional and yet related in virtue of their expressing a love of order—hence the choice of "conscience" rather than the continued use of "pity." In *Emile* and with regard to civilized men generally, "pity" stands for only one thing, the sentiment of commiseration. As such it is a manifestation of the principle of soul called conscience.

Nevertheless, even when it is conceived as this one thing, as a sentiment, pity turns out to be the stuff of several things, for it is a sentiment that takes multiple shapes and forms. In a passage in which he speaks of pity as a sentiment, Rousseau contends, "[F]rom this quality alone flow [many] social virtues," and asks ... "In fact, what are generosity, clemency, humanity, if not pity applied to the weak, to the guilty, or to the human species in general? Benevolence and even friendship are, rightly understood, the products of a constant pity fixed on a particular object: for is desiring that someone not suffer anything but desiring that he be happy?" (*SD* 131–32). Excepting only romantic passion, pity would seem to be the direct source of all nonexploitative social feelings.

If the "social virtues" flow directly from pity, many other good things flow from it indirectly. This we may conclude from the case of Emile, whose elaborate education in pity, a wide-ranging enterprise replete with field research as well as much study of history and fables, culminates in a state that falls little short of moral perfection.[55] Upon completing his description of Emile's education in pity, Rousseau catalogs some of its far-reaching effects:

---

55. This moral and sentimental education is recounted in detail in *Emile* IV:221–49.

I have first given the means, and now I show the effect. What *great views* I see settling little by little in his head! What *sublime sentiments* stifle the germ of the petty passions in his heart! What *judicial clarity*, what *accuracy of reason* I see forming in him, as a result of the cultivation of his inclinations, of the experience which concentrates the wishes of *a great soul* within the narrow limit of the possible and makes a man who is superior to others and, unable to raise them to his level, is capable of lowering himself to theirs! The true principles of the just, the true models of the beautiful, all the moral relations of beings, all the ideas of order are imprinted on his understanding. He sees the place of each thing and the cause that removes it from its place; he sees what can do good and what stands in its way. Without having experienced the human passions, he knows their illusions and their effects. (IV:253; emphasis added)

As pity is the sentimental source of nearly all social virtue and fellow feeling, a proper education in pity amounts to a wide-ranging social education. And a successful education in pity yields all the excellences—moral, intellectual, and aesthetic—that Rousseau cites in this interior portrait of the maturing Emile. To be sure, neither pity nor even conscience (of which, to repeat, pity is a manifestation) deserves full credit for Emile's sound judgment, for his "judicial clarity" and "accuracy of reason." These intellectual virtues—and indeed, the social virtues as well—require reason as well as conscience in order to develop. But neither could Emile have developed so well as thinker and judge without conscience's help, for it is conscience that inspires him with wholesome motives and that thereby virtually inoculates him against the passions that distort most men's judgment. Without "sublime sentiments" and "great views," which are incontestable manifestations of conscience and that appear only as a result of his education in pity, Emile would have been less sound of mind, not to mention less sound of spirit. The "love of order ... when developed and made active" comes to nothing less than intellectual, moral, and aesthetic superiority.

Emile's education in pity does not come close to completing his comprehensive natural education. He still needs to learn of God, Woman, and politics, and he has yet to acquire refined taste and incorruptible virtue. (These are things that can be well learned only with the motive power of romantic love.) His incipient sexual passion still needs to be sublimated, first into longing and then into sustainable love. But his education in pity has successfully prepared him for all of this: conscience has fitted him, as it were, with a template—or rather, conscience is itself a template, so shaping the further development of his soul as to ensure that newly emerging inclinations will not contradict the principle of harmony that lies at the heart of all naturalness. That is to say, conscience, the active love of order, will keep Emile's sexual and social passions from becoming vessels of disorderly *amour-propre*. It is in this—in the fact that conscience plays the decisive role and, even more, in the *way* that it plays this role—that Rousseau's understanding of sublimation differs most clearly from other understandings.

In the cases of Plato and Freud sublimation is conceived in terms of a particular psychic actor (reason and the ego, respectively) acting upon—that is, elevating—desire. The elevation of desire is explained, even if only metaphorically, as the consequence of a positive act. For Plato, reason apprehends the superiority of higher objects of desire and so lures desire upward; for Freud, the ego determines what might serve as the best available substitute object and redirects instinctual energy accordingly. Rousseau, by contrast, does not put forward a comparable positive act. One cannot say, even metaphorically, that conscience does any positive work, that it actively elevates desire. Rather, the process of Rousseauan sublimation is best explained in negative terms. The job of conscience is not to scout the terrain and discover better objects but rather to keep psychic energy from overflowing its natural channels, which is essentially negative work. As a principle of soul, conscience is less an intrapsychic actor than a developmental template whose task is to keep psychic energy from dissipating, thereby leaving it no choice but to rise as the higher mental faculties develop. In the passage just quoted, Rousseau supplies, almost in passing, a concise summary of his conception of sublimation. He speaks of "the experience which *concentrates the wishes of a great soul within the narrow limit of the possible* and [so] makes a man who is superior to others." The "experience" to which he refers is "the cultivation of [Emile's] inclinations," by which he means Emile's preadolescent education. But if education is the proximate cause of this elevation to superiority, conscience is the immediate as well as the formal cause. Conscience, then, is what concentrates the wishes of this great soul; conscience is the true sublimator.

To switch from the engineering metaphor (conscience as developmental template) to a horticultural one, one might liken the basic principle of Rousseauan sublimation to pruning a tree. Pruning is a negative task, but one that encourages a positive phenomenon—that is, vertical growth. A comparable process takes place in Emile's soul. By activating and nourishing his conscience, Emile's education snips and otherwise discourages lower growth, thereby ensuring that all growth will take place in the higher regions. The whole thrust of the "negative education" of his youth is to prevent the premature (and hence distorting) development of such faculties as imagination and foresight or, in the rare event that a characteristic does develop too early, to squelch it.[56] To those who might object to this comparison on the grounds that pruning interferes with nature whereas Emile's education is supposed to cultivate it, we need only respond that naturalness in civilization is such a difficult attainment that it requires at least as much artifice as is involved in pruning. An education in civilized naturalness requires strict and constant, even if hidden, governance: "Instinct is good as long as it acts by itself; it is suspect from the moment it operates within man-made institutions. It must not be destroyed, but it must be regulated" (*Emile* IV:333–34). "One must use a great deal of art to prevent social man from being totally artificial" (*Emile* IV:317).

Emile's education in pity, then, yields an impressive array of excellences, and much that it does not yield directly, it at least makes possible by activating and cultivating conscience in the broadest sense of that word (which, as we have seen, is very broad indeed). This ostensible education in pity is in truth much more than an education in pity, for it activates and cultivates the love of order at all levels. And along with this love, it equips Emile with knowledge to match. As Rousseau states in the passage quoted above, "The true principles of the just, the true models of the beautiful, all the moral relations of beings, all the ideas of order are imprinted on his understanding" (IV:253).

The latter is a most extraordinary and revealing statement in several respects. In the first place, it is an enormous claim of success: Rousseau points to knowledge that any philosopher would be pleased to have and proclaims that such is the yield of the education in pity that he has given to an ordinary fifteen-year-old boy.[57] Second, and by necessity, it is a claim on behalf of

---

56. The only case in which a characteristic appears too early in Emile and thus needs to be eradicated is the first appearance of vanity in his soul. After upstaging a magician at a fair, Emile experiences the literally dizzying delight of the crowd's acclaim; vanity has been awakened. Fortunately for him, however, vanity's untimely emergence has been foreseen and so is met with the best possible response: humiliation (the magician thwarts his next attempt at glory), which routs this vanity and sends it back into the subterranean tunnels of latency. Thus does a "negative education" serve him even at its harshest. "How many mortifying consequences are attracted by the first movement of vanity! Young master, spy out this first movement with care. If you know thus how to make humiliation and disgrace arise from it, be sure that a second movement will not come for a long time" (III:175). See also "*Amour-Propre*'s Inevitability," in Chapter 4. (It bears noting that the tutor not only *foresaw* the first appearance of vanity but *arranged* it, a fact that speaks to the subtlety and the difficulty of a successful "negative education.")

57. Emile's ordinariness lies in his native endowments, not in the person he becomes—which, of course, is precisely Rousseau's point.

conscience: whatever belongs to pity belongs to conscience, of which pity is but the first expression. Third, Rousseau's words effectively convey conscience's role as developmental template: Emile still has much to learn, but the principles that will guide his future learning have now been "imprinted" (*se gravent*) on his mind; they will govern the ways in which he assimilates future experiences both of the world and of his own fast-maturing soul. Finally, at the risk of reading too much into Rousseau's formulation, we seem to find in it an indication of his metaphysics—that is, an indication of his understanding of life's moral order. We seem to find an implied statement about the relationship between the just, the beautiful, the moral, and the very idea of order itself.

Let us take note of the sequence in which Rousseau lists the results of Emile's education in pity. Listed first are "the true principles of the just." That principles of justice should be mentioned first seems natural enough, given the close and obvious relation between conscience and justice (Rousseau at times defines conscience as "an innate principle of justice").[58] But the reasoning behind the remainder of the sequence may not be as obvious. Indeed, that the remaining acquisitions should appear in *any* sequence is remarkable: that conscience, through an education in pity, should account for knowledge of beauty and the rest is an extraordinary notion unique to Rousseau. But what of the sequence? What significance if any can we find in the list that proceeds from "the true principles of the just" to "the true models of the beautiful" to "all the moral relations of beings" to, finally, "all the ideas of order"?

The answer I would suggest is that the list proceeds from that which is an expression to that which is the source, from that which is subsumed to that which subsumes, and from the more narrowly specific to the more general. Or, to use Platonic language, it may be that in Rousseau's understanding the just participates in the beautiful, which in turn participates in the moral relations of beings, which themselves participate in the idea(s) of order. This interpretation becomes all the more plausible as we notice the absence of a conjunction in the sentence. The sequence proceeds not in the manner of "first, second, third, *and* fourth" but, rather, "first, second, third, fourth." The absence of a conjunction seems to imply that with each successive reformulation, Rousseau means to correct himself by expanding his object, that each successive element is presented as being larger than and subsuming its predecessor.[59] This much, at any rate, is incontrovertible: an individual who has grasped "all

---

58. See, for example, *Emile* IV:289 and *LM* 1108.

59. Omitting a conjunction for the purpose of suggesting a more expansive reformulation is not unknown in world literature. Consider, for example, the conjunctionless sequence in Prospero's famous speech in *The Tempest*:

the ideas of order," the final element of the list, will necessarily have grasped all of the preceding elements, since those other elements are but specific cases (social, aesthetic, and so on) of order. Moral relations, beauty, and justice are respectively defined as one or another expression of order, and so we are entitled to say that conscience, which is itself defined as the love of order, is the source of Emile's (or anyone's) recognition of and attachment to the just and the beautiful.

So we now have a second reason to attribute all human excellences, and not just the obviously moral ones, to conscience. (The first reason, which we have already discussed, was Rousseau's explicit attribution of "all the excellence of [human] nature" to conscience.) And there are even more reasons still— beginning with the simple fact that these excellences develop in Emile. Emile is presented as (civilized) naturalness incarnate. It does not seem unreasonable, therefore, to infer that his every trait is natural (in the civil sense). If Emile acquires good taste and a love of beauty, that is significant reason to consider these acquired qualities natural. And if one is prepared to consider these traits natural, it is but a small and perfectly logical step to attribute them to conscience, since conscience is the only part of nature that embraces spiritual phenomena, which these traits certainly are.

But we need not rely only on such inferential reasoning to establish that these excellences are natural and arise from conscience. For we have Rousseau's explicit declaration, first, that good taste has a basis in nature and, second, that there is a causal, sequential relationship between taste, ideas of beauty, and, finally, moral notions. We have from him a series of unambiguous statements that establish the naturalness of qualities that one has traditionally regarded as the distinguishing marks of high civilization.

Emile journeys to Paris for an extensive education in taste. In the course of this education, he learns a truth with which few Parisians, despite their refinement—or, rather, because of it—are acquainted: "All the true models of taste are in nature" (IV:341). Armed with that understanding, Emile is able to acquire the Parisians' delicacy without the grotesquerie and spiritual distortion that all too regularly accompany it. What does it mean to say that all the true models of taste are in nature? Surely, given Rousseau's view of nature as essentially harmonious, it means that good taste is a taste for harmonious order. Thus

---

And, like the baseless fabric of this vision,
The cloud-capp'd towers, the gorgeous palaces,
The solemn temples, *the great globe itself*,
Yea, all which it inherit, shall dissolve. (4.1)

we may surely say that it is a manifestation of conscience. A good aesthetic sensibility, of which good taste is the first sign, is as much a product of conscience as is a strong and just moral sense. Indeed, these two products are directly related: "By means of taste the mind is imperceptibly opened to ideas of the beautiful of every sort and, finally, to the moral relations related to them" (*Emile* V:375). What is the connection? It would seem that appreciating (the beauty of) order in one context awakens the mind to appreciate it in others. "The love of the beautiful," Rousseau writes, "is a sentiment as natural to the human heart as the love of self. . . . Whatever the philosophers may say of it, this love is innate to man and serves as principle to his conscience" (*d'Alembert* 23).

The moral and aesthetic sensibilities, if wholesomely developed, are intimately related. They are different expressions of the same basic principle, the love of order—different expressions, that is, of conscience. And they are not even so very different at that. For the respective peaks of morality and beauty are in fact one and the same thing. The "supreme *beauty*," says the Rousseau of the *Dialogues*, is none other than *virtue* (II:127; emphasis added). It is as "an idolater of the beautiful in all its genres" that Jean-Jacques cherishes virtue. "Order, harmony, beauty, perfection are the objects of his sweetest meditations," and it is precisely because virtue so perfectly embodies these qualities that he considers it the preeminent good among human things. Emile, too, learns to prize virtue for its beauty. On the one occasion on which he is asked to resist inclination so that he might develop virtue, the case for virtue is made at least in part on aesthetic grounds. "Do you want, then, to live happily and wisely?" asks his tutor. "Attach your heart only to imperishable beauty"—that is, to virtue (V:446).

Thus may a man reared in civilization achieve the inner state that will enable him to remain natural. His social and sexual passions are sublimated by an education that funnels them through the developmental template of conscience. This education, Emile's education, is full of artifice. It entails much manipulation—not of his will, to be sure, but of the surrounding environment. This management of Emile's surroundings perhaps amounts to an even greater intrusion upon his freedom, in that it guides his will without his knowing it. But this education, for all its calculated manipulation, is nevertheless a natural education, for it ensures that all his higher capacities will accord with the lower ones; it ensures that Emile's soul will be as internally harmonious as that of the savage in the state of nature, or at least very nearly so.[60] Sublimation is

---

60. The manipulative aspects of Emile's education might even be seen as preserving the integrity and authenticity of his experience: "The point of the tutor's so-called manipulations is to keep Emile

natural. It meets the criteria for naturalness that were enunciated at the start of this chapter: it produces sentiments and inclinations that constitute a deepened and extended *amour de soi*, and it thereby ensures that the *amour-propre* that is unavoidable even in Emile will be limited in extent and benign in character. Or, to apply a different test, one we encountered in the previous chapter, sublimation succeeds in making a life that "consists in the closest possible approximation to the state of nature which is possible on the level of humanity."[61] And it does so, moreover, while at the same time elevating the soul to a level at which it partakes of the sublime, for the "level of humanity" is potentially a very high level.

There can be no natural life in civilization without sublimation. The point is not so much that sublimity is a necessary aspect of naturalness as that only sublimation, only the upward channeling of psychic energy and especially sexual passion, can keep desire from roaming in unnatural and miserable directions. Only true beauty can continuously command the gaze of desire and so keep it from straying to more easily available but corrupting objects; only true love can prevent debauchery. There is no middle course. And so while sublimity is not a necessary aspect of naturalness, it is necessary to naturalness after all—if not as a constitutive element then as a means to it.

But not everything about the civilized natural man is sublime. That is to say, sublimation, though necessary for reconciling civilization and naturalness, is not by itself sufficient to the task. In the intrapsychic drama that culminates in the development of the civilized natural man, sublimation does indeed play the starring role, but not even the most virtuosic star could make a success of so complex a production as this without assistance from a worthy supporting cast. Our elaboration of the meaning of naturalness amid civilization would not be complete, even in outline, without our considering the aspects of naturalness that arise in some way other than through sublimation.

What Else Is Natural, and Why

As we have seen, the naturalness of sublimation is indicated in several ways. It is suggested by the realization that sublimation is the work of conscience,

---

from being shaped by that which is not him, but it is not precisely to manipulate *him*. All mediation must be, will be, Emile's own." Strong, *Politics of the Ordinary*, 109–10.

61. Strauss, *Natural Right and History*, 282.

which Rousseau explicitly labels natural, and it is betokened by Rousseau's many pronouncements that this or that consequence of sublimation—be it romantic love, the love of beauty, even the love of virtue—is natural in the civil state.[62] But all this evidence really just confirms a judgment whose primary basis lies elsewhere. The primary and sufficient reason for considering sublimation natural is that it deepens and extends *amour de soi*. Indeed, that it promotes or preserves *amour de soi* is the primary and sufficient reason (and a necessary condition) for considering *any* human attribute natural, whether it arises from sublimation or not.

Included among the natural characteristics that arise through some process other than sublimation are many that not only diverge from but actually contradict the characteristics of the savage. (Characteristics that do arise through sublimation tend to be more highly evolved than, but still continuous with, savage characteristics, as, for example, romantic love is more highly evolved than but continuous with savage sexuality.) Emile's naturalness consists at least in part of traits that would have been unnatural for the savage. Whereas the savage was indolent, Emile is highly active throughout his life, enjoying and profiting from manual labor (I:56, III:195–203). In fact, Rousseau comments on the unhealthfulness of laziness in civilized man (*Corsica* 323). Whereas the savage is unreflective, spending most of his free time asleep (*SD* 112), Emile is reflective, even meditative. "He must work like a peasant and think like a philosopher so as not to be as lazy as a savage" (III:202). Emile even develops honor, which, being a manifestation of *amour-propre*, was unknown to the savage but is nevertheless said to have a natural basis (IV:417). And he develops virtue, perhaps the characteristic of this natural man most alien to the savage.

Obviously virtue is unnatural in the strict sense. It represents the subordination of inclination to duty (*Reveries* VI:96), and if it is too much to say that virtue exists for the purpose of suppressing nature, it surely is not too much to say that it becomes necessary precisely where nature, in the form of goodness, proves inadequate as a behavioral guide. "I have made you good rather than virtuous," says Jean-Jacques to the newly and passionately social Emile. "But he who is only good remains so only as long as he takes pleasure in being so. Goodness is broken and perishes under the impact of the human passions.

---

62. Note that it is not virtue but rather the love of virtue to which Rousseau accords natural status. Jean-Jacques, a purer example of naturalness than Emile (because unlike Emile, Jean-Jacques lives on the margins of society), lacks virtue, but he does love it. (See *Dialogues* II:126–27.) As for virtue itself, Rousseau does not pronounce *it* natural. Nevertheless, one could make the case (as I attempt later in this chapter) that even virtue can be natural, albeit only in the civil state.

The man who is only good is good only for himself" (V:444). To be good for others—to be natural in the civil state—one needs virtue. Nevertheless, virtue is clearly less natural than goodness. Is it natural at all?

The logic of the present interpretation would answer in the affirmative. Emile requires virtue precisely in order to maintain the psychic balance and harmony that constitute the heart of his naturalness. Without virtue, without this peculiar acquisition that seems so alien to everything natural, the balance between desires and faculties will be destroyed.

> How pitiable you are going to be, thus subjected to your unruly passions! There will always be privations, losses, and alarms. You will not even enjoy what is left to you. The fear of losing everything will prevent you from possessing anything. As a result of having wanted to follow only your passions, *you will never be able to satisfy them.* You will always seek repose, but it will always flee before you. You will be miserable, and you will become wicked. How could you not be, since you have only your unbridled desires as a law? (V:444; emphasis added)

There is nothing natural about virtue, except that it serves nature, which makes it natural after all, so long as it remains essentially personal rather than civic in its purpose and orientation.[63]

With the case of virtue we have encountered a very important feature of Rousseau's understanding of nature. In the previous chapter we observed that different versions of natural men correspond to different levels of naturalness. Although what is natural in the savage state and what is natural in the civil state have significant elements in common, the two categories are distinct. Now, in our elaboration of the second of these categories, we find that there are degrees of naturalness *within* that group. All that is natural in the civil state is not *equally* natural in the civil state. Romantic love, for example, though not natural in the strict sense—Rousseau claims to have shown in the *Second Discourse* that love "is not as natural as is thought" (*Emile* V:430)—nevertheless is a matter of involuntary attraction and inclination and so seems believably natural in our everyday sense of things. Virtue, on the other hand, entails the overcoming of inclination by will and so strikes us, by any commonsense standard, as much less natural. Indeed, in a certain sense, virtue entails the *overcoming* of nature. But because it helps to maintain psychic order and balance

---

63. *Civic* virtue is not natural. It serves the purpose of denaturalization in that it expresses and supports patriotism, which is a species of *amour-propre* rather than *amour de soi*.

and thereby protects *amour de soi*—because it serves nature's purpose—it merits inclusion among those things that are natural in the civil state. In the acquisition of virtue, nature is no guide: "It abandons us to ourselves" (*Emile* V:445). Yet nature requires that virtue be acquired. Nature calls for and, in the case of Emile, receives virtue's service. And that, even if only in a technical sense, makes virtue natural, just as enlistment makes soldiers out of even the most improbable civilians. It is purpose that determines identity.[64]

In the end, there is only one criterion for determining whether a characteristic or activity is natural in the civil state: Does it promote or protect *amour de soi?* If it does, it is natural; if it does not, it is not. How, though, shall we know? It is not an easy thing to recognize just what does and what does not serve *amour de soi.* Indeed, given the futile records of even the most renowned philosophers (according to Rousseau's assessment, at least), one might justifiably despair of ever discerning which of our myriad impulses and activities are natural.[65] One might despair, that is, if one were left to one's own abstract reasoning—which, fortunately, we are not.

Nature is beneficent and provides much guidance to those who have not lost the ability to sense its promptings. Most of that which is natural, even that which is natural only in the civil state and to the barest degree, has a way of making itself known—or rather, has a way of making itself felt. Rousseau is in earnest when he exclaims in the concluding paragraph of the *First Discourse,* "O virtue! sublime science of simple souls, are so many difficulties and preparations needed to know you? Are not your principles engraved in all hearts, and is it not enough in order to learn your laws to commune with oneself and listen to the voice of one's conscience in the silence of the passions? That is true philosophy" (64).[66]

Those people and those societies that live in closer proximity to nature (we are referring here largely to savage and peasant societies) do not do so as a result of superior reasoning. If anything, they benefit from *not* being sophisticated

---

64. That there are degrees of naturalness applies not only to attributes but also to needs. See *Fragments* 529–30. See also Schwartz, *Sexual Politics*, 14–15.

65. Rousseau's contempt for the achievements of philosophy is perhaps most vividly expressed in *FD* 60–61. See also *Dialogues* III:239n, where Rousseau says philosophers are particularly untrustworthy when they purport to identify what belongs to nature.

66. The same sentiment is expressed in the fifth of the *Lettres morales* and by the Vicar at *Emile* IV:286: "I do not draw these rules [of conduct] from the principles of a high philosophy, but find them written by nature with ineffaceable characters in the depth of my heart. I have only to consult myself about what I want to do."

I take Rousseau's reference to virtue to include goodness. See note 28 to this chapter.

thinkers. They remain close to nature because they have not allowed anything to obscure the principles that nature has engraved in all human hearts. Neither interest nor passion nor the obfuscatory power of a sophisticated but amoral reason has been permitted to choke or drown out the voice of nature. And this is good news for us as well, who *have* allowed interest and passion (with the assistance of their handmaiden, reason) to remove us from nature. It is good for us because we can find in the examples of these more natural people much guidance as to the substance, the concrete actualities, of civilized naturalness. In our quest for knowledge of what would constitute a natural life in civilization we need not begin our search from scratch; we need not search at random for the traits and ways of life that would bring us closer to nature. Instead, we can learn something of what is natural by observing those who have remained close to nature. We can grant to their particular characteristics and activities the tentative presumption of naturalness and then test the merit of that presumption with our reason. (We do need reason, we reflective beings who would know what is natural.) In this way one can employ reason in the service of nature, which is where it belongs but where it has all too seldom been. One can take one's philosophical bearings from nature. Which is exactly what Rousseau claims to have done.

The strongest signal—one might even call it presumptive evidence—that a given characteristic is natural and worth (re)attaining is that it is universally present among primitive peoples but is not so common among modern peoples.[67] Most of the many such characteristics are negative, though there are critically important positive ones as well.[68] The negative characteristics are of the sort that one typically associates, in our everyday discourse, with the phrase "getting back to nature." In fact, though he does not use exactly that term, Rousseau provides in the sixth of the *Lettres morales* a handbook for just that purpose. (He is surely the spiritual father of the modern version of this idea, though, to be sure, children have a way of creatively reinterpreting their parents' intentions.) In the *Lettres*, Rousseau advises periodic retreats from the material and social entanglements of Paris to the rustic simplicities of the country. The Comtesse d'Houdetot, his addressee, is advised that she will find

---

67. It goes without saying that characteristics that are found in both primitive and modern societies are to be presumed natural. An example would be the prohibition against incest. See *Languages* IX:272n.

68. By "negative characteristics" I simply mean those that are defined in terms of absence. An absence of luxury, for example, is a negative characteristic. By "positive characteristics," conversely, I simply mean those that are defined by some presence—such as the presence of a particular custom. The words are used only for the sake of convenience. They express no judgment as to the significance or the relative value of the characteristics at hand.

in the country a freedom and happiness that will diminish her attachment to the vain cares and amusements of corrupt civilization. A physical return to nature will initiate a spiritual return: "Eyes struck solely by the sweet images of nature reconcile it better with our heart" (1114). Soon the voice of conscience, the voice of nature, will make itself heard. Neither the Comtesse nor we modern readers can reach Emile's level of naturalness, but one does stand to achieve, through simplicity, greater closeness to nature. (Other portraits of a civilized simplicity that falls short of *Emile*'s perfection are found in both the *First* and the *Second Discourse*, in the *Letter to d'Alembert*, and in the more idyllic scenes of *Julie*.)

Among the positive characteristics that Rousseau deems to have been universally present in simpler societies but scorned (unnaturally) in more highly developed ones, the most prominent are those that have to do with sexual mores. Modesty, shame, and chastity; male "attack" and female "defense"; masculinity and femininity that define themselves in complementary terms, seeing in one another their own fulfillment—these are phenomena (as Rousseau tells it) that once upon a time were woven into the social fabric, giving it both strength and warmth, but that lately, and with great consequence, have fallen into disrepute. Obviously none of these things is natural in the pure sense. Sex in the pure state of nature was no more emotionally complicated than eating or drinking: all appetites were merely physical (*SD* 134–37). Just as obviously, however, they *are* natural in the civil state. Rousseau makes the point repeatedly and unequivocally in *Emile*, the *Letter to d'Alembert*, and the *Lettres morales*—works that evince a practical intention to lend support to the cause of civilized naturalness.[69]

That sexual modesty and the rest are natural is presumptively established, in Rousseau's view, by their being the rule among all who have not suffered the distortions of a noxious education. It is only by the unnatural exertions of a corrupted reason that what we now regard as traditional sexual mores have lost ground. Do you not sense the falseness of those who deny that modesty is natural, Rousseau asks the Comtesse d'Houdetot, when "you see it in all its force among the ignorant and rustic peoples and [when you see that] its sweet voice is not stifled in the more cultivated nations except by sophisms of reasoning?" (*LM* 1110). This near universality ought to be enough to convince one of the naturalness of modesty and shame, especially if one experiences them within oneself. To those who ask, "Why should we blush at the needs which nature has given us? Why should we find a motive for shame in an act

---

69. See *Emile* V:357–65; *d'Alembert* 83–90; and *LM* 1110–11.

so indifferent in itself and so beneficial in its effects as the one which leads to the perpetuation of the species?" and who ask why men and women should be governed by different rules in sexual matters, Rousseau responds with his own question: "Is it not absurd that I should have to say why I am ashamed of a natural sentiment, if this shame is no less natural to me than the sentiment itself? I might as well ask myself why I have the sentiment. Is it for me to jus- tify what nature has done? From this line of reasoning [that is, the reasoning of those who view chasteness as a convention imposed by and for the sake of fathers and husbands], those who do not see why man exists ought to deny that he exists" (*d'Alembert* 83). That modesty and shame arise within us, says Rousseau, that they are overcome if at all only by the determined assault of decadent philosophy or education, ought to tell us these qualities are natural and therefore worth maintaining in all their force. As far as Rousseau is con- cerned, that ought to be enough: "Is it for me to justify what nature has done?"

But in fact, Rousseau does justify what (he thinks) nature has done.[70] He begins to do so in the very next paragraph of the *Letter* and he does so in much greater depth and detail in the opening section of book V of *Emile*. And in so doing he confirms the thesis to which this chapter is devoted, namely, that the definitive criterion of what is natural in the civil state is that it promote or preserve benign self-love, or *amour de soi*. To be sure, Rousseau does not make the case in those terms. Instead, he explains in intricate detail how it is that these traditional mores serve to strengthen and sweeten social bonds. (The strengthening is in part a result of the sweetening.) But that purpose is itself subservient to the larger purpose that we have here identified.

In the passages devoted to sexual mores, Rousseau argues at one and the same time toward two conclusions: that traditional mores are good for us and that they are natural. The same evidence and the same arguments advance the two conclusions equally. All of these things—modesty, shame and chastity; the psychological interdependence of the sexes, according to which women are to judge the merit of men and men the merit of women; the differentiation of male and female roles not just in matters of love but in all of social life—all of these things are good for us (both as individuals and as societies) because they enhance the affectional ties between men and women. They enhance the ties from which loving families are made and that represent the only alternative in

---

70. Indeed, just as one can read the *Second Discourse* as a justification of nature or a kind of theod- icy, so too can one read the whole of Rousseau's writings on civilized naturalness as a general justifi- cation of nature. Note the very first line of book I of *Emile*: "Everything is good as it leaves the hands of the Author of things" (37). (Regarding the *Second Discourse*, see Scott, "Theodicy of the *Second Discourse*," 696–711, and Starobinski, *Transparency and Obstruction*, 20–21.)

the modern world to the harsh and resented chains of egotistic self-interest. And they are natural for the same reason.

The universality of these phenomena among rustic peoples is seen by Rousseau as a fair indication of their naturalness. So too is the fact that most civilized people experience impulses toward them, even if many of us repudi- ate them on the basis of ill-conceived ideas. But the *argument* for their natu- ralness is based on the purpose they serve, on their enhancing affection. The details of Rousseau's argument are beyond the purview of this inquiry and, in any case, have been explicated elsewhere.[71] What is relevant, though, are the criteria, both explicit and implicit, by which the judgment of naturalness is made. Rousseau explicitly argues for the naturalness of traditional sexual mores on the grounds that they create and support an affectional basis for male- female relations. Female modesty and chastity, for example, are said to be nec- essary in order to stimulate male desire for and attachment to a single woman. They stoke male desire and then, by denying it easy satisfaction, create the conditions under which desire can be sublimated into passionate longing. They also enhance the pleasure of sexual relations, not only in anticipation but also in consummation. Here Rousseau purports to trump the hedonistic case for sexual liberation and demystification: without modesty and chastity, the passions would languish "in a boring freedom" (*d'Alembert* 84); with them, by contrast, great passions are ignited that intensify pleasure and that them- selves contribute mightily to the possibility of a beautiful and nobly enchant- ing love.

Without modesty, chastity, and the rest, according to Rousseau, sex would not be moralized and so would be less pleasurable and less meaningful. If desire remained unsublimated, sexual attraction would be dissociated from affection, leading to a world in which relations between the sexes would be (if they are not already) relations of exploitation. And exploitation, even when mutual, is a corrupt and dispiriting basis for social relations—and how much more so when it occurs within the family, where one might have enjoyed "the sweetest sentiments known to men" (*SD* 146–47).

Rousseau's explicit reason for considering traditional sexual mores natural is that they promote romantic and conjugal love and discourage debauchery and exploitation. There is much intricate reasoning, there are many intermediate steps and subsidiary conclusions, but all of that reasoning is aimed at estab- lishing that these mores do in fact promote affection between men and women (and, consequently, that they promote loving families). Affection is the announced standard of naturalness. Understandably, Rousseau does not bother

---

71. See Schwartz, *Sexual Politics*, chap. 2.

to justify this standard: his interest is in persuading his readers of the enormous value of these mores and of the love that they can help create. If he succeeds at that task, he will have brought his readers nearer to nature, and they will have been persuaded by inner experience, the best of all possible evidence, that the path he recommends is indeed the road of nature. We, however, who seek to uncover and articulate the underlying unity of Rousseau's philosophy of nature need to consider the unspoken but critical connections within it. We do need to examine the standard and look into its basis. Why affection? Why should Rousseau adopt as his explicit test of naturalness the question of whether something promotes affection between men and women? What we find is that Rousseau uses this more wieldy standard as a way of determining whether various mores promote or protect *amour de soi*, which is his ultimate standard for judging naturalness in civilization. Affection promotion is a practicable and reliable stand-in for Rousseau's more abstract ultimate standard.

To demonstrate that something promotes affection is less obscure, and is bound to have greater emotional and persuasive force, than demonstrating that it serves the cause of *amour de soi*. But we still need to uncover the substantive relation between the two standards, that is, the subsumption of the former by the latter. How does promoting affection between men and women also promote or protect *amour de soi*?

It does so both indirectly and directly. It tempers *amour-propre*, ensuring that this morally ambiguous variety of self-love will not, weedlike, overrun the ground occupied by benign *amour de soi*: mutual affection is mutual recognition, and such recognition satisfies and tames *amour-propre*. And it deepens and extends *amour de soi* directly by adding to the absolute—which is to say, the nonrelative, nonrivalrous, noncombative—love of existence that constitutes the real meaning of that thoroughly natural form of self-love.

Affection between lovers is perhaps unique in the extent to which it engages both sorts of self-love. In no other sphere do conquest and recognition (prizes sought by *amour-propre*) mingle so extensively with selflessness and sympathy (expressions of *amour de soi*). But romantic love is not unique in the dual nature of its service to *amour de soi*. Most things that qualify as natural in the civil state—certainly most interesting things that so qualify—do so because they serve *amour de soi* both directly and indirectly: directly, by deepening the absolute love of existence; indirectly, by limiting *amour-propre*. Of the two, the indirect means is by far the more difficult and complex, both to achieve and to comprehend. It is also the more important means from a practical standpoint: The direct enhancement of *amour de soi* will tend to take care of itself, or, rather, it would take care of itself if it were not obstructed by the intrusion of *amour-propre*—which is exactly why the tempering of *amour-propre* is so important from a practical standpoint. Good governance of *amour-propre* is the sine qua non of civilized naturalness. It is, one might almost say, *the* moral and political problem for Rousseau.[72]

Whatever promotes or preserves *amour de soi*, whether directly or indirectly, is natural in the civil state. Our effort in this chapter has been to explicate the meaning of this formula and, in so doing, confirm that it is indeed an accurate representation of Rousseau's view. The examples, especially those drawn from the realm of sex and love, were selected because they serve these purposes particularly well. These examples are not unique, but rather paradigmatic. An examination of any other phenomena that Rousseau attaches to Emile or otherwise calls natural would reveal that they, too, serve the cause of *amour de soi* in one way or another.

The limits of our efforts are suggested by that catchall "one way or another." The phrase covers a multitude of intricacies. One could devote many chapters to explaining the ways in which different natural characteristics and activities promote or preserve *amour de soi*. Short of that, our rendering of Rousseau's philosophy of nature must remain a sketch rather than a detailed portrait. But there also remains a more serious gap, one that keeps even the sketch from being complete and that therefore needs to be addressed: we need to take up the relation between the two kinds of self-love.

I have repeatedly referred to the regulation of *amour-propre* as an indirect but necessary support of civilized naturalness. That support, it turns out, needs to be positive. However much *amour de soi* is threatened by a lawless *amour-propre* (and the threat is devastating), it actually *needs* the support of a wholesome *amour-propre*. Naturalness requires more than just that *amour-propre* not run wild. It also requires that *amour-propre* lend its force to the cause of naturalness. If this is so—if, as I am suggesting, the preservation of *amour de soi* in the civil state requires that *amour-propre* be well governed—not extirpated, not transcended, not even diluted, but rather well governed—then our sketch will not be complete until we have examined the nature of that governance and its results. Here we have arrived at one of the deeper paradoxes in Rousseau's thought. How can the psychic force that constitutes denaturalization in the citizen and that foments perverse unnaturalism in the Parisian be made to support naturalness in Emile? This is the question whose answer will supply the final lines of our sketch.

---

72. Good governance of *amour-propre* is as important to the denaturalized civic life as it is to the natural life. The solutions embodied by these lives are radically different, but the problem to which they respond is the same.

4

The Problem of Self-Love

Although barely distinguishable from the animals, the inhabitant of the pure state of nature was a human being. Notwithstanding that he was a solitary being who lacked speech, that his mental abilities differed not at all in kind and only marginally in degree from those of his nonhuman neighbors—notwithstanding even that he was unable to make meaningful use of his freedom and perfectibility, the very capacities that distinguished him from those neighbors—he was a natural *man*. Underlying this determination is Rousseau's substitution of freedom and perfectibility for reason and speech as the defining human attributes, a reconceptualization that has proved to be one of the more significant turns in intellectual history. Whether Rousseau intended or even could have foreseen all the paths he opened is doubtful. Yet even if we subtract the unintended effects and look only at Rousseau's own apparent purposes, his redefinition of humanity still marks a highly consequential departure from the earlier prevailing view. To cite just one major effect, one that we have already encountered in previous chapters, his redefinition justified his using the creature he called "natural man" as a standard against which to measure the species in its present state. If natural man was indeed a man, then we today can be justly compared to him, and his goodness and happiness are conditions that we might legitimately seek to replicate in whatever way and to whatever extent we can.

But the real radicalism of Rousseau's departure, at least from an anthropological point of view, lies less in his according human status to the creature who inhabited the state of nature than in his account of man's leaving that state. For it was in leaving the state of nature and becoming civilized that man became what he now is, what he now *irrevocably* is.[1] And what he is—what we are—is a peculiar combination of benign self-sufficiency and perilous, unquenchable need.

A transformation of indescribable proportions has taken place: the solitary has acquired sociability. It is not just that civilized man lives with others and speaks to them and thinks about them, or even that he desires their voluntary recognition. Rather, man has become a social creature in the most fundamental sense. More than just living *with* others, he lives *in* and *through* them: "the sociable man, always outside of himself, knows how to live only in the opinion of others; and it is, so to speak, from their judgment alone that he draws the sentiment of his own existence" (*SD* 179).

We are perhaps accustomed to interpreting this observation as a disparaging one. And indeed, the context of the remark would seem to confirm that reading. In fact, though, sociality in and of itself is not an undesirable thing; living through others, drawing the sentiment of one's existence from one's fellows, is not inherently bad in Rousseau's view. The socialization of humanity need not have played out as badly as it has—or badly at all. Rare though they have been, good communities and good men and women attest to this fact. Moreover, even corrupt societies offer something infinitely valuable to those who have remained decent enough to accept it: "O Emile," says the young man's soon to be retired governor; "where is the good man who owes nothing to his country? *Whatever country it is*, he owes it what is most precious to man—the morality of his actions and the love of virtue" (*Emile* V:473; emphasis added).[2] Rousseau's

---

1. There can be no going back to an earlier state of development: "human nature does not go backward, and it is never possible to return to the times of innocence and equality once they have been left behind" (*Dialogues* II:213).

2. Rousseau elaborates on the preciousness of acquiring morality—that is, on the value of entering the civil state—at SC I-8:55–56.

praise of the potential benefits of social life yields little even to the likes of Aristotle. (Indeed, Rousseau could almost agree that an asocial man must be either less than or more than human.[3]) Still, given the complete facts of the case—given that it was socialization that opened the way for all of the evil and nearly all of the misery that have so marred the human experience in subsequent ages—we must consider that transformation to be at best a mixed blessing. In truth, it is a *very* mixed blessing. And we must deem the quality of soul that emerged with this transformation at best morally ambiguous. That quality of soul, of course, is *amour-propre*.

Many other characteristics appeared with the socialization of the species. A veritable panoply of new capacities and inclinations—by and large the whole realm of the distinctively human—made their entrance onto the stage either contemporaneously with or as a consequence of that transformation. But of all these new phenomena, *amour-propre* was the decisive one, for it was *amour-propre* that redefined the human problem. In ways that we shall explore in this chapter, *amour-propre* redefined the fundamental needs experienced by every civilized human being. The other characteristics that appeared with the socialization of man, as important as they are, were not comparably decisive. They have had great influence both on the way that needs and desires are felt and on the repertoire of available responses to those now deep and complicated passions. But these other characteristics have not given rise, on their own, to new needs. Only the birth of *amour-propre*, only the emergence of a second variety of self-love, reaches deep enough in the soul to have had that kind of effect.[4]

In according human status to the inhabitant of the pure state of nature, Rousseau rejected the naturalness of any kind of moral or psychological dualism. Together with his self-sufficiency, natural man's outstanding characteristic was his wholeness. He utterly lacked internal conflict. He suffered no conflict between inclination and duty because he knew nothing of—indeed, had no—

---

3. Aristotle, of course, states that it is the *apolitical* man who must be either less than human or more than human: "He who is without a city (*polis*) through nature rather than chance is either a mean sort or superior to man" (*Politics* 1253a3–5). (Strong makes the same point, only without my qualification: "Politics is ... for Rousseau, as it had been for Aristotle, constitutive of the human" [*Politics of the Ordinary*, 76].) Readers should also note one other discrepancy between Rousseau's appreciation of social life and Aristotle's: for Rousseau the highest human type is the solitary dreamer, the man who lives an indolent life of contemplation on the fringes of society. See "Beyond Amour-Propre? Prospects and Possibilities," later in this chapter.

4. Self-love, we recall, is not only a passion but also the source of other passions. This is as true of *amour-propre* as of *amour de soi*, as we shall soon see.

duty. He suffered no conflict *among* inclinations because these inclinations, deriving from the same, orderly source (namely nature, as expressed in *amour de soi*), were themselves perfectly well ordered with respect to one another. This self-sufficiency and wholeness combined to produce his perfect, even if premoral, goodness. But we who are civilized are no longer whole. In fact, at the deepest level, at the level of primary passions or principles of soul, we are divided in two. In the souls of all but the true citizen (who is virtually nonexistent today) and the thoroughly corrupt man (also a rare personage, for most of us are corrupt but are not without some vestige of humane feeling), there exist, side by side, two different kinds of self-love.[5] Some portion of original self-love, some portion of *amour de soi*, remains. But the rest of *amour de soi*— which in most people means most of it—has been converted into *amour-propre*. And almost always these very different variants of self-love find themselves at odds with one another in their respective objects of desire and in the very ways in which they shape one's experience of life.

So it would seem that Rousseau is a kind of dualist after all. Man as he is now constituted is possessed of two (and only two) competing motive forces. Moreover, one of these forces is good and thus constitutes the central goal of good education (*Emile*) and worthy moral reform (*Lettres morales*), while the other, though not always and necessarily evil, never stops being dangerous— indeed, potentially calamitous—and hence needs to be sternly and thoroughly governed.[6] Two principles: one good; the other, if left ungoverned, bad. Formally, at least, the opposition between *amour de soi* and *amour-propre* is comparable to the reason-versus-appetite and soul-versus-body polarities found in classical and Christian moral philosophies. Rousseau's scheme is as dualistic as those. To be sure, Rousseau rejects the notion that a moral or psychological dualism exists *by nature*. But that is precisely the point. Nature is a unity, but nature is only one part of the human soul.

As we shall soon see, there is nothing stark or simple, nothing Manichaean, about Rousseau's dualism. For one thing, the respective dimensions of *amour de soi* and *amour-propre* in the soul are not predetermined. For another, *amour-propre* admits of myriad possibilities: besides being the source of the worst human evils, it has also been the source of the greatest accomplishments. Patriotic citizenship, an altogether glorious human possibility in Rousseau's view and one that has been realized in the world, is built out of a certain kind of *amour-propre*. And even in the world beyond the virtuous republic, *amour-propre*

5. Although most people are corrupt, very few are entirely so. See *LM* 1107.
6. That *amour de soi* is the centerpiece of naturalness and hence the goal of natural education (*Emile*) and moral reform (*Lettres morales*) was the main point established in Chapter 2.

has produced some wonderful results. To the "furor to distinguish oneself," Rousseau writes, "we owe what is best and worst among men, our virtues and our vices, our sciences and our errors, our conquerors and our philosophers" (*SD* 175). If it turns out that the worst has outweighed the best—and it has, for "what is best and worst among men" turns out to mean "a multitude of bad things as against a small number of good ones"—that still does not mean that a better outcome is impossible. Finally, it may be possible for some people to transcend *amour-propre* and thereby to acquire a kind of natural wholeness that is purer even than Emile's. This may be dualism, but it is a dualism whose range of possibilities can be painted only with a full palette and not merely with shades of gray, let alone just black and white.

I stated in the preceding chapter that the good governance of *amour-propre* should be considered *the* political problem for Rousseau. (It is also the foremost moral and psychological problem, which is what makes it so politically consequential.) We shall begin our study of *amour-propre* by examining why that is so—that is, by exploring just what is at stake in governing or failing to govern *amour-propre*. Then, in the second section of the chapter, "What *Amour-Propre* Is and How It Arises," we shall inquire into the precise natures of *amour de soi* and *amour-propre* and into the relation between them. In this section we shall attempt a more precise understanding of these critical but none-too-well understood concepts and their respective roles in a well-ordered soul. Finally, the third section, "Beyond *Amour-Propre?* Prospects and Possibilities," explores the possibility of transcending *amour-propre*, the possibility represented by Jean-Jacques and the one that Rousseau seems to consider the highest available to man.

The Stakes

Why is the good governance of *amour-propre* so important? The answer is threefold. First, the appearance of *amour-propre* is inevitable in every socialized human being. In fact, not only *amour-propre* but even vanity, its most obnoxious expression, is inevitable in everyone. Second, *amour-propre* is morally ambiguous. As we have seen, it can produce either great evil or great good depending on how it is educated. Third, the specific character of one's *amour-propre* will be the decisive factor in determining one's character and behavior, including political behavior. It is passion that determines behavior, and self-love that determines passion—and not just any self-love but *amour-propre* in particular. Although *amour de soi* gives rise to a variety of sentiments, it is *amour-propre* that is the source of virtually all strong social and political passions. *Amour-propre* admits of myriad forms—it is not just a question of pride versus vanity but also a question of what *kind* of pride or vanity—and the specific form that it takes will ultimately determine the things that one does.

Amour-Propre's Inevitability

That Rousseau believes in the inevitability of *amour-propre* in every socialized human being is indisputable. What is at issue in the lives of men is not whether *amour-propre* will make its appearance, but when and in what form. And even these questions are undecided only to a point. It is possible to prevent *amour-propre*'s emergence in a child, but once adolescence has begun and has given the young person an irresistible interest in others, it is only a matter of time before sexual desire and self-consciousness combine to stimulate its appearance: "This species of passion, not having its germ in children's hearts, cannot be born in them of itself; it is we alone who put it there, and it never takes root except by our fault. But this is no longer the case with the young man's heart. Whatever we may do, these passions [pride and vanity, the two branches of *amour-propre*] will be born in spite of us" (*Emile* IV:215).[7]

As for the question of what form this nascent *amour-propre* will take, it seems that this too is only partly controllable even by the best education. One might prefer to raise a child who will be completely free of vanity and whose *amour-propre* will express itself only in the form of a wholesome pride, but this is simply not possible. Regarding vanity, emulation, and glory, Rousseau says: "These dangerous sentiments will, I am told, be born sooner or later in spite of us. I do not deny it. Everything has its time and its place. I only say that one ought not to assist their birth" (*Emile* IV:226). The goal of a natural education is not, therefore, to prevent the birth of *amour-propre*. The goal, rather, is to delay its appearance and to shape it into as wholesome a form as possible. (The hope is to delay *amour-propre*'s appearance until adolescence, by which time reason and conscience will have developed sufficiently to manage it.) No one, not even the man in whom *amour-propre* is least present, is *utterly* free of it.[8]

---

7. Rousseau's reference to pride and vanity as "the two branches of *amour-propre*" appears at *Corsica* 326.

8. The evidence is quite clear that Jean-Jacques, who is that man, has at the very least a residual, latent *amour-propre*. (See, for example, *Dialogues* II:145.) That Jean-Jacques is the man in whom *amour-propre* is least present, and that he does yet have some *amour-propre*, will be further established in "Beyond *Amour-Propre*? Prospects and Possibilities," later in this chapter.

The inevitability of *amour-propre* and the difficulty in delaying it are suggested by Rousseau's choice of language to describe its initial appearance. The verb he most commonly uses to describe the appearance of *amour-propre* is "awaken" (*éveiller*).[9] And in the lines quoted above he speaks of *amour-propre* as something that will inevitably "be born." Birth of course implies gestation. The suggestion conveyed by both terms is that *amour-propre* is somehow ready to appear, that is, that it awaits only some triggering circumstance to precipitate its appearance. And indeed this is exactly Rousseau's view. It seems that *amour-propre* is latent almost from infancy. And it is, so to speak, only barely latent, at that. It is not a deep slumber but rather a very light sleep from which *amour-propre* is awakened. It is a sleep that can be interrupted easily and early. And it is not a sleep that, once seriously interrupted, can be resumed. That is why Rousseau warns repeatedly against doing anything that might prematurely awaken *amour-propre*—as, for example, when he admonishes parents not to submit to the small child's arbitrary will: "Dominion awakens and flatters *amour-propre*" even in the young innocent (*Emile* I:68).[10] That is also why Emile's governor arranges for the young man's first expression of vanity to be met with stunning humiliation: "How many mortifying consequences are attracted by the first movement of vanity! Young master, spy out this first movement with care. If you know thus how to make humiliation and disgrace arise from it, be sure that a second movement will not come for a long time" (*Emile* III:175).[11] By doing nothing that might incite the taste for dominion and by ensuring that a first stirring of vanity will not soon be followed by a second, the parent or governor can see to it that *amour-propre* is not awakened until late adolescence, by which time the basis of a good moral character—one in which *amour-propre* might be well governed—will have been laid.

Delay is necessary: the child in whom *amour-propre* awakens early will likely be dominated by unwholesome *amour-propre* later in life. Only when reason and conscience have had time to develop sufficiently is it possible to steer *amour-propre* into wholesome channels.[12] But delay is not enough: to ensure

9. See, for example, *Emile* I:68 and III:178.

10. Rousseau offers parents several maxims aimed at maintaining *amour-propre*'s sleep in the small child: (1) let him use all his strength; (2) help him in all that is connected with physical need; (3) limit this help to the truly useful—grant nothing to whim; and (4) study his language and signs in order to distinguish which of his desires come from nature and which from opinion. "The spirit of these rules is to accord children more true freedom and less dominion" (*Emile* I:68).

11. The story of Emile's first vanity and his resulting humiliation is told at III:173–75. Note that the tutor's role in arranging Emile's humiliation is hidden. Emile must never knowingly experience punishment or any other coercive expression of his tutor's will.

12. That reason is to be *amour-propre*'s guide is noted at *Emile* II:92.

that *amour-propre* will assume a wholesome form (a pride founded on virtue), *amour-propre* must be educated once it has begun to develop. Prior to adolescence, Emile's education is largely aimed at preventing the early awakening of *amour-propre*: that is the essential meaning of Rousseau's maxim that "the first education ought to be purely negative" (II:93). But with the onset of adolescence—with the first inchoate stirring of sexual desire—negative education must be replaced by something else. The tutor must now become something of a Mentor.[13] To be sure, the tutor still does not teach by conventional precept (or even by unconventional precept, for that matter), but he now educates in a much more positive way. With the threads of the young man's new and as yet indeterminate longing, the tutor weaves for him—and weaves *into* him— an image of beauty. He makes Emile fall in love with an ideal woman. (How much further from negative education can one get?) This causes Emile to search for the embodiment of this ideal and then, after he finds her, to seek her favor. As a consequence of this quest, his *amour-propre* manifests itself in a wholesome way, for Sophie is of such character that her recognition cannot be won—and thus Emile's *amour-propre* cannot be satisfied—except by his exhibiting pride and virtue rather than vanity. Sophie and the tutor, in other words, reinforce the resistance to vanity that Emile's negative education has already sown.

Amour-Propre's Ambiguity

Amour-propre needs to be so extensively educated precisely because it is so protean a force in the soul. Protean and potent: it can be good or bad; it can be good *and* bad; it cannot be neutral. Its moral ambiguity is the ambiguity of a high-octane fuel. Once ignition occurs, *amour-propre* can be used either for productive or for destructive purposes, depending upon the quality of the engine (that is, the quality of the psyche that was produced by early education) and upon the skill and wisdom of the operator (that is, the character of the person's will). What it cannot do is nothing.

Would it be best if it *could* be made to do nothing? Should we look upon *amour-propre* as an unavoidable evil? Clearly it serves an important purpose in the citizen: his patriotism, the source of his identity, is but a particular form of extended or generalized *amour-propre*. But what about for the natural man in the state of society? He, after all, has been defined in the previous two chapters as one in whom not *amour-propre* but rather *amour de soi* is the predominant

---

13. The comparison to Mentor, tutor to Telemachus, is Rousseau's own. See *Dialogues* II:90.

principle of soul. Is *amour-propre* simply a burden or obstacle for him—and for us, for whom he serves as a model?

The answer, in brief, is no: *amour-propre* is not simply an unavoidable evil from the standpoint of the civilized natural man. For all its evils, *amour-propre* is a necessary condition for many good things—things that give his life much of its pleasure, most of its meaning, and virtually all of its nobility. To begin with, a certain measure of *amour-propre* is necessary for him to be able to know "the sweetest sentiments known to men: conjugal love and paternal love" (*SD* 146–47). A domestic life infused with the sweetness of conjugal and familial love is possible only on the basis of romantic attraction—which is to say, only where sentiments of preference and the desire to be preferred have appeared—which is to say, only after *amour-propre* has been born. In a hypothetical world without *amour-propre*, there could be friendship and there still would be sexuality; there might even be sexual friendships. But there could be no true romance, for that would require efforts aimed at and satisfactions gained from being beloved, from being preferred. The lover's pleasure comes less from favors granted than from the granting—less from the favors in themselves than from his being chosen as the one to receive the favors of his beloved. Minus *amour-propre*, being so chosen would have no meaning and thus would be enormously less pleasurable. Without *amour-propre*, then, there would be no romance—surely a loss in itself, notwithstanding the agonies that frequently attach to it; and there would be no conjugal or paternal love, an even surer loss in Rousseau's view (surer in that familial love poses much less risk of pain than does romance), for those "sweetest sentiments" can arise only from a nuptial bed that has been made by romance.[14]

We might also recall in this connection that the historic period that Rousseau considers "the happiest and most durable epoch," "the best for man," was an era in which *amour-propre* was present (*SD* 151). Rousseau is referring, of course, to the epoch of nascent society. During that period the souls of men and women were possessed of a newborn and as yet moderate *amour-propre*, which enabled them to enjoy one another immensely and did not lead them into the chronic rancor that a more perversely developed *amour-propre* would

14. Rousseau does not say that conjugal love exists only where it has been preceded by as intense a romance as Emile's and Sophie's. It may be possible to replicate the experience of men and women in the stage of nascent society, a period that seems to have included conjugal love but perhaps not so much romantic ecstasy. Yet even these relationships entailed a certain amount of romance. And surely conjugal love itself, apart from the romantic love that might or might not have preceded it, depends on *amour-propre*. Even where love is quiet and calm, as long as it has a sexual dimension, it involves sentiments of preference and so requires *amour-propre*. It is not only in the heated early stages of a relationship that one wants to be desired.

produce among their descendants. The men and women of that era had enough *amour-propre* to make them appreciate being loved, but not so much that they were plagued by its worst ills. They suffered as yet only minimal quantities of vanity, contempt, shame and envy, the "new leavens" that only later, in consequence of "some fatal accident," would ferment into "compounds fatal to happiness and innocence" (*SD* 149, 151). Their small portion of *amour-propre* was on balance a boon.

We, of course, who are so much more materially and psychologically interdependent than our ancestors, are not likely to reduce *amour-propre* to the modest proportions it assumed in them; even Emile's *amour-propre* is larger and more refined than theirs. (Emile "is a savage made to inhabit *cities*," not the tribal villages of that earlier period [III:205].) Nevertheless, their example is enormously significant, for it demonstrates that the existence of *amour-propre* does not in principle preclude happiness and decency. And it is this knowledge that serves as Rousseau's crucial premise, for it makes Emile plausible. And Emile, as it turns out, enjoys an even better condition with regard to *amour-propre* than our ancestors did. Although his *amour-propre* is indeed larger and more refined than theirs was, it is *wholesomely* refined and so produces an even more enviable soul. Whereas they represent the happiest epoch known *so far*, Emile, I believe, represents the happiest we might yet be.[15]

Romantic and familial love are not the only goods that depend upon *amour-propre*. Virtue is another. Given that virtue is exercised only against inclinations, it should not be surprising that its source is found outside of the realm of nature, outside the realm of *amour de soi*. Why does one practice virtue? Why would one repudiate desire in favor of an abstract principle?[16] The only answer that conforms with Rousseau's belief that all behavior is motivated by self-love is that those who practice virtue do so because they derive, or at least expect to derive, more satisfaction from doing so than from not doing so. This is in fact Rousseau's view, as we saw in Chapter 1. What we can now add to

15. The happiness that Emile represents is the happiest available to "ordinary minds." That which is available to someone with the natural gifts of Jean-Jacques would seem to be the greatest of all.

16. Virtue always is the servant of abstract principle: Rousseau defines it as "obedience to law," or conforming to the general will. (The description of virtue as obedience to law appears at *SC* I-8:56. The description of virtue as the conformity of one's private will to the general will is found at *PE* 218.) Lest one think that these descriptions apply only to the virtue of the denatured citizen, it bears noting that when Emile is sent away in order to develop virtue, what he studies is political right, whose central principle, of course, is law, or the general will (V:459–67). Regarding the connection between Emile's virtue and his political education, see Lorna Dawson Knott, "The Transpolitical Moral Education in Rousseau's *Emile*" (paper presented at the annual meeting of the American Political Science Association, Washington, D.C., 1997), 21–28.

that earlier discussion is that the satisfaction achieved by the practice of virtue is a satisfaction that derives from a certain kind of *amour-propre*. In fact, virtue can bring at least two different satisfactions, each of which is rooted in *amour-propre*. For most who are virtuous, the satisfaction of practicing virtue is the satisfaction of receiving recognition. "What was the motive of the virtue of the Lacedaemonians if not to be esteemed virtuous?" (*Fragments* 501).[17] Unless a society has reached the depths of corruption, there will remain in it many who, although not virtuous themselves, at least admire virtue when they see it. The other satisfaction of practicing virtue is more rare; it is the reward and motivation of those who practice virtue amid a thoroughly corrupt, unappreciative society. There, where practicing virtue does not win the esteem of others, the satisfaction of practicing virtue is a wholly interior one. The virtuous man has enough *pride*, and the right kind of pride (that is, a pride based on his attaining a certain level of virtue), that the conditions of his self-esteem require him to practice virtue. He cannot satisfy the demands of his *amour-propre*—he cannot succeed in loving himself—unless he practices virtue.

Rousseau's works are full of instances in which *amour-propre*, always in the form of pride, is put to good moral use. "Let us extend *amour-propre* to other beings," he writes. "We shall transform it into a virtue, and there is no man's heart in which this virtue does not have its root" (*Emile* IV:252). The virtue to which he refers in this case is beneficence, which is a kind of generalized and rationalized pity. Pity itself, being an expression of *amour de soi*, is an instance of goodness rather than virtue. But with the help of *amour-propre*, pity can be transformed—can be rationalized and generalized (that is, moralized)—into beneficence. "To prevent pity from degenerating into weakness, it must ... be generalized and extended to the whole of mankind. Then one yields to it only insofar as it accords with justice, because of all the virtues justice is the one that contributes most to the common good of men. For the sake of reason, for the sake of love of ourselves, we must have pity for our species still more than for our neighbor, and pity for the wicked is a very great cruelty to men" (253). Like all other virtues, beneficence is rooted in self-love. It offers "inner enjoyment," Rousseau tells us in the next paragraph, in that exercising it makes us feel good about ourselves.

In fact, *amour-propre* not only helps to generalize and extend pity, it also helps to cultivate pity in the first place. Pity, as we saw in the previous

17. It is not only the citizen whose practice of virtue is motivated by the desire for recognition. Even the wise man "is not insensitive to glory" (*FD* 58).

chapter, is an expression of *amour de soi*, not *amour-propre*. Nevertheless, it seems that *amour de soi* in this case requires the service of *amour-propre*; pity may be natural, but this is a case in which "[o]ne must use a great deal of art to prevent social man from being totally artificial" (*Emile* IV:317). Emile *can* pity—first, because he understands himself to be vulnerable to suffering and thus identifies with those who do suffer and, second, because he does not suffer much himself and thus is not overtaken by envy.[18] But he *does* pity, at least in part, because it feels good to do so. Pitying others confirms his good opinion of himself: it buttresses or enhances his self-esteem. "[C]ommiseration ought to be a very sweet sentiment," Rousseau tells us, "*since it speaks well of us*" (*Emile* IV:229; emphasis added).[19]

Nor is Emile alone in being made better by *amour-propre*. Sophie is another who benefits from it, and in ways unique to her sex. (Presumably she also benefits in all the non-sex-specific ways Emile does.) She needs *amour-propre*, as Rousseau tells it—specifically, she needs pride—to maintain her chastity. It is only her proud sense that she merits a man as meritorious as herself that keeps her from yielding to the advances of lesser men and even from yielding too soon to Emile. It takes pride to resist the impulses of so passionate a nature as hers. "Possessing the temperament of an Italian woman and the sensitivity of an Englishwoman, Sophie combines with them—in order to control her heart and her senses—the pride of a Spanish woman, who, even when she is seeking a lover, does not easily find one she esteems worthy of her" (V:402). Both Sophie and Emile are proud, and each has a sense of honor, as well (V:417–18). In each, *amour-propre* enriches and safeguards the fruits of a natural education.

Amour-propre also has moral uses in people who lack the integrity and naturalness of an Emile or a Sophie. Rousseau's various accounts of his own life testify to this. In *Emile*, for example, we hear the story of how the Savoyard Vicar deliberately and successfully used the young Rousseau's *amour-propre* to save him from complete corruption. The vicar encountered a young man whom injustice and misfortune had degraded and depraved nearly beyond hope of recovery.

18. Emile's education in pity is described at IV:221–31. For a concise summary of Rousseau's four-part psychic mechanism of compassion, see Bloom, introduction to Rousseau's *Emile*, 18.

19. That *amour-propre* plays such an important role in inculcating the habit of pity does not alter the fact that the source of pity—that is, the "stuff" of which it is made—is *amour de soi*. *Amour-propre*'s role is that of buttress and facilitator. Others have made the same general point, albeit with different notions of the particulars. See, for example, Horowitz, *Rousseau, Nature, and History*, 237, and Melzer, *Natural Goodness of Man*, 93.

> To protect the unfortunate young fellow from this moral death to
> which he was so near, the priest began by awakening *amour-propre* and
> self-esteem in him. He showed him a happier future in the good
> employment of his talents. He reanimated a generous ardor in his heart
> by the account of others' noble deeds. In making the boy admire those
> who had performed them, the priest gave him the desire to perform like
> deeds. To detach him gradually from his idle and vagrant life, he had
> the boy make extracts from selected books; and, feigning to need these
> extracts, he fed the noble sentiment of gratitude in him. He instructed
> him indirectly by these books. He made the boy regain a good enough
> opinion of himself so as not to believe he was a being useless for any-
> thing good and so as not to want any longer to make himself con-
> temptible in his own eyes. (IV:264)

The vicar used *amour-propre* to combat self-contempt in the young Rousseau
and awaken in him a pride that demanded that he have integrity if he wanted
to have a good opinion of himself. The particulars of this usage were utterly at
variance with the techniques that this same young man would one day use
upon his imaginary Emile. Emile is deliberately kept from the kind of heroic
reading that the vicar assigned to Rousseau. But that is only a measure of how
different were the needs, and how different the remaining potentials, of these
two young men—one of whom was already compromised by a rampant and
mostly ugly *amour-propre*, while the other has been kept free of such taint
throughout childhood and youth. The difference between the vicar's inculcation of pride in the young Rousseau and Emile's negative education is the
difference between treating a virus and preventing one.

We also find instances of *amour-propre*'s moral usefulness in the *Confessions*.
By his own admission, Rousseau was not a virtuous man. But he recounts occasions in his life on which he was led by *amour-propre* to behave virtuously. In
one such instance he was inspired by the sight of a Roman ruin to pass up a
fairly seamy assignation. After several hours of "ravishing contemplation" of
the ruin, the Pont du Gard, and then days of agitated reflection, he resolved to
pass up an encounter that would have been unworthy of the noble aspirations
inspired by the ruin.

> I executed [this resolution] courageously, with some sighs, I admit; but
> also with that internal satisfaction that I tasted for the first time in my
> life of saying to myself, "I deserve my own esteem, I know how to pre-
> fer my duty to my pleasure." This is the first genuine obligation that I

had from studying. It was studying that had taught me to reflect, to compare. After such pure principles that I had adopted such a short time before; after the rules of wisdom and virtue that I had made for myself and which I had felt myself so proud of following; the shame of being so little consistent with myself as to give the lie to my own maxims so soon and so emphatically won out over voluptuousness: *pride might perhaps have as great a part in my resolution as virtue; but if this pride is not virtue itself it has such similar effects that it is pardonable to mistake it for virtue.* (VI:217–18; emphasis added)

Pride, a form of *amour-propre*, produced in Rousseau a moment of moral reformation—and not just one moment. In fact, pride would later produce a moral transformation of six years' duration, a period in which "the noblest pride sprang up on the ruins of uprooted vanity" (IX:350)—and a period during which the passion for virtue, if not virtue itself, would find expression in some of the most inspired political writings the world has seen.[20] Thus, just as it can serve a vital moral purpose in an Emile or a Sophie, *amour-propre* can also be instrumental in improving a more checkered character.

Nor are *amour-propre's* moral contributions limited to nay-saying virtue. Without *amour-propre*, there would be no moral heroism or even strong moral passion. We are inclined, as readers of Rousseau, to look upon virtue as a necessary substitute for lost goodness. But virtue—or at least virtue fueled by passion—goes much further than goodness. As a moral force, goodness is largely negative. The merely good man does no harm, but neither does he fight injustice; his main response to injustice is sadness and disdain. Moral passion requires a sense of indignation, but indignation, as the root of the word implies, arises only when one cares about having one's self-worth or one's values respected by others. Only *amour-propre* gives rise to that kind of concern. Thus the passion for justice that is great enough to battle for it is born not of *amour de soi* but only of *amour-propre*. This point emerges with great clarity from the following description of Rousseau's own self-love: "It [my self-love] began by revolting against injustice but finished by disdaining it. By withdrawing into my soul and severing the external relations which make it demanding, by renouncing comparisons and preferences, it was satisfied with my being

---

20. The period of Rousseau's moral transformation lasted "almost six years" (*Confessions* IX:350)—from 1749 to 1754 or 1755—during which time he composed both the *First* and the *Second Discourse* and conceived of his entire philosophical system. Not everyone, of course, is willing to accept Rousseau's interpretation of his transformation. For a different (and somewhat harsher) interpretation of *amour-propre's* role in Rousseau's transformation, see Carol Blum, *Rousseau and the Republic of Virtue* (Ithaca: Cornell University Press, 1986), 40–43.

good in my own eyes. Then, *again becoming amour de soi*, it returned to the natural order" (*Reveries* VIII:115–16; emphasis added). Only while it was *amour-propre* did Rousseau's self-love lead him to raise his hand against injustice. As it was transformed back into *amour de soi*, it lost its moral passion.

The lesson of Rousseau's experience is confirmed by that of two other exemplars: Cato and Socrates. Cato, Rousseau's exemplary citizen, was the embodiment of the finest kind of *amour-propre*. Socrates, by contrast, though not as free of *amour-propre* as Jean-Jacques would later be, was still free of its grip to a remarkable degree.[21] Both men found themselves living under tyranny, but they responded altogether differently. Cato hated his tyranny and fought against it. As a citizen, as a man whose self-love was actually love of self as part of a greater whole, he could not tolerate corruption of that whole. Socrates, on the other hand, did not fight against the tyranny he faced, though he certainly did disdain it and willingly risk his life by disobeying its commands. Socrates' self-love was much more a love of self as a self-sufficient whole. Consequently, the corruption of the city, while lamentable, did not taint him personally. Nor did it impinge upon his most important freedom, his natural freedom: he "was able to live under the Tyrants because he was very certain of conserving his freedom everywhere."[22] Certainly Rousseau admires Socrates. But if we want evil to be combated, Rousseau suggests, we need Cato's virtue more than Socrates'—we need the moral passion that only *amour-propre* can inspire.[23]

Understanding that the psychological seat of virtue and moral passion is *amour-propre*—more specifically, pride—Rousseau advises those who hope to achieve good republican government to encourage pride. Pride alone can provide the basis for widespread civic virtue and public-spiritedness. Rousseau's prescriptive political writings, most notably the *Constitutional Project for Corsica*, advise measures explicitly aimed toward this effect.[24]

21. For a discussion of Rousseau's views of Cato and Socrates and how they compare with himself, see Kelly, *Rousseau's Exemplary Life*, 50–57, 64–75.

22. This fragment appears in *Jean-Jacques entre Socrate et Caton*, ed. Claude Pichois and René Pintard (Paris: José Corti, 1972), 54.

23. See Melzer, *Natural Goodness of Man*, 256–61, for a discussion of the necessity of *amour-propre* for moral action. Melzer interprets Rousseau's authorial activity in this light.

24. See *Corsica* 325–29. What is explicitly advised in *Corsica* is implicitly advised elsewhere. As Ruth W. Grant observes, "Rousseau hopes to use pride precisely in order to inculcate integrity." See *Hypocrisy and Integrity: Machiavelli, Rousseau, and the Ethics of Politics* (Chicago: University of Chicago Press, 1997), 167. Indeed, the inculcation of pride as a source of public-spiritedness can be seen as the centerpiece of the civic ethos, that is, as the key to successful republicanism, in Rousseau's view. As Shklar writes, "The civic ethos . . . redirects *amour-propre* from pursuing personal exploitation to positive public enterprises. The whole political structure of Sparta has no other end" (*Men and Citizens*, 19).

Nevertheless, the case should not be overstated. Certainly all of the foregoing is true: *amour-propre* has its uses. But these uses and the benefits derived therefrom have not outweighed the harm done by *amour-propre* in every era subsequent to the epoch of nascent society. Rousseau tells us this explicitly, as we have already observed. Moreover, it cannot be denied that most of the problems *amour-propre* can help to solve by promoting virtuous behavior are themselves products of *amour-propre*. *Amour-propre* may be a source of virtue, but it is also the source of vice. Rousseau's genius is to find *amour-propre*-based remedies for the moral ills caused by *amour-propre*, much as the framers of the American Constitution purported to offer "a republican remedy for the diseases most incident to republican government."[25] But alas, Rousseau's *amour-propre* is not as fundamentally decent a thing as the republicanism of Madison and his associates. The situation is more grave; the prospects grimmer.

How, then, should one assess the situation? How should *amour-propre* be viewed? In the end, very simply, we are left with a great and momentous ambiguity. *Amour-propre* produces more bad than good, but at least some of the good that it produces is essential to a good life, or at least to the variants of the good life that are available to an ordinary person. Without it we would not know the pleasures of romance and marriage. Without it we would be stripped of the special dignity that comes with virtue; for virtue does more than just counter vice, it also elevates one's level of existence. And, finally, there is this: even if it turns out that the best life possible for man is one in which *amour-propre* plays no role (and such, I think, is Rousseau's view), that life can only be realized by passing through and then transcending *amour-propre*. Even if *amour-propre* is eventually not present in such a life, it once *was* present, and necessarily so. For the central activities of this life entail the use of faculties that could only have developed amid society, which means, amid the presence of *amour-propre*. But that is a matter to which we shall return in the final section of this chapter.

Amour-Propre's Influence on Character and Behavior

As we observed in Chapter 2, Rousseau believes that there is a universal, fixed human nature. "Man," he writes, "is the same in all stations" (*Emile* IV:225). "Our true study" in *Emile*, he says, "is that of the human condition" (I:42)—a single condition common to all members of the species. He even maintains

---

25. *The Federalist Papers*, no. 10, introduction by Clinton Rossiter (New York: New American Library, 1961), 84.

that standards of right and wrong, deriving as they do from this fixed nature, are themselves fixed: "Throughout the ages the natural relations do not change, and the standards of what is or is not suitable that result from them remain the same" (V:391).

But there is also tremendous variation of character among individuals, and much variation across national borders and across the centuries as well. Rousseau refers to "the almost infinite division of characters" among individuals of the same class and nation (*Emile* IV:226–27). He marvels at "how much one individual can differ from another due to the force of education" (IV:254). He claims men differ considerably according to nationality (he even ridicules the adage that "men are everywhere the same"[26]), and he contends they have differed still more considerably according to the age in which they lived (V:453–54). Fixed or not, human nature permits enormous individual variation—indeed, more variation than has yet been realized: "We do not know what our nature permits us to be" (I:62). Accordingly, Rousseau urges the legislator and other political actors to proceed almost as if human nature were not in fact fixed and one. The legislator is advised to act as if it were malleable: "One who dares to undertake the founding of a people should feel that he is capable of changing human nature, so to speak" (SC II-7:68). And those concerned with the good governance of a particular people are counseled to be mindful of the particular character of that people rather than some general idea of human nature: "Man is one; I admit it! But man modified by religions, governments, laws, customs, prejudices, and climates becomes so different from himself that one ought not to seek among us for what is good for men in general, but only what is good for them in this time or that country" (*d'Alembert* 17).

What is the cause of all this variation? In the lines quoted above, Rousseau cites education, nationality, culture, even climate. But if we were to search out the medium through which each of these factors exerts its influence on human character, we would find *amour-propre* at the center every time, for *amour-propre* is the major constitutive element of our characters and the source of most of our behavior. "The great springs of human conduct come down, on close examination, to two, pleasure and vanity; and what is more, if you subtract from the first all that appertains to the second, you will find in the last analysis that everything comes down to practically pure vanity" (*Corsica* 325). If nearly all behavior is motivated by *amour-propre* (vanity), then no effort to reform behavior is likely to succeed except insofar as it acts upon *amour-propre*.

26. SD 211n. j.

Only the good governance of *amour-propre* is apt to render any significant benefit.

Amour-propre's significance in Rousseau's interpretation of human character and behavior can be established by any number of textual citations. The lines quoted from the *Constitutional Project for Corsica* are exceptional only in their combination of simplicity and categorical scope. The basic idea they express is not exceptional: it finds voice in all of Rousseau's major works. But perhaps the most effective way to demonstrate *amour-propre*'s significance, certainly more effective than heaping up quotations and citations that have been lifted from their contexts, lies in another direction. For all its complexity, Rousseau's motivational psychology is built around a small handful of simple and unambiguously stated propositions. Taken together and stated in the following way, these propositions constitute something close to a formal proof of *amour-propre*'s predominance in human affairs.[27]

The first proposition is that "passions are the motive of all action"; "it is only passion which makes us act" (*Dialogues* I:9; *Emile* III:183). This is not a merely formal or truistic tenet. With it, Rousseau pointedly denies that unaided reason can rule in the soul. Reason, he contends, cannot be made to direct behavior unless it has first enlisted passion into its service, and this it can only have done on passion's own terms.[28]

The second proposition is that all passions derive from self-love. Self-love (of either variety) is itself a passion, but a passion so basic and general that it ordinarily expresses itself through other, more specific passions: "The source of our passions, the origin and the principle of all the others, the only one born with man and which never leaves him so long as he lives is self-love—a primitive, innate passion, which is anterior to every other, and of which all others are in a sense only modifications" (*Emile* IV:212–13). The term translated as "self-love" in this passage is *amour de soi*. But what Rousseau says here about *amour de soi* is also partially true of *amour-propre*. Originally, or by nature, self-love is exclusively *amour de soi*. *Amour-propre*, like every other passion, grows out of, or is a modification of, *amour de soi*. Yet *amour-propre* is fundamentally different from all those other passions and is functionally similar to *amour de soi*. Although it is born of *amour de soi*, *amour-propre* immediately assumes the status of rival rather than servant or minister. Like *amour de soi*, *amour-propre*

---

27. I have already discussed the importance for Rousseau of the question of self-love broadly understood. (See "Five Human Types ..." in Chapter 2 above.) What we want to establish now is the singular importance of one kind of self-love: *amour-propre*.

28. Here is the complete sentence, of which we read only the second part: "In vain does tranquil reason make us approve or criticize; it is only passion which makes us act" (*Emile* III:183).

is so basic and general that it ordinarily needs to express itself through other, more specific passions. (At times Rousseau does seem to speak of *amour-propre* as the immediate source of behavior, but this occurs only when he drops his careful philosophical usage in favor of conventional usage, according to which "*amour-propre*" is roughly synonymous with "vanity.")

The third proposition is that there are indeed only two basic varieties of self-love. Every passion and behavior arises from either *amour de soi* or *amour-propre*—or from both: many passions are complex and express tendencies born of both varieties of self-love. (The most obvious example of such complexity is surely the sexual passion, in which the physical element and the gentle element arise from *amour de soi* while the parts that entail preference or the desire for preference, what Rousseau calls the "moral" side of love and attraction, arise from *amour-propre*.) But the strands of even the most tangled passions grow out of only two sources. Rousseau never makes reference to a third possibility. Nor *could* he make reference to a third kind of self-love, for the way in which he defines *amour de soi* and *amour-propre* and the way in which he characterizes the difference between them leave no room for any other kind of self-love. The difference between the two kinds of self-love centers on the question of absoluteness versus relativity or comparison. An impulse of self-love is either absolute, meaning that one desires one's good without regard to one's standing relative to others—in which case it is *amour de soi*—or else the impulse is in some way relative or comparative, meaning that it does entail considerations of one's standing—in which case it is *amour-propre*. This is as exhaustive a set of possibilities as the set whose members are A and not A. An impulse of self-love is either absolute or it is not; it is either *amour de soi* or it is *amour-propre*. The latter begins precisely where the former ends, leaving no room for anything else.[29]

If all activity is motivated by passion and all passion is an expression of either *amour de soi* or *amour-propre*, then all activity can be attributed either to *amour de soi* or to *amour-propre*. But in what proportions? The fourth proposition has to do with the relative force of *amour de soi* and *amour-propre* in shaping the passions. The contest is not close. *Amour-propre* is the dominant form of self-love in most people. In the disorderly polity of the soul, *amour-propre* is the ruling council's junior member only in length of service. Whereas passion can arise from either variant of self-love, most passion arises from *amour-propre* rather than from *amour de soi*. That this is so is easily determined by a process of elimination. Only passion that is wholesome and benign, that expresses

29. See *SD* 221–22n. o; *Emile* IV:213; and *Dialogues* I:9.

nature's order, derives from *amour de soi*: "*Amour de soi* is always good and always in conformity with order" (*Emile* IV:213). Whatever is not wholesome and benign, whatever does not express nature's order, does not derive from *amour de soi*. Such passion must derive from *amour-propre*. Now it is quite clear that, on Rousseau's reading, most of the passion that animates human beings is *not* wholesome and benign. On the contrary, it is either competitive to the point of malevolence, or based on prejudice, or both. Hence, most passion stems from *amour-propre*.

We are now able to draw our conclusion. If *amour-propre* is the chief source of passion, it is very likely the chief source of behavior as well: if all behavior is motivated by passion, and most passion derives from *amour-propre*, then it seems very likely that most behavior is motivated by *amour-propre*.[30]

Moreover, besides playing the leading role in shaping behavior, *amour-propre* exercises similar influence over character and experience. Rousseau makes several statements regarding the influence of *amour-propre* on our inner lives. Some of these statements we have already discussed; some we have not. If our examination of Rousseau's core psychological propositions has left any doubt as to the importance of governing *amour-propre*, a brief look at some of these statements should lay that doubt to rest.

It is important to notice how categorical Rousseau is in attributing evil to *amour-propre*. In the *Second Discourse* he contends that *amour-propre* "inspires in men all the harm they do to one another" (221–22). Similarly, in *Emile*, drawing a contrast between the two varieties of self-love, he insists: "the hateful and irascible passions are born of *amour-propre*" (IV: 214). One might also recall that he attributed to *amour-propre* "what is worst among men" (*SD* 175). (To be sure, he also attributes our virtues to it, but these pale in comparison with our vices, as we observed earlier.) Rousseau does not equivocate. Although *amour-propre* is not always bad, all bad comes from *amour-propre*. Even when *amour-propre* is not fingered explicitly, its lurking presence is not hard to discern. Consider the following example. In a statement as simple

---

30. This reasoning does not quite measure up to the standards of a formal proof. Hence the qualifying statement "it seems *very likely*" (rather than "I conclude") in my conclusion. This qualification is needed because it is impossible to know for certain that the passion motivating behavior is representative of passion at large, that is, that the passion acted upon reflects the same ratio of *amour-propre* to *amour de soi* that is found in felt passion, or passion at large. It is conceivable that passion that is acted upon differs somewhat from passion that is felt. This is a technical point, however: there is no substantive reason to suppose that any significant difference exists between passion that is acted upon and the total reservoir of felt passion. Thus, although we must qualify our conclusion, we can state it with real confidence. On the basis of the four propositions we reviewed, it *does* seem very likely that most behavior is motivated by *amour-propre*.

and categorical as any other that he makes, Rousseau claims : "All wickedness comes from weakness" (*Emile* I:67). *Amour-propre* is not mentioned. But one who knows what "weakness" means to Rousseau—that it is an essentially relative thing, measured by the distance between one's desires and one's ability to satisfy those desires—will immediately recognize *amour-propre* as the unindicted co-conspirator.[31] For if all wickedness comes from weakness, all weakness, at least weakness of the sort that leads to wickedness, comes from *amour-propre*. The common effect of all *amour-propre*, whether governed well or ill, is to open a wealth of new needs, and the defining effect of ill-governed *amour-propre* is that these new oceans of desire are unnavigable—either too turbulent, or too vast, or both—and thereby the cause of weakness.

This raises another point of no small significance. In causing weakness, *amour-propre* produces not only wickedness but also unhappiness. As we discussed in Chapter 1, happiness is determined by one's ability to satisfy one's desires. When one's desires far outstrip one's capacities, the result is unhappiness. "Our unhappiness consists ... in the disproportion between our desires and our faculties," Rousseau instructs, and "the road of true happiness" consists "in diminishing the excess of the desires over the faculties and putting power and will in perfect equality" (*Emile* II:80). The way to diminish the excess of desires is to temper its source, which is *amour-propre*.[32] One whose judgment has not been distorted by ill-governed *amour-propre* will not be consumed by unending desires. "One has pleasure when one wants to have it. It is only opinion that makes everything difficult and drives happiness away from us" (*Emile* IV:354)—and opinion can have this effect only where *amour-propre* has sunk its poisonous roots. Emile is happy because he is never tyrannized by *amour-propre*. When *amour-propre* finally does make its appearance in him, it is regulated and, by being invested in the passion for virtue, is ultimately made to be self-correcting: since passion yields only to stronger passion, a strong passion for virtue is the only reliable means for rooting out whatever new shoots of unwholesome *amour-propre* might appear.[33] And, beyond Emile, there

31. "This word 'weak' indicates a relation, a relation obtaining within the being to which one applies it. He whose strength surpasses his needs, be he an insect or a worm, is a strong being. He whose needs surpass his strength, be he an elephant or a lion, be he a conqueror or a hero, be he a god, is a weak being" (*Emile* II:81).

32. In the passage cited, Rousseau aims his cautionary remarks at imagination rather than at *amour-propre* per se. But imagination, a faculty, is dangerous only because it works with and upon *amour-propre*. Imagination is dangerous because it incites excessive passions, but those passions are manifestations of, and therefore depend wholly upon, *amour-propre*. Thus, in Rousseau's investigation of the causes of unhappiness, *amour-propre* is implicated every bit as much as imagination.

33. For discussions of the uses of passion in controlling passion, see *Emile* IV:327 and V:445.

is Jean-Jacques, who recovers "peace of soul and almost felicity" by finally subduing *amour-propre*. The lesson of his case applies to us all: "In whatever situation we find ourselves, it is only because of *amour-propre* that we are constantly unhappy" (*Reveries* VIII:116).

For all these reasons, the good governance of *amour-propre* is the thing most needful. And there is one more reason. Once unwholesome *amour-propre* has taken root, its effects can probably never be undone. "The sole folly of which one cannot disabuse a man who is not mad is vanity" (*Emile* IV:245). As with the species, so with the individual: there can be no going back.[34] Mistakes are irreversible, which makes it all the more imperative that we understand exactly what *amour-propre* is and how it arises.

What *Amour-Propre* Is and How It Arises

Amour-propre is one of those concepts—nature is another—whose centrality to Rousseau's thought is widely understood but whose full meaning is obscure. Few readers would dispute that *amour-propre* is implicated as a major source of evil and that virtually all of Rousseau's ameliorative efforts are aimed at tempering its influence.[35] *Amour-propre* would turn up on every attentive reader's list of Rousseau's major concerns. Asked to define *amour-propre,* however, these same readers would find themselves at subtle but significant variance with one another, for there is a common tendency to overlook some important distinctions—to mistake a part of *amour-propre* for the whole or a common but not universal characteristic for its defining feature.

Our effort in this section will thus be similar to our earlier effort with regard to Rousseau's concept of nature. We shall seek to replace the prevailing partial and approximate interpretations of Rousseau's *amour-propre* with a more comprehensive and precise understanding. There will be one significant difference

34. Regarding the impossibility of reversing the moral development of the species, see *Dialogues* III: 213.

35. Even those who caution against placing blame on *amour-propre* per se would not deny that *amour-propre* is the stuff—the material cause—of vice and that Rousseau's ameliorative efforts are very much aimed at governing it. N. J. H. Dent, for example, argues that it is not *amour-propre* per se but rather inflamed *amour-propre* that is dangerous. (See *Rousseau: An Introduction*, 4, 52–67, 70–85; see also the entry for "*amour-propre*" in *A Rousseau Dictionary*, 33–36.) Similarly, Melzer observes, correctly, that it is not *amour-propre* per se but rather personal dependence that Rousseau regards as the true villain. (See *Natural Goodness of Man*, 70–85.) But neither of these ills, neither inflamed *amour-propre* nor corrupting personal dependence, can exist without *amour-propre*.

between the following discussion and the earlier one, however. Whereas the complexity and the subtlety of Rousseau's conception of nature are obvious to anyone who has read *Emile* and the *Second Discourse*, the complexity and subtlety of his conception of *amour-propre* are often overlooked. (The complexity of which I am speaking is not the complexity of *amour-propre*'s development, which generally *is* appreciated, but rather the complexity of *amour-propre*'s very nature, which generally is not.) Whereas very few readers believe they fully understand Rousseau's concept of nature, a much greater interpretive confidence prevails—unjustifiably—regarding *amour-propre*. Thus our task is twofold. Besides arriving at a new and improved interpretation, we must also demonstrate the need for one.

Answers and Rebuttals: An Attempt at Dialectic

What is *amour-propre*? It is a kind of self-love. It is a relative or comparative self-love.[36] It is the successor to *amour de soi*, it is transformed *amour de soi*. This much we know already. We also know that it is inevitable in civilized human beings, that it is aroused by social comparisons, and that it is morally ambiguous. But none of these observations, either individually or collectively, quite adds up to an accurate definition or a full and fair characterization. What is *amour-propre*? It is the self-love of a being whose estimate of his own worth is contingent, whose self-esteem is neither absolute nor assured by nature. Like *amour de soi*, *amour-propre* is the desire for one's own good. The great difference between it and *amour de soi* is simply that in *amour-propre*, the desire for one's own good necessarily includes the desire to esteem oneself.

Good witness of oneself is one of only three true needs, the others being strength and health (*Emile* II:81). In the savage, this first need was not problematic. Like the beasts, he had no need to establish his self-worth; he took his worthiness (of preservation and other goods) for granted. In us, however, the need for good witness certainly has become problematic.[37] It has been complicated by self-consciousness. And it is this complication that has given birth to *amour-propre*. With self-consciousness, human beings acquired the ability—and with the ability, the need—to evaluate themselves. Our need for self-worth

36. But what is self-love? Sometimes it is described as a passion and sometimes as a principle. In reality, it is both. For more on Rousseau's understanding of "principles of soul" and how self-love can be both a passion and a principle of soul, see "Sublimation in Rousseau . . ." in Chapter 3 above.

37. The savage could never have understood, for example, Julie's gratitude to Wolmar for giving her "everything that can give me some value in my own eyes" (*Julie* IV-12:402). Such a sentiment —such a concern—occurs only in civilized human beings.

has come to require that we meet certain standards of worthiness—or rather, that we *believe* that we are meeting such standards—and in so doing it has caused us to pass from savages (and small children) into the interesting, problematic creatures that we are.

Valuation—more specifically, self-valuation, or the need for self-esteem—lies at the heart of *amour-propre*. Does Rousseau state the matter thus? He does not. Rather than identify its abstract, purposive essence, his discussions of *amour-propre* are more phenomenological; they concentrate on more evident, less abstract matters—*amour-propre*'s genesis, its potentials, its comparative quality. Rousseau does not offer the sort of philosophical definition or characterization that I am attempting here. Nevertheless, the characterization I am outlining comprehends the many aspects and expressions of Rousseau's *amour-propre* and is not contradicted by any of them. There are many phenomena that *generally* appear with *amour-propre* or that in some other way are associated with it. But none of these other features truly defines or even perfectly correlates with *amour-propre*.

Before going any further in elaborating on valuation as the defining feature of *amour-propre*, let us review some of these other things: let us examine some of the qualities, activities, and attitudes that are imperfectly associated with *amour-propre* but that, being more obvious and more often mentioned by Rousseau, are often mistakenly identified as its defining feature. A catalog of some of these things will both reveal their insufficiency as defining features and open the way for a fuller appreciation of *amour-propre*'s valuational essence.

1. *Amour-propre* is not accurately defined as self-love that is self-conscious or self-reflective. Such self-love *may* be *amour-propre*—in fact, it usually is—but it also could be *amour de soi* instead.

2. *Amour-propre* is not simply defined as the self-love of sociable or civilized men. *Amour-propre* often brings people into relations with one another, but so does, or at least so can, *amour de soi*.

3. *Amour-propre* is not perfectly synonymous with the desire for recognition. In certain instances, *amour-propre* disregards others' opinions. Moreover, the desire for recognition does not always indicate *amour-propre*: a certain desire for recognition also emanates from *amour de soi*.

4. *Amour-propre* is not exactly the same thing as psychological dependence on others. Dependence does normally indicate *amour-propre*, but *amour-propre* does not always entail dependence.

5. *Amour-propre* is not always indicated by the desire to have and to exercise

power. That desire, so long as it does not become the desire for dominion over other wills, can derive from *amour de soi*.

6. *Amour-propre* is not indicated by every variant of what, in English, we call pride. A child in whom *amour-propre* has yet to be born can feel pride in his or her skills and accomplishments.

7. *Amour-propre* is not always indicated by competitiveness. Competitiveness certainly may signal *amour-propre*, but, depending on the nature of the competition, it does not always do so.

8. *Amour-propre* does not always express itself as the desire to see others laid low. Although often cruel or malicious, *amour-propre* is not invariably so. Neither does it constantly view the social world in zero-sum terms.

Each of these characterizations hits upon something that is generally, but not perfectly, associated with *amour-propre*. In no case is there an absolute correlation between the characteristic cited and *amour-propre*. In two cases, the cases of psychological dependence and ill will, the cited characteristic always indicates *amour-propre*, but *amour-propre* does not always entail *them*. Two other characteristics—sociality and self-consciousness—are always found with *amour-propre* but may also be found with *amour de soi*. And as for the remaining four, their connection to *amour-propre* is even less dependable. The desire for recognition, the enjoyment of power, taking pride in self-improvement, competitiveness—despite their general association with *amour-propre*, none of these is always present in *amour-propre* or always betokens *amour-propre*. In no case is there a perfect overlap that would allow us to say that one or another of these characteristics is the defining feature, or even *a* defining feature, of *amour-propre*. So says the textual evidence.

Three of the characterizations are rebutted by the example of Jean-Jacques. The Jean-Jacques of the *Dialogues* and the *Reveries* is a man largely free of *amour-propre*.[38] As the generally reliable "Rousseau" of the *Dialogues* says, "The man who is not dominated by *amour-propre* and who does not go seeking his happiness far from himself is the only one who knows heedlessness and sweet leisure, and [Jean-Jacques] is that man as far as I can determine" (II:144). *Amour-propre* does maintain a kind of shadowy presence in Jean-Jacques's soul, but for the most part it remains dormant: it is awakened only by rare circumstances and does not stay awake for long (*Reveries* VIII:117–18). Thus, absent any evidence to the contrary, we are entitled to assume that the dominant elements

---

38. We shall refer to the Jean-Jacques of the *Dialogues* and the author of the *Reveries* as one and the same person. There are some differences between the two characters, but the differences are negligible with regard to the matter at hand.

of Jean-Jacques's character are manifestations of *amour de soi* rather than *amour-propre*—even if these elements are generally associated with *amour-propre*.

Jean-Jacques is reflective, self-conscious, sociable, and desirous of others' recognition—thus establishing that none of these traits is exclusive to *amour-propre* or its defining feature.

(1) That he is reflective about himself is apparent on every page of the *Dialogues* and the *Reveries*. Indeed, the *Reveries* are nothing *but* an exercise in self-reflection: the author describes and comments upon his character and his experience, examining who he is and how he relates to the world around him. And although Jean-Jacques never makes a direct appearance in the *Dialogues*, what emerges from the lips of "Rousseau" and "the Frenchman" is a portrait of a man who is so penetrating on the subject of himself that he has been able to ascertain important facts about the essence of human nature (namely, its inner goodness) from his self-study. Jean-Jacques lacks *amour-propre* yet is as self-conscious and reflective a man as has ever lived—from which we conclude that while self-consciousness may generally be associated with *amour-propre*, the former is not the latter's defining feature.[39]

(2) Jean-Jacques's sociability is only slightly less apparent than his self-reflectiveness. Although not mentioned on every page, it is mentioned frequently—and memorably. One hears repeatedly of his longing for "the sweetness of true society" (*Dialogues* III:225).[40] That this longing goes unfulfilled only clinches the point: rather than resign himself to an asocial life, he takes to populating his world through imagination. When his enemies, through their slander and scheming, deprive him of the opportunity for true friendship, he is able to compensate himself by spending "five or six hours a day in [the] delightful company" of imaginary friends and mistresses (*Dialogues* II:119).[41] So strong is Jean-Jacques's need for love and friendship that he "socializes" his solitude, and so powerful is his imagination that he achieves happiness in doing so. Jean-Jacques lacks *amour-propre* yet is "the most sociable and loving of men" (*Reveries* I:27). Hence, one can conclude that, while sociability is indeed associated with *amour-propre*, the former is not the latter's defining feature.

---

39. That self-consciousness and reflection can occur without *amour-propre* is also demonstrated by the denizens of Rousseau's "ideal world" (*Dialogues* I:9–12). Like Jean-Jacques, they are deeply conscious of and thoughtful about themselves but free of the disposition to compare themselves with others—free, that is, of *amour-propre*. As Starobinski describes their condition, "consciousness ceases to be separate from the world ... yet the self is certain that it exists" (*Transparency and Obstruction*, 82).

40. See also *Dialogues* II:118 and 165.

41. Further autobiographical descriptions of the uses of imagination appear at *Reveries* III:28 and *Confessions* I:34 and IX:358–59. For elaboration on this theme, see Schwartz, *Sexual Politics*, 98–102, and Kelly, *Rousseau's Exemplary Life*.

(3) If there is a single quality that one tends to equate with *amour-propre*, it is the desire for the esteem of others. Undoubtedly the most commonly endorsed of the characterizations listed above is the characterization of *amour-propre* as the desire for recognition. Yet the simple fact is that Jean-Jacques, in whom *amour-propre* barely breathes, has this desire. In a passage depicting the delights of his imaginary friends and mistresses, we are told that part of his happiness comes from his being "known, esteemed, and cherished in these elite societies" (*Dialogues* II:119). In an even more striking passage from the same work, "Rousseau" reports from first-hand knowledge that Jean-Jacques has insistently expressed this desire: "He told me a hundred times that he would have been consoled about the public injustice if he had found a single human heart that opened up to his, felt his sorrows, and pitied them. The frank and full esteem of one single person would have compensated him for the scorn of all the others" (*Dialogues* III:225). If Rousseau is consistent in his autobiographical works, if Jean-Jacques truly is without much *amour-propre*, then we must conclude that not even the desire for others' esteem is a perfect indicator of the presence, let alone the essence, of *amour-propre*.

When is the desire for recognition not an indicator of *amour-propre*? The answer has to do with the larger purpose of the desire. If a person craves the esteem of others in order to enhance or safeguard his or her own self-esteem, then this desire is indeed born of *amour-propre*.[42] If a person desires esteem for some other reason, however—for its own sake, for the sake of nonegoistic pleasure or commiseration—then it is apt to be an expression of *amour de soi* rather than *amour-propre*. Doubtless most instances of the desire for recognition are instances of *amour-propre*. One way to know this is to consider what

---

42. Why should one's self-esteem depend on others' esteem? Rousseau does not say. (Since the question goes to the purposes behind our being constituted as we are, it may be that Rousseau sees the question as lying beyond the scope of science and hence beyond his capability to answer. For further discussion of Rousseau's unwillingness to speculate on such matters, see the section in this chapter titled "The Birth of *Amour-Propre*," below.) But if Rousseau does not answer the question, others do—most notably Hegel and his interpreter, Alexandre Kojève. Hegel's answer has to do with the subjective nature of self-esteem. Without others' express recognition, one is apt to lack "subjective certainty" of one's human worth or dignity. Even if one is inclined toward pride or self-esteem, one cannot be sure of one's worthiness without the express recognition of another consciousness. A person making so subjective a judgment as the one that gives rise to self-esteem requires, if not objective confirmation (in the form of some scientific measure or divine signal), at least the confirmation offered by others' subjective judgment. For the full argument, which is as much epistemological and metaphysical as psychological, see G. W. F. Hegel's *The Phenomenology of Spirit,* trans. A. V. Miller (New York: Oxford University Press, 1977), sections 166–96, pp. 104–19, and Kojève, *Introduction to the Reading of Hegel* (New York: Basic Books, 1969), 4–11. Aristotle similarly notes that those who desire honor (from good and knowing men) aim at having their own good opinion of themselves confirmed. See *Nicomachean Ethics* 1159a22.

is at stake in most cases. When one's feelings are on the line—when the failure to gain desired recognition results in anger or shame, or, conversely, when gaining recognition brings about pride—we may be certain that the desire is an expression of *amour-propre*. Anger, shame, and pride appear only where the demands of self-esteem have made themselves felt. Anger is aroused when one is refused desired respect. Faced with such a denial, the person with strong self-esteem will feel contemptuous indignation, while the person with weaker self-esteem (for example, a vain or insecure person) is apt to feel resentment. But whatever the specific variety, anger is provoked only when one's self-love is offended by the denial of respect. As for shame and pride, their relation to self-valuation or self-esteem is even more intimate. In fact, it is more than intimate, for it is a relation of identity: shame *is* the loss of self-esteem that we suffer when we fail to live up to our sense of self-worth, and pride *is* the enhancement of self-esteem we gain from real achievement or recognition of real achievement.[43]

When Jean-Jacques is denied the recognition he desires, he suffers sadness and a sense of loss. But he does not become angry, nor does he feel shame. What is at stake for him is joy and sadness, not self-esteem or its lack. His desire for recognition arises from a source other than *amour-propre* and so proves that the characterization of *amour-propre* as the desire for recognition is not accurate.

There is also another reason not to consider *amour-propre* synonymous with the desire for others' recognition, a reason exemplified not by Jean-Jacques but by the outstanding citizen, his counterpart across the nature-citizenship divide. As we have seen, virtuous citizens are very much creatures of *amour-propre*. The outstandingly virtuous citizen, a Cato, is no exception to this rule. But precisely because he is so virtuous—and especially if those around him no longer are virtuous at all, as was the case with Cato—he will not care much for their recognition. Peerless, he sees no one whose respect could much matter to him; indeed, he sees many whose respect he surely would disdain. Such a person is too proud, has too noble an *amour-propre*, to seek recognition from his own society. Perhaps he acts with an eye toward future, morally revitalized generations, or perhaps he has in mind the virtuous figures of generations past, or possibly the gods. However, even if he does act with some such audience in mind, he certainly is not motivated by the prospect of any applause he might hear. His immediate focus is on worthiness as such, on an objective, impersonal

43. See Francis Fukuyama, *The End of History and the Last Man* (New York: Avon Books, 1992), xvi–xvii, 164–65.

standard, rather than on any audience that he can see. As a person with great *amour-propre,* he certainly is intent on safeguarding his self-respect. But precisely because his *amour-propre is* so great, so noble, its gaze is perforce directed away from those around him to the interior realm of his own high standards. Thus he, like Jean-Jacques, illustrates the inaccuracy of simply equating *amour-propre* and the desire to be recognized by one's fellows.

(4) The same reasoning that refutes the characterization of *amour-propre* as the desire for recognition also invalidates the characterization of *amour-propre* as psychological dependency. Cato's commitment to unrewarded virtue at the expense of recognition proves that he was not dependent on others (or, at the very least, that any dependence he did have was outweighed by his greater attachment to virtue). The *amour-propre* of the truly exemplary citizen transcends psychological dependence on his fellow citizens. Doubtless even Cato began life dependent on others' approval and support.[44] And even at the peak of his virtue Cato would have continued to see and judge himself from outside, from the perspective of others' eyes, as it were, just as the psychologically dependent person does. But whereas the psychologically dependent person judges himself from the perspective of other people's opinions, the exemplary citizen judges himself from the perspective of the nation's true needs. As a citizen, Cato was in a very definite sense "other-directed," but his "other" was the good of the nation, not the judgment of its citizens—which is why he sounds to us so much like the model of "inner-directed" integrity.

In the *Second Discourse,* Rousseau seems to say that all social men are psychologically dependent on others. "[T]he social man," he says, "always outside of himself, knows how to live only in the opinion of others; and it is, so to speak, from their judgment alone that he draws the sentiment of his own existence" (179). But the *Second Discourse* is about savages and their corrupt descendants; it is not about citizens—and it is certainly not about exemplary citizens like Cato. The description does not apply, and is not meant to apply, to one such as Cato. The description does fit the exemplary citizen in part: he does exist outside of himself in the sense that he still looks at himself and judges himself from the perspective of the city. But this depiction fits him *only* in part, for he surely does not "live only in the opinion of others."

---

44. A technical clarification: In Rousseau's view the psychological need for support and approval appears not at birth but with the onset of self-consciousness and *amour-propre.* In most people this occurs soon after birth. But it need not occur until many years have passed. The preadolescent Emile exhibits no need or desire for others' support or approval. His dependence on others would seem to be strictly physical.

Thus far, three of the characterizations of *amour-propre* have been rebutted by Jean-Jacques, and a fourth by the outstanding citizen. The remaining four are easily dispatched by the example of Emile.

(5) One of the most reliable indications of *amour-propre*, and without a doubt its most unfortunate expression, is the desire for power. Yet Emile exhibits a taste for power or mastery long before he shows the first hint of *amour-propre*. Referring to a young Emile in whom the birth of *amour-propre* is still years away, Rousseau notes: "It belongs to every age, especially his, to want to create, imitate, produce, *give signs of power and activity*" (II:98; emphasis added).[45] Clearly it is inaccurate to attribute all variants of the taste for power or mastery to *amour-propre*. The young Emile's joyful mastery of tasks and even of nature—the context of Rousseau's observation is the story of Emile's first attempt at gardening—derives from *amour de soi*.

Of course, some variants of the taste for power do always indicate *amour-propre*. Every desire for dominion over other people comes from *amour-propre*. Still, it would be inaccurate to see the desire for dominion, or any other variant of the desire for power, as the defining feature of *amour-propre*. For even after he does develop *amour-propre*, Emile never exhibits any desire to rule anyone but his wife (and he happily obeys her as much as he rules her).

(6) All expressions of *amour-propre* can be classified as either pride or vanity.[46] But not everything that we call pride (in English) is an expression of *amour-propre*. Although the noun *orgueil* (the principal French equivalent of "pride") does not appear in connection with the preadolescent Emile, the verb *se piquer* (appropriately translated as "to pride oneself") does appear. Speaking for Emile and himself, the tutor states: "*we pride ourselves* not on knowing the truth of things but only on not falling into error" (III:206; emphasis added).[47] The young Emile does not feel the kind of pride that is based on comparisons with others. His is not the pride of superiority. Still, at least according to contemporary English usage, his experience does include some kind of pride and therefore invalidates the notion that all pride is a species of *amour-propre*.

(7) The same thing that is true of *amour-propre*'s relation to pride is also true of its relation to competitiveness. Just as the experience of pride does not always derive from *amour-propre*, so too competitiveness, the desire not just to

45. Even the toddler seeks to project his power into the surrounding world: "he senses in himself, so to speak, enough life to animate everything surrounding him. That he do or undo is a matter of no importance; it suffices that he change the condition of things" (I:67).

46. See the section in this chapter titled "How Much *Amour-Propre* ...," below.

47. "Nous ne nous piquons ni lui ni moi de savoir la vérité des choses, mais seulement de ne pas donner dans l'erreur" (OC IV:485).

be good but to be *better,* does not always indicate *amour-propre.* Competitiveness relative to other people surely does indicate *amour-propre,* but competitiveness oriented toward oneself, competitiveness oriented toward outstripping one's own previous achievements, does not. Thus, even as Rousseau warns against inculcating the one, he endorses the other:

> [L]et there never be any comparisons with other children, no rivals, no competitors, not even in running, once he has begun to be able to reason. I prefer a hundred times over that he not learn what he would only learn out of jealousy or vanity. However, every year I shall note the progress he has made; I shall compare it to that which he will make the following year. I shall tell him, "You have grown so many inches. That is the ditch you jumped over, the load you carried, the distance you threw a pebble, the course you ran before getting winded, etc. Let us now see what you will do." Thus I arouse him without making him jealous of anyone. He will want to outdo himself. He ought to. I see no problem in his being his own competitor. (III:184)

Competitiveness, like pride and like the desire for mastery, does not derive from *amour-propre* and so need not be feared—as long as its focus is something besides other people. Like those other two, competitiveness is a relative or comparative sentiment. Competition cannot exist without an other, the competitor. But what counts is not comparativeness per se but rather the nature— that is, the object—of the comparison. As the child becomes a youth, as he develops reason, he will begin to make comparisons, for comparison is what reasoning is all about. The trick—the way to make those comparisons serve the child's development and keep from awakening *amour-propre*—is to ensure that the referents of his relative evaluations are not other people.

What about competitiveness that *is* oriented toward other people? Can we not define *amour-propre* as the desire to be better than other people, as the desire for first place among men and women? Certainly many commentators have endorsed just this definition. They have interpreted Rousseau's description of *amour-propre* as "a relative sentiment" (*SD* 220 n. o) to mean *amour-propre* causes one to care only about one's standing relative to other people.[48] But as generally true as this definition might be, it is not perfectly true. *Amour-propre* always wants preeminence, but in its "larger" varieties it wants more

---

48. See, for example, John Charvet, *The Social Problem in the Philosophy of Rousseau* (New York: Cambridge University Press, 1974), 69. See also Horowitz, *Rousseau, Nature, and History,* 93.

than preeminence. A person with great pride, or even a person with moderate pride but great skill, will want to be not only the best but also excellent or great. A Cato will not be content to be the most virtuous citizen. Surrounded by corrupt compatriots, he will be satisfied only by meeting a higher and more objective standard of moral excellence. Similarly, an artist or craftsman who is unrivaled by his fellows will likely continue to prod himself to greater achievement, not in order to be the best—he is already the best—but to be even more excellent by an objective, suprasocial standard. Thus, while *amour-propre* may begin as the desire for preeminence—and while for most of us it may never go beyond this—for some, at least, it does seek further goals.

(8) If the example of the pre-adolescent Emile refutes the simplistic identification of *amour-propre* with competitiveness, pride, and the desire for mastery, the example of the older Emile, an Emile *with amour-propre*, refutes the characterization of *amour-propre* as universally ill-intentioned toward others.[49] The birth of *amour-propre* effects significant changes in Emile. Many new passions take shape in his soul, but ill will is not among them. His sense of honor is not prickly or pugnacious, but requires only that others not mistreat him with impunity.[50] His pride (and we are now talking about *orgueil*, not just *se piquer*) is based on his virtue and achievements rather than on his superior natural authority and attractiveness.[51] He envies no one and needs to defeat no one. And the one conquest he does attempt is both successful and bloodless.[52] Emile, in short, exemplifies the ideal upheld by most contemporary moral and psychological thought; he is the goal of all but the most marginal of our psychotherapies. He is not without *amour-propre*, but he *is* without the zero-sum mentality, alternately offensive and defensive, that characterizes those whose *amour-propre* has been less well educated than his. The example of Emile thus disproves the characterization of *amour-propre* as universally

49. The idea that *amour-propre* always entails ill intentions might seem to be refuted by the example of the virtuous citizen as well. However, even the most exemplary citizen is problematic in this regard: his virtue ensures he will be well disposed to his fellow citizens but does not guaranty that his stance toward members of other communities will be as beneficent. On the contrary, "[e]very patriot is harsh to foreigners. They are only men. They are nothing in his eyes" (*Emile* I:39). One need only recall the actual histories of Sparta and the Roman Republic. Home to the type of citizen Rousseau admires, these communities were far from peaceful toward their neighbors. (Consider, too, Socrates' comparison of ideal guardians to "noble dogs," who are "as gentle as can be with their familiars and people they know and the opposite with those they don't know." See *Republic* 375d.)

50. See IV:250.

51. Emile's superiority is palpable to other men, even if it means little to him. By virtue of this superiority, Rousseau tells us, Emile could easily ascend to political authority if he wanted to. See IV:335.

52. The reference of course is to Sophie, who, though conquered, also governs him.

ill-intentioned toward others. Ill will, to be sure, is common in *amour-propre*. But as it is not universal, it is no more a defining feature of *amour-propre* than any of the others we have reviewed.

Here perhaps, if anywhere, the skeptical reader will object. Does not Rousseau maintain in the most unambiguous terms that *amour-propre* is by its very nature rivalrous and discontented? In fact, he does. *Amour-propre is* always rivalrous: "Remember that as soon as *amour-propre* has developed, the relative 'I' is constantly in play, and the young man never observes others without returning to himself and comparing himself with them" (*Emile* IV:243). And it is always discontented: "*amour-propre*, which makes comparisons, is never content and never could be, because this sentiment, preferring ourselves to others, also demands others to prefer us to themselves, which is impossible. This is how the gentle and affectionate passions are born of *amour de soi*, and how the hateful and irascible passions are born of *amour-propre*" (*Emile* IV:213–14). There is no getting around the categorical nature of these statements. Once *amour-propre* appears, the young man "never" ceases to compare himself competitively with others. And although *amour-propre* can be the source of much that is admirable in human beings, "it is *never* content, and never could be." Even in Emile, *amour-propre* is rivalrous and discontented.

Nevertheless, rivalrousness and discontent do not necessarily imply ill intentions toward others. The rivalrousness and discontent of Emile's *amour-propre* is the rivalrousness and discontent of the superior competitor. Like the runner who is leading the race and who knows that the other runners will not catch up to him, Emile compares himself with others but is sufficiently pleased with his relative position not to wish them any harm. Rivalrousness, in his case, means only that he continues to compare himself with others. And discontent in his case means simply that his self-esteem is not absolute and without requirements, but rather contingent upon his acting in such a way as to sustain his own good witness. This is worlds away from the gnawing discontent of one who is, or who feels himself to be, trailing in life's race.[53] Emile would not want to trade places with anyone; he feels himself—with justice—to be ahead of the game. Recognizing that the celebrated are apt to be the

---

53. Those who lack Emile's satisfaction with their place in the scheme of things often find themselves unable to enjoy even the things they have. *Amour-propre* "is irritated by the advantages someone else has over us, without being appeased by those for which it feels compensated. The feeling of inferiority in a single respect therefore poisons the feeling of superiority in a thousand others, and what one has more of is forgotten in devoting attention only to what one has less of" (*Dialogues* II:113). For an interesting discussion of the inevitable dissatisfaction of those who are afflicted by such sensitive *amour-propre*, see Anthony Skillen, "Rousseau and the Fall of Social Man," *Philosophy* 60 (1985): 105–21.

most dependent and therefore the most miserable of men, and that the lives of "the great" amount to little more than the anxious pursuit of vain triumphs, he feels no inclination to prefer their lot to his own (IV:242–44). He knows he has no reason to envy anyone, and so his *amour-propre*, far from malevolent or resentful, is benign to the point of beneficence.

Emile's *amour-propre* is beneficent because the young man is able to compare himself favorably with other people from the very first—that is, from the moment that his *amour-propre* is born. The birth of *amour-propre* gives rise to a host of new passions. "But to decide whether among these passions the dominant ones in his character will be humane and gentle or cruel and malignant, whether they will be passions of beneficence and commiseration or of envy and covetousness, we must know what position he will feel he has among men, and what kinds of obstacles he may believe he has to overcome to reach the position he wants to occupy" (IV:235). Because Emile is pleased with his relative standing, his *amour-propre* becomes the source of "humane and gentle" passions rather than "cruel and malignant" ones. As the reference to "beneficence and commiseration" indicates, his *amour-propre* forms an alliance with his natural sympathy by making him feel good about himself as one who cares for others. He pities those who suffer not just because pity is natural and so feels good in its own right but also because in pitying and in rendering assistance to the suffering, he confirms his good opinion of himself.

This alliance in Emile's soul between *amour-propre* and natural pity points to the deeper, more philosophical reason for the harmlessness of his *amour-propre*. To say that there is an alliance between Emile's *amour-propre* and natural pity is to say that there is an alliance between his *amour-propre* and his *amour de soi*, since pity is an expression of *amour de soi*. To put it a little differently, it is to say that there is an alliance in him between *amour-propre*, the characteristic that most represents and accounts for man's departure from nature, and nature itself. The unnatural in Emile is in sync with the natural; the discontinuity between nature and human nature is overcome.

The birth of *amour-propre* marks the end of original naturalness. But *amour-propre*'s alliance with *amour de soi* achieves another kind of naturalness: the alliance between the two is precisely what constitutes civilized naturalness. Earlier we defined Emile's naturalness, the naturalness of "the natural man living in the state of society," in largely quantitative terms: the natural man is one in whom there is still much *amour de soi*, one in whom *amour-propre* has not supplanted too much of the original, nonrelative self-love. But civilized naturalness is more than just a quantitative matter. Indeed, the quantitative fact—the survival of a high degree of *amour de soi*—is made possible only by a qualitative element: an *amour-propre* that is beneficent. That beneficence comes from Emile's correct belief that no one's position in life is more enviable than his. The good governance of *amour-propre* as exemplified by Emile's education is thus less a matter of limiting its extent than of shaping its character. It is only because he feels himself so fortunate, so much like a winner, that Emile is able to forget about the race, about winning and losing, as much as he does. It is only because his *amour-propre* is soothed by his self-assessment that he is able to avoid worrying about self-assessment and to dwell instead in the sweet ease of *amour de soi*.

Such are some of the more common mischaracterizations of Rousseau's *amour-propre*. That they are more often implicit than explicit does not make them any less needful of correction. Perhaps it makes the task of correction *more* imperative: nothing is more potentially damaging to an edifice, after all, whether architectural or interpretive, than hidden structural flaws. But pointing out some common errors has obviously not been the sole purpose, or even the main purpose, of the foregoing review. We have examined these characterizations not so much because they are somehow wrong but because they are also somehow right. Each fastens upon some characteristic or phenomenon that is generally associated with *amour-propre*. In so doing, each illuminates some of the practicalities of *amour-propre*. Even if they fail to isolate *amour-propre*'s essence, they still have shed considerable light on it, for in (meta)psychological matters such as these, it is only by wading through the practicalities of a thing that one ultimately reaches its essence.

That essence, to repeat, is valuational. *Amour-propre* is the source of all feeling and behavior that concern the individual's need to establish, maintain, or confirm his or her sense of self-worth—in today's popular language, self-esteem. The existence of *amour-propre* is perfectly coextensive with the problem of self-esteem. *Amour-propre* exists only when, to the extent that, and for as long as self-esteem is problematic or contingent.

Amour-propre is born only when, in consequence of incipient self-consciousness, self-esteem ceases to be absolute and unconscious and becomes instead problematic. The infant, like the savage, is free of *amour-propre*. Having no meaningful self-consciousness, no awareness of his moral relations with others, his sense of self-worth is not problematic; and so in him there is only *amour de soi*.

Once it has been born, *amour-propre* exists only to the *extent* that self-esteem has become problematic. That is to say, the extent of *amour-propre*'s "takeover" of the soul, the extent to which it supplants *amour de soi*, depends upon just how problematic self-esteem has become. In most people the takeover is total, or very nearly so. But it need not be. As the case of Emile illustrates, the birth of *amour-propre* need not mark a complete break with all that went before: a good deal of *amour de soi* can survive and coexist with *amour-propre*. As we noted earlier, the extent to which *amour-propre* gains hold of the soul is determined by the specific quality of the *amour-propre* concerned. Whereas some kinds of *amour-propre* inevitably become all-consuming (one thinks of the vanity of Jean-Jacques's enemies), other kinds (the pride of an Emile or a Sophie, for example) are less aggressive in their appetite to rule the soul.[54] Thus any hope of limiting *amour-propre*'s scope—and thereby achieving civilized naturalness à la Emile—depends on our inculcating the right kind of *amour-propre*, or what one may be forgiven for calling the good kind of bad self-love.

Finally, *amour-propre persists* only for as long as self-esteem *remains* problematic. If a person should somehow free himself of the need to earn or safeguard his sense of self-worth—and presumably this would require a transcendence of ordinary self-consciousness, since it was the advent of self-consciousness that made self-esteem problematic in the first place—then that person would have achieved freedom from *amour-propre*. Such, in fact, is the condition of Jean-Jacques, at least at his best.

In all these respects—in its birth, in its character and extent, and in its persistence—*amour-propre* reflects the problem of self-valuation. Let us address each of these points in turn.

The Birth of *Amour-Propre*

Following Rousseau, we have spoken of the "birth" of *amour-propre* and of its being "aroused" or "awakened." But it is important not to lose sight of another, perhaps more descriptive terminology. When he is not merely referring to the event but is actually describing it, Rousseau speaks of the appearance of *amour-propre* as a transformation: "This is the point where *amour de soi turns into amour-propre*" (*Emile* IV:235); and, "that is how *amour de soi*, which is a good and absolute feeling, *becomes amour-propre*" (*Dialogues* I:9). What occurs is not an acquisition so much as a conversion.

What brings about this conversion? Rousseau offers several accounts—one in the *Second Discourse*, one in the *Dialogues*, and two in *Emile*. These accounts are not entirely consistent with one another, though they are not irreconcilable

---

54. The outstanding characteristic of Jean-Jacques's enemies is their all-consuming vanity, which reveals itself in their obsession with him. See, for example, *Dialogues* II:154–55.

either. Each, moreover, shares a central element, for in each account of the transformation of *amour de soi* into *amour-propre*, which is of course a passionate or sentimental transformation, what propels the process is cognitive development. The process begins when circumstances conspire to stimulate and refine the rational faculty, which is really nothing more than the ability to perceive and consider relations of various sorts.[55] Once launched, cognitive development continues apace until, eventually, self-consciousness—the awareness that one is a separate self related to others and that those others have desires and wills of their own—is attained. Then the decisive change, no longer merely cognitive, takes place: as one gains awareness of being a separate self related to other selves, needs that had been simple and absolute become complicated and relative. Most significantly, the need for good witness of oneself, originally a largely unconscious and easily satisfied need, gets socialized and relativized. Good witness of oneself, the only one of man's three "true" or natural needs that is cognitive, inevitably is transformed by cognitive development. One's sense of self-worth comes to depend upon what others think and upon one's place vis-à-vis those others, at which point *amour-propre* has been born. *Amour-propre* is made possible—and inevitable—only by cognitive development, by the knowledge of one's separateness from and relatedness to others.[56]

55. Although Rousseau gives no single definitive characterization of reason, what he seems to mean by it is the capacity to compare, analyze, and draw inferences—that is, to consider relations between things. (See, for example, *LM* 1090.) That is why he is able to ascribe a certain (albeit minimal) rational capacity to children and even to animals (*Emile* II:108; *SD* 114).

56. One might perhaps object to the idea that the need for good witness of oneself even existed in original man, since that would seem to impute a moral need to a premoral being. I have nevertheless chosen to speak of this need as present in original man for the following reasons. First, Rousseau does call this a *true* need, which suggests that it was in fact present, even if in a primitive or unconscious form. That it is characterized as a true need suggests that even if it was entirely unfelt by the savage, it still should be thought of as existing in potentiality or latency rather than as not existing at all (recall that Rousseau assumes that many psychic phenomena did in fact exist in latency in the soul of original man; see *Emile* II:80). Second, in saying that the savage enjoyed good witness of himself, I am perhaps doing what Rousseau does when he ascribes pity to the savage: although in a certain, strict sense the savage did not have good (or any) witness of himself, his behavior was the same as that of a being who did have it. Indeed, just as his repugnance at seeing other sensitive beings suffer can be seen as a kind of protopity, so might the savage be seen as enjoying a kind of proto- or premoral self-esteem as well. Rousseau knew that we see among the animals behavior that is akin or analogous to what he recognized as moral behavior in human beings. (See, for example, *Emile* IV:286–87n.) Just as submoral or proto-*amour-propre* is seen in some animals (see note 14 to Chapter 5), so, it seems to me, can one see a submoral version or analogue of self-esteem in pre- or nonmoral beings. A dog that has been cowed, for example, seems not only skittish but also, somehow, "demoralized." Thus it seems permissible—indeed, useful—to say that this need that is moral and hence complicated and problematic for civilized man existed in a premoral and hence uncomplicated and unproblematic way for the savage.

This is certainly the case in the account offered in the *Second Discourse*. There, Rousseau provides a historical narration that admittedly is partly speculative but whose major elements he affirms with confidence.[57] What initiates the process of man's great inner transformation is something utterly circumstantial and without moral content: natural phenomena such as "great floods or earthquakes" and the breaking up of "portions of the continent into islands ... forced [men] to live together" (148). What was physical and hence submoral in itself is anything but submoral in its ultimate effects, however. The connection between the physical and the moral is the cognitive. "A permanent proximity cannot fail to engender at length some contact between different families. Young people of different sexes live in neighboring huts; the passing intercourse demanded by nature soon leads to another kind no less sweet and more permanent through mutual frequentation. People grow accustomed to consider different objects and to make comparisons; imperceptibly they acquire ideas of merit and beauty which produce sentiments of preference" (148). What has occurred thus far? Accidental circumstances (being forced to live in close proximity to one another) have prompted cognitive change: people have acquired both the ability to make comparisons and the standards (ideas of merit and beauty) by which to make those comparisons. Only now, in consequence of these cognitive steps, does the first sentimental change take place: their "ideas of merit and beauty ... produce sentiments of preference."

From this point the process gathers steam. Everything changes, and changes quickly. But even now, the process of sentimental development, the development that will culminate in the birth of *amour-propre*, proceeds only as far and as fast as cognitive development allows:

> In proportion *as ideas and sentiments follow upon one another* and as mind and heart are trained, the human race continues to be tamed, contacts spread, and bonds are tightened. People grew accustomed to assembling in front of the huts or around a large tree; song and dance, true children of love and leisure, became the amusement or rather the occupation of idle and assembled men and women. Each one began to look at the others and to want to be looked at himself, and public esteem had a value. The one who sang or danced the best, the handsomest, the strongest, the most adroit, or the most eloquent became the most highly considered; and that was the first step toward inequality and, at the same time, toward vice. From these first preferences

---

57. See note 2 to Chapter 1.

were born on one hand vanity and contempt, on the other shame and
envy; and the fermentation caused by these new leavens eventually
produced compounds fatal to happiness and innocence. (149; emphasis
added)

The continued enhancement of man's cognitive capacity brings about the full
flowering of *amour-propre*. The plant has not yet become a wild, choking
vine—vanity and contempt, shame and envy are as yet nascent and thus only
slightly noxious—but it has taken firm and virtually unextractable root. The
great moral and sentimental transformation of the species, the true launching
of human history, has been brought about by the expansion of man's cognitive
horizons.

Such is Rousseau's account of the genesis of *amour-propre* in the species.[58]
The accounts given in the *Dialogues* and in *Emile* address the genesis of *amour-
propre* in the individual. The account that appears in the *Dialogues* comes
from the mouth of the "Rousseau" character, but it accords with—indeed, it
succinctly summarizes—views elsewhere expressed by his namesake. Like the
story told in the *Second Discourse*, the *Dialogues* account emphasizes the cognitive source of *amour-propre*'s awakening.

> If you ask me the origin of this disposition to compare oneself, which
> changes a natural and good passion into another passion that is artifi-
> cial and bad, I will answer that it comes from social relations, from the
> progress of ideas, and from the cultivation of the mind. So long as we
> are occupied solely by absolute needs, we confine ourselves to seeking
> what is truly useful to us, we scarcely cast an idle glance at others. But
> as society becomes more closely knit by the bond of mutual needs, as
> the mind is extended, exercised, and enlightened, it becomes more
> active, embraces more objects, grasps more relationships, examines,
> compares. In these frequent comparisons, it doesn't forget either itself,
> its fellows, or the place it aspires to among them. (II:113)

It is impossible to miss the centrality of the cognitive in this account. Circumstance, in the form of social intercourse, surely plays a role. But its role, as
in the *Second Discourse*, is to stimulate cognitive development—"the progress
of ideas," "the cultivation of the mind." And it is this progress, which consists

---

58. The foregoing account is of vanity's genesis. Pride had already made its first appearance a
little earlier. See *SD* 144.

in the comprehension of more and more relationships, that brings about the inclination to compare self to others, the inclination that signals the arousal of *amour-propre*.

The reader may have noticed an apparent contradiction. Earlier, we made a point of dissociating ill will from the core of *amour-propre*. However often *amour-propre* is in actual fact ill-intentioned toward others, the example of Emile, we observed, proves that it need not always be. Yet the passage just quoted seems to imply just the opposite. Rousseau characterizes the transformation of *amour de soi* into *amour-propre* as the transformation of "a natural and good passion into another passion that is artificial and *bad*." Nor is this the only such remark. Rousseau frequently depicts *amour-propre* as the bad form of self-love.[59] Consider again, for example, the following celebrated passage from *Emile*: "*Amour de soi*, which regards only ourselves, is contented when our true needs are satisfied. But *amour-propre*, which makes comparisons, is never content and never could be, because this sentiment, preferring ourselves to others, also demands others to prefer us to themselves, which is impossible. This is how the gentle and affectionate passions are born of *amour de soi*, and how *the hateful and irascible passions are born of amour-propre*" (IV:213–14; emphasis added). This is not quite as harsh a treatment of *amour-propre* as simply calling it bad, but it is nearly so. Nothing good is attributed to *amour-propre*. That, combined with the fact that good things *are* attributed to *amour de soi*, implies that *amour-propre* is simply the dark half of Rousseau's dualistic psychological scheme. Which version is true? How shall we resolve the contradiction between our earlier, more ambiguous portrait of *amour-propre* and the present, darker one?

We might begin by noting that the less ambiguous of the two depictions, the one in which the word "bad" is actually used, is not said in the author's own name. Rather, it comes from the mouth of a character in the *Dialogues*. And while that character, as his name implies, surely does represent Rousseau's own general outlook, Rousseau advises us not to consider any of his characters completely reliable when it comes to interpreting the details of his philosophical system—not even when the character goes by the same last name as the author (*Dialogues* I:69–70). But that only makes the contradiction less sharp. To resolve it altogether, we need to consider the contexts in which the passages appear and Rousseau's purposes in those passages.

---

59. So much so that some commentators call it just that. See, for example, Bloom, *Love and Friendship*, 51. Another harsh depiction appears at *Dialogues* I:9, where the "Rousseau" character says that *amour-propre* "demands preferences, whose enjoyment is purely negative, and it no longer seeks satisfaction in our own benefit but solely in the harm of another."

To put it simply, the *amour-propre* that Rousseau disparages in the passages quoted above is bad *amour-propre*, not all *amour-propre*. The *amour-propre* to which he is referring there is the *amour-propre* that *does* generate hateful and irascible passions. Why, then, does he not say so? Why condemn *amour-propre* in such an apparently universal way? Because in point of fact, the great majority of *amour-propre is* bad. In most people it manifests itself as vanity and envy rather than as virtue. Doubtless it would have made our task as interpreters easier had Rousseau been more precise and supplied a qualification like "usually" or "generally." But sometimes precision has the effect of temporizing: had Rousseau explicitly exempted some forms of *amour-propre* from his condemnations, he would have sacrificed rhetorical power and thus risked diluting the moral effect he hoped to achieve. Rather than weaken the force of his words, he leaves it to the reader to recognize that an author who praises some *amour-propre* only a few pages after seeming to condemn all of it means that condemnation to apply to most but not all *amour-propre*. Only about twenty pages after he decries *amour-propre* as the source of "hateful and irascible" passions, Rousseau acknowledges that *amour-propre* can be the source of "humane and gentle" ones as well.[60] One who knows how to read, he might have said, will surely come to the proper interpretation. An author cannot be blamed if his readers have so little regard for context that they fail to resolve a conflict as resolvable as this one—especially when the author has instructed his readers that to understand his full meaning requires "consistent attention" and much effortful rereading (*Dialogues* III: 211).

As it turns out, the acknowledgment that *amour-propre* can be the source of "humane and gentle" passions appears in the fourth and last of Rousseau's accounts of the birth of *amour-propre*.[61] This account depicts the genesis of *amour-propre* not as it typically is, but rather as it might and ought to be—as it *will* be in Emile. This is a singular discussion; nowhere else does Rousseau recount the birth of good *amour-propre*, which makes his narration all the more weighty as evidence for our interpretive thesis. Whatever the difference between Emile's (good) *amour-propre* and the (bad) *amour-propre* of nearly

60. As John Plamenatz notes, "It was seldom [Rousseau's] way to weaken the effect of his condemnations by qualifying them at the time he made them. He preferred another method; he preferred to unsay in one place what he had said in another." See *Man and Society*, vol. 1 (London: Longman Group, 1963), 422. The contradictory descriptions of *amour-propre* appear at *Emile* IV:214 and 235, respectively. Other scholars have replied differently to this inconsistency. J. I. MacAdam, for example, argues that it indicates an unresolved contradiction, and one that detracts from the coherence of Rousseau's work. See "The *Discourse on Inequality* and the *Social Contract*," *Philosophy* 50 (1975): 17.

61. The third account, which I addressed elsewhere in this chapter, appears at *Emile* IV:213–15.

everyone else, his, exactly like theirs, owes its birth to cognitive development. Just as was the case with the savage, it is only after making comparisons—only in *consequence* of making comparisons—that *amour-propre* appears in Emile. "Since my Emile has until now looked only at himself, the first glance he casts on his fellows leads him to compare himself to them. And the first sentiment aroused in him by this comparison is the desire to be in the first position. This is the point where *amour de soi* turns into *amour-propre* and where begin to arise all the passions which depend on this one" (IV:235). "The point where *amour de soi* turns into *amour-propre*" in Emile is a point defined by cognitive development, the point at which self-consciousness has achieved critical mass, as it were.

The primacy of cognitive development among the causes of *amour-propre* often goes unrecognized. The more common practice is to point a finger at sexuality. As with Adam and Eve and the rest of us, the end of Emile's original innocence, the birth of his *amour-propre*, is said to be connected to the emergence of adult sexuality. This is entirely true: *amour-propre* and sexuality *are* connected. But sexuality is not the primary cause of *amour-propre*'s birth. If it were, then the savage would have had *amour-propre*—which, of course, he did not (*SD* 222). Rather, *amour-propre* is awakened only with the emergence of moralized, self-conscious sexuality, which is possible only for those whose cognitive development has advanced far enough to include an acquisition that the savage lacked: an awareness of oneself as a separate self related to other selves. In fact, the story of Adam and Eve, read correctly, makes the same point. What brings about their loss of innocence, after all, is a cognitive acquisition, not a sexual one. They eat of the fruit of the tree of the *knowledge* of good and evil. Only then do they become aware of their sexuality and lose their innocence.

The emergence of his sexuality is the condition that prompts the birth of Emile's *amour-propre*. Indeed, sexuality makes this birth inevitable: it inspires in him the irresistible need to consider his attractiveness to others. Nevertheless, there are two reasons to view cognitive development, the emergence of self-consciousness, as the more basic cause of *amour-propre*'s arousal. First, *amour-propre* can and usually does awaken long before sexual development. Emile is the exception: Rousseau's celebrated discourse on babies' tears indicates that most people's *amour-propre* begins to be stirred in infancy; and that while it can only develop so much in those early months (because the sense of separate self is only so far advanced), it clearly reaches large and corrupting proportions in most children long before the age at which they develop sexual interest in others. Second, *amour-propre* is *defined* in essentially cognitive terms. In the *Dialogues*, Rousseau refers to *amour-propre* as the "disposition to compare oneself" (II:113). *Amour-propre* always involves comparison; it does not always involve sexuality. Sexual relations (whether actual or merely desired) do tend to be the most intense social relations and those in which *amour-propre* is most deeply invested. But that does not speak against the primacy of cognitive development in arousing *amour-propre*. Indeed, it only confirms it, for the intensity of sexuality is itself owed to cognitive development. Savage sexuality was not intense. It is only the self that is conscious of its separateness that will passionately crave the overcoming of separateness that sexual relations represent.

The primacy of the cognitive in Rousseau's developmental scheme is more than a little ironic. No previous philosopher had elevated the passions and sentiments to such heights. Rousseau not only accords them their due respect as the sole source of human behavior, he celebrates them as well, at least the good ones among them, as the essential content and goal of the good life. He even defines human existence in terms of feeling: it is no mistake to see in Rousseau a sentimental reformulation of Descartes' *cogito*. And yet, for all that, cognitive development has priority in writing the terms of the human condition, for it is cognitive development that gives rise to the birth of *amour-propre*, the single greatest influence on our feelings. The decisive "moment" in human development occurs when self-consciousness is achieved, when one perceives one's separateness from and relatedness to others.[62]

The significance of self-consciousness in Rousseau's thought has not been appreciated as much as it deserves to be. Every major step in human development, and every distinctively human trait, is connected to the development of self-consciousness. It is only by developing a sense of oneself as a separate self that one really begins to live: "strictly speaking, the life of the individual begins" when "he gains consciousness of himself" (*Emile* II:78). And it is only by acquiring a more highly developed self-consciousness that one can claim one's full human birthright. We have just examined the role of self-consciousness in awakening *amour-propre*. Earlier, in Chapter 3, we explored its role in awakening conscience and noted that "conscience is only developed and only acts from enlightenment" (*Beaumont* 936)—that is, from an awareness of one's relations with others. Thus, not only *amour-propre* but also the more advanced manifestations of *amour de soi* owe their genesis to self-consciousness. Moreover, it

62. The intellectual perception of oneself as a separate and related self obviously does not require a very highly developed rational faculty: what is required for the birth of *amour-propre* is only a perception of separateness (and of the fact that other people have independent wills), not a *conception*. That is why even a small child can have *amour-propre*. He may not understand his relatedness to others, but he does perceive it—in a way that the pre-adolescent Emile does not.

is self-consciousness that gives real meaning to freedom, one of the defining attributes of humanity. Freedom that is not conscious of itself is only a formal freedom, a freedom without content. A self that is unaware of its separateness cannot think about itself; it has inclination but no will and so cannot exercise its freedom in any meaningful sense. The measure of one's capacity for a fully human life is the measure of one's self-consciousness.

But the capacity for a fully human life necessarily entails the capacity for vice and misery as well. If self-consciousness opens the way to a full flowering of human nature, it also provides fertile soil for the flowers of evil. *Amour-propre*, the source of all the world's evil and most of its misery, arises with the onset of self-consciousness and could almost be defined as aggressive, worried self-consciousness—what is *amour-propre* if not the self's response to its vulnerability as a limited, separate self? Self-consciousness, in other words, though morally neutral, lies at the heart of all evil and most misery.

Accordingly, it is by overcoming this keen sense of separateness that evil and misery are mitigated. Each of Rousseau's theoretical solutions to the human problem can be easily formulated in terms of overcoming separateness. The citizen avoids separateness by being connected to the city—not just legally but in the most personal sense. He is part of a larger whole. Jean-Jacques avoids separateness by becoming a whole unto himself: he achieves a level of consciousness at which other people are no longer meaningfully present and at which he is at one with nature. And Emile first *avoids* separateness by being kept ignorant of his moral relations with others and then *overcomes* it by falling in love and marrying.

Before attaining self-consciousness, man is less than fully human. But attaining self-consciousness is hardly an end in itself. Indeed, it is not a fulfillment at all, but a problem, and only when this problem is solved can full, flourishing humanity be achieved. The attainment of self-consciousness gives rise to the human condition as we now know it by reconstituting the requirements of man's well-being.[63]

Our inquiry into the birth of *amour-propre* has yielded considerable results. Self-consciousness, we have learned, makes self-esteem contingent and relative and

---

63. The major interpreter who has most highlighted the import of self-consciousness in Rousseau's thought is probably Starobinski. Starobinski does not talk much about self-consciousness per se, but he interprets Rousseau's project—and Rousseau's life—as the pursuit of totalistic, transparent relations with others, that is, as the overcoming of separateness and the alienating reflectiveness that goes with it.

so causes *amour-propre* to be born. But for all we have learned, one very major question remains unanswered. A comprehensive explanation would tell us not only what triggers the birth of *amour-propre* but also why it can be triggered at all. Why should the awareness of one's relatedness to others confer on those others such enormous significance? Why should it relativize self-esteem, transforming what had been an absolute need for good witness of oneself into the need to compare favorably to others? Why should the experience of other people's wills incite willfulness, such that a small taste of dominion gives rise to a lust for rule?[64] We know what awakens *amour-propre* from latency. What is still wanted is an explanation of the latent potential itself.

But what is wanted is not available. Rousseau never explains why *amour de soi* is so easily transformed into *amour-propre*. His various accounts of the genesis of *amour-propre* do not explain the original existence of the potential that is activated.[65] What should we make of this? Does it indicate a deficiency in Rousseau's treatment of self-love? I suggest the following: Rather than constituting a weakness in Rousseau's account, the absence of such an explanation reflects a kind of intellectual integrity and humility. If Rousseau neglects to explain the potential for *amour-propre*, it is simply because he refuses to speculate about things he knows he cannot apprehend. To offer an explanation of an innate, latent potential would be to claim knowledge of God's intention in creating man. And that is a species of knowledge that Rousseau, whose every tenet is based entirely on human experience, would not purport to have.

Rousseau, as we know, eschewed speculative metaphysics and theology. When he did discuss God, his focus was usually our experience of him rather than his specific purposes—as in the "Profession of Faith of the Savoyard Vicar," for example. On the rare occasions when he did speak to God's intentions, as in his letter to Voltaire on Providence, his goal was less to propound his own view of divine will than to refute those who in effect had indicted God

64. How easily *amour-propre* is awakened and how hopeless it is to try to put it back to sleep is discussed in "The Fixedness of Man's 'Present Nature'" in Chapter 2 above.
65. As Grant demonstrates, the appearance of *amour-propre* cannot be explained as a consequence of self-interest or inequality or anything else that preceded it historically; *amour-propre* is an independent and in some ways inexplicable psychic force (*Hypocrisy and Integrity*, 155–61). (Grant also illuminates the enormous political implications of this independent status.) Probably the most that we can say regarding the causes of the relativization of self-love is that it would seem to be a consequence of the development of conscience. The need for good witness of oneself as it appears in civilized human beings can be understood as the product of the interaction between conscience and self-love—that is, as conscience, or the love of order, informing the requirements of self-love, just as conscience informs so much else. But this is only a partial explanation. We still do not know why self-esteem should have become *so* problematic nor, for that matter, why so many should seek it through means that are repugnant to conscience.

for indifference to human suffering (OC IV:1059–75). And even in these works the scope of his arguments was limited: Rousseau's theodical writings, including the *Second Discourse* and even *Emile*,[66] justify God's ways by proving the goodness of creation as it was before man fouled it; there is no attempt to justify human suffering as somehow serving God's purpose. ("Everything is good as it leaves the hands of the Author of things; everything degenerates in the hands of man" [*Emile* I:37].)

Rousseau did break new epistemological ground. He supplemented the Enlightenment's naturalistic approach with introspective investigation; he introduced a subjective dimension hitherto unseen among his contemporaries. But the subject of these investigations is himself, his own mind and experience, not God. Hence he comments upon every question concerning *amour-propre* except the one regarding which his own experience remains silent—the question of *amour-propre's* presence as a latent potential.[67] Unless one is prepared to make the sort of teleological inductions that modern science rejects, one cannot purport to know why any particular disposition is present in man, least of all one that is unnecessary for the species' survival and that causes so much destruction. One is of course entitled to find fault with Rousseau for neglecting to explain *amour-propre's* presence. One should realize, however, that one's complaint is with modern scientific naturalism and not just with Rousseau.[68]

How Much *Amour-Propre*, and What Kind?
Gentleness Versus Cruelty, Pride Versus Vanity

Once *amour-propre* has been born, two critical questions remain to be settled. The first is the question of its character. In some people *amour-propre* becomes

66. See note 70 to chapter 3 .

67. Regarding another, similarly obscure matter, Rousseau wrote the following lines in the first draft of *Emile*: "If I am asked how it is possible for the morality of human life to emerge from a purely physical revolution, I will answer that I do not know. *I base myself throughout on experience and do not seek the reasons for the facts*" (emphasis added). See editorial note 2 to book IV of *Emile*, p. 488.

68. A point that does particularly pertain to Rousseau is the implication of his understanding of the origin of *amour-propre* for the principle of natural goodness. *Amour-propre* is most striking for being a disorderly factor in an otherwise orderly universe. Its appearance spells the end of nature's (pre)historic reign. Yet it can only appear because its latent potential exists *by nature*. Nature, characterized above all by order, contains within itself the potential for disorder. Does not this latent potential speak against the interpretation of nature as altogether harmonious? If the potential for *amour-propre* exists by nature, and especially if the actualization of that potential was easy (as we have seen) and was precipitated by circumstances that were themselves natural (as we shall see), then nature would seem to point beyond its original goodness. This issue will be addressed in Chapter 5.

pride; in others, vanity; in still others, probably in most, a mix of the two. Nor is the question of *amour-propre*'s character just a question of how much pride versus how much vanity. It is also a question of what kind(s) of pride and what kind(s) of vanity. There are as many varieties of pride and vanity, of *amour-propre*, as there are of personality.

The second question is that of extent. How much, what proportion, of original *amour de soi* will be transformed into *amour-propre?* This is not an issue that Rousseau addresses explicitly, but it is obvious from a cursory survey of the personages populating his works that the extent of *amour-propre*, not just its character, varies among people. Emile, for example, is much more a proud young man than a vain one, but he is not nearly as proud as the citizen. Emile's pride is of a different sort from the citizen's—it has a different character—but it is also smaller. Pride simply does not play the same dominant role in Emile— does not dictate as much thought, feeling, and behavior—as it does in the citizen. The questions of character and extent are separate but of course they are also intimately related to one another. Emile is able to maintain a substantial reservoir of *amour de soi* precisely because his *amour-propre* assumes the character that it does.

Actually, the foregoing formulation is not quite accurate: the questions of *amour-propre*'s character and extent do not remain to be settled after its birth; they are settled (at least for a while) as *amour-propre* is being born. Birth and character formation are simultaneous, because they stem immediately from a common source. *Amour-propre* is born with the first comparison of self to others, and its basic character is determined by the result of that comparison. Rousseau introduces the question of *amour-propre*'s character at the very moment that he describes its birth in Emile:

> Since my Emile has until now looked only at himself, the first glance he casts on his fellows leads him to compare himself with them. And the first sentiment aroused in him by this comparison is the desire to be in the first position. This is the point where *amour de soi* turns into *amour-propre* and where begin to arise all the passions which depend on this one. But to decide whether among these passions the dominant ones in his character will be humane and gentle or cruel and malignant, whether they will be passions of beneficence and commiseration or of envy and covetousness, we must know what position he will feel he has among men, and what kind of obstacles he may believe he has to overcome to reach the position he wants to occupy. (IV:235)

In this passage Rousseau poses the question of *amour-propre*'s character in terms of whether it will be gentle or cruel. As we discussed earlier, the question can also be put in terms of whether or not *amour-propre* will form an alliance with *amour de soi*. When *amour-propre* is gentle and humane, it is because it has aligned itself with and even supports natural pity, which is an expression of *amour de soi*. When *amour-propre* is cruel and malignant, it is because it has effectively overcome natural pity. Everything depends upon the results of that first comparison of self to others. When the initial comparison is favorable, *amour-propre* assumes a gentle character and moderate proportions and allies itself with the considerable remaining reservoir of *amour de soi*. When the comparison is not favorable, *amour-propre* sours and grows.

But gentleness versus cruelty is only one way to pose the question of *amour-propre*'s character. There is another way. Far more often than he speaks of gentleness and cruelty, Rousseau speaks of pride and vanity. Pride versus vanity is the most basic polarity within the universe of *amour-propre*. Unlike gentleness versus cruelty, it refers to the substance of self-love and not just its aspect.

Just as *amour de soi* and *amour-propre* comprise the totality of possibilities in the realm of self-love, so pride and vanity comprise the whole of *amour-propre*. Rousseau refers to pride and vanity as "the two branches of *amour-propre*" (*Corsica* 326). Thus they constitute a second dualism—a dualism within a dualism. And this second dualism is only slightly less complex than the first. It is, however, considerably less morally ambiguous.

Beginning with the *First Discourse*, all of Rousseau's writings reflect a subtle consciousness of *amour-propre*'s moral ambiguity. But it is only in his later writings, beginning with *Emile*, that a meaningful distinction between pride and vanity is maintained.[69] The first direct comparison is a telling one. Self-love, Rousseau observes, "becomes pride in great souls, vanity in small ones" (*Emile* IV:215). This is not a Manichaean statement, for it does not categorically smile upon pride. Pride is associated with greatness of soul, but greatness of soul is not thoroughly unproblematic: there is much about it that is morally ambiguous at best. But the statement *is* definitive in its disparagement of vanity. Whereas the greatness of soul that is associated with pride is an ambiguous thing, the smallness of soul associated with vanity is altogether contemptible. As we saw in Chapter 1, Rousseau judges the quality of lives and souls—or at least expresses his judgments of them—in quantitative terms. The goodness

---

69. Even in the later writings, the distinction is not maintained with perfect consistency. See note 72 to this chapter.

of a good life lies in the maximization, the largeness, of its existence; similarly, the badness of a bad life is manifest in the smallness of its existence. There is nothing redeeming about smallness of soul, not even the fact that small souls host only petty vices: petty vices, to judge from Rousseau's assessment of modern life, are all too capable of producing great injustice—if not individually then in the aggregate.[70] So goes Rousseau's first pronouncement comparing pride and vanity. Pride, by virtue of its association with great souls, is accorded a wary but definite respect. Vanity, by contrast, is accorded no such respect: it is the mark of a contemptible state of soul.

But what *are* pride and vanity? What is the difference between them? Some have argued that Rousseau offers no clear and workable distinction between the two forms of *amour-propre*.[71] Certainly he never does so in a thorough and systematic way. Nevertheless, his usage is relatively consistent, and it is possible to deduce a fairly specific and sustainable distinction.[72] As subspecies of *amour-propre*, both pride and vanity are essentially concerned with the need for a sense of self-worth. The proud man must tend to his need for self-esteem every bit as much as the vain man; each, being self-conscious and comparing himself to others, needs to acquire and maintain a sense of self-worth. How the two men will go about trying to satisfy this need, though, will be very different. The difference between pride and vanity is found in the character of the pursuit of self-worth. It is revealed by the "objects" that are sought as a means to self-esteem or, to put it another way, by the standard that governs the effort to gain and or keep self-esteem. When the standard governing an individual's pursuit of self-esteem is rooted in reality—when one's sense of self-worth depends upon achieving something whose value is real and not merely the product of opinion—pride is at work. When the standard is rooted in appearance or opinion, one is ruled by vanity.

70. "I do not accuse the men of this century of having all the vices; they have only the vices of cowardly souls; they are only rogues and knaves" (*Last Reply* 72). "Vile and cowardly even in their vices, they have only small souls" (*Emile* IV:335).

71. See, for example, Plamenatz, *Man and Society*, I:420–23.

72. Admittedly, Rousseau is not perfectly consistent in his use of the terms "pride" and "vanity." What he lacks in semantic consistency, however, is largely made up by conceptual consistency. That is, it is possible to discern what kinds of *amour-propre* he approves of and what kinds he does not approve of, and why—and that is the distinction that matters most. (Even Plamenatz, who complains that Rousseau is unclear on the distinction, admits that Rousseau "might have distinguished vanity from pride if he had ever troubled to do so." See *Man and Society*, I:420–23.)

For purposes of clarity, I shall refer to the kinds of *amour-propre* that Rousseau does endorse as pride and to the kinds of *amour-propre* that he condemns as vanity. This does not seem unreasonable, since Rousseau himself generally uses the two terms in just that way, especially when he is comparing good and bad *amour-propre*.

The essential difference between pride and vanity has to do with the difference between reality and appearance, between being and seeming, but not in the most direct or obvious way. It would be incorrect to say that vanity cares about opinion and that pride does not. Vanity *does* care about opinion—"vanity is the fruit of opinion; it arises from it and feeds upon it" (*Corsica* 326)—but so does pride. Pride too desires respect, at least under normal conditions. Pride, however, seeks respect only in recognition of accomplishments whose value is real, that is, independent of opinion; pride does not want recognition for accomplishments whose whole value is the product of opinion. Like vanity, pride seeks praise; but unlike vanity, it seeks to *deserve* praise. What pride most wants, even more than praise, is praiseworthiness.

The difference between pride and vanity concerns the grounds on which respect, including self-respect, is sought. In the following passage from the *Constitutional Project for Corsica,* Rousseau explains how opinion acts as the source of the difference between pride and vanity even as he acknowledges the respective ways in which each is tied to opinion.

> Opinion which lays great store by frivolous objects produces vanity; but that which lights on objects intrinsically great and beautiful produces pride. You can thus render a people either proud or vain, depending on the choice to which you direct its judgments.
>
> Pride is more natural than vanity, since it consists in deriving self-esteem from truly estimable goods; whereas vanity, by giving value to that which is valueless, is the work of prejudices which are slow to arise. (326)

The distinction between pride and vanity can be resolved into the following elements. Pride is a feeling of, or desire for, self-worth that is (a) earned and (b) based on something truly praiseworthy. "Praiseworthy" is used here to mean something intrinsically valuable, either as an end in itself or as a clear means to an end that is valuable in *itself*; if a thing is valuable only on the basis of opinion, it is not praiseworthy. If either of these two conditions is absent, what we have is vanity, not pride. Vanity is a feeling of, or desire for, self-worth that is either (a) unearned or (b) based on something that is not truly praiseworthy, or both. If a person applies himself to learning a useful trade and succeeds in learning it well, the feeling of satisfaction he experiences is pride. If he attempts to pass himself off as being more skilled than he actually is—if he seeks unearned credit—he has violated one of the two defining criteria of pride and so has shown himself to be vain. Similarly, if he seeks credit for something that is good but that has come to him through no effort of his own—if he derives a sense of self-worth on the basis of noble birth or good looks or native intelligence, for example—he has violated the same criterion, that is, he has sought to establish his worth on something that is unearned and so has exhibited vanity. Among those who fail to meet the first requirement of pride, the requirement that their worth be earned, are the fops and phonies who are a staple of French literature, from La Rochefoucauld to Molière to the novels of Balzac and Flaubert. (Among great French-language writers, only Rousseau, it seems, neglected to portray this kind of vanity. Whatever their shortcomings, none of the characters in his *Julie* quite meets the prevailing standard.)[73]

If a person seeks credit for something that he has in fact accomplished but that is not praiseworthy, he has failed to meet the other requirement of pride, and so he too is vain. This holds true even if the accomplishment is impressive. Few if any accomplishments have been as impressive as Caesar's, for example, but it is Aristides and Brutus who are put forth as exemplars of pride—Caesar is associated with vanity.[74] If the first kind of vanity is displayed most memorably in satires and novels, the best portrait gallery in which to view the second kind would probably be Plutarch's *Lives*. When Emile finally reads biographies of "the great," he pities them as discontent creatures of vanity. Far from finding inspiration or models to emulate, he finds in most of Plutarch's lives confirmation of the superiority of his own condition (IV:242). (Here we observe a major difference between the two kinds of vanity. Rousseau does not depict Caesar and his ilk as small-souled. His association of vanity with small souls clearly was intended to apply only to vanity of the first sort and not the second. Those who are vain in the second sense may be as deficient in wisdom as those who are vain in the first sense, but they often exhibit other virtues, as well as a certain largeness of spirit—which surely accounted at least in part for Rousseau's abiding love of Plutarch.)[75]

---

73. Rousseau similarly observes that in *Julie* he "sustained interest through six volumes without the help of a single wicked person or a single bad action" (*Dialogues* II:149). See *Confessions* IX:361–62 for descriptions of his characters' universal charm and amiability.

74. See *Confessions* I:20–21.

75. Rousseau's enjoyment of Plutarch highlights his distance from an otherworldly perspective, the perspective from which critiques of "the great" have usually come. From the latter point of view, the difference between a Caesar and a Cato is ultimately not very great: "Vanity of vanities, saith the Preacher, vanity of vanities; all is vanity" (Ecclesiastes 1:2). What counts for the Preacher and those like him is the paltriness of whatever does not partake of God's glory. Rousseau's critique of Caesar and of mastery in general bears a certain surface resemblance to this view, as seen in Emile's pity for the emptiness of Caesarian ambition. But Rousseau's admiration for virtuous pride reflects his fundamental disagreement with otherworldliness of any kind. Emile disdains the false goods of opinion—for example, conquest and glory—but the goods he regards as true are very much of this world.

And of course it is possible to qualify as vain on both counts; one can seek to establish one's worth on the basis of something that is neither earned nor praiseworthy. The obnoxious heir to an illicit fortune or to a conqueror's throne would exemplify this combination. Such doubly vain individuals enjoy the rare distinction of being both hated and despised by the same people.

Such is the theoretical distinction between pride and vanity in Rousseau's work. Theoretical distinctions, of course, frequently lose their clarity, if not their entire meaning, when they are applied to reality. Neither of the two criteria by which we have distinguished between pride and vanity is without problems. Earned versus unearned, to take the first criterion, is less an either-or choice than a continuum with an infinite number of points between the two poles. It is the rare achievement in which fortune has not supplemented skill; indeed, skill itself more often than not owes something to fortune. More-over, individual psychology further complicates the matter by distorting judg-ment—leading some to believe that they deserve credit for what really came to them by chance and others to believe just the reverse, that what they really have achieved is somehow not valid or valuable. As for the second criterion, it is, if anything, even more subject to ambiguity. One need not be a moral rel-ativist to recognize that praiseworthiness is a standard that varies considerably —among peoples, among persons, across situations, and even according to mood. To say the least, the theoretical distinction between pride and vanity is not always easy to apply in reality.

Nevertheless, it is a valid one. The two criteria, whatever their ambiguities, convey real meaning and, what's more, they are widely and intuitively per-ceived to do so. True, the precise proportions of skill and fortune may elude our analysis of an accomplishment, but that does not mean that we are kept from a rough sense of whether and to what extent the accomplishment is a true achievement, that is, has been earned. Recognizing the role of fortune in human affairs need not—and typically does not—keep one from estimating the part played by skill; it only makes analysis more sophisticated. (When Machiavelli carefully disentangles *virtù* and *fortuna*, he is doing systematically and subtly what people normally do intuitively and roughly.)[76] True, too, judg-ment is often distorted by the individual's psychology. But the fact that we consider the sources of these distortions to be pathologies and that we even

76. Machiavelli's confidence in our ability—or at least *his* ability—to discern the respective roles of skill and fortune is evident from the title of chapter 25 of *The Prince:* "How Much Fortune Can Do in Human Affairs, and in What Mode It May Be Opposed" (trans. Harvey C. Mansfield Jr. [Chicago: University of Chicago Press, 1985]).

have names for them (such as narcissistic and borderline disorders) underscores how confident we are in our ability to make rough judgments of earned achievement. As for praiseworthiness, the second criterion, the fact that it is the most hotly disputed of standards does not keep us, individually and as societies, from applying it again and again—and usually with more confidence than doubt, however misplaced that confidence might sometimes be. (In fact, Rousseau would hold that our confidence in our moral judgment is eminently justified, at least when it is based on the universal and divinely inscribed dictates of conscience.)

Doubtless there are times when it is difficult, perhaps even impossible, to determine whether an instance of *amour-propre* should be considered pride or vanity. The distinction between pride and vanity is not as sharp, even in theory, as the distinction between *amour-propre* and *amour de soi*. But the existence of gray areas does not negate the general validity of a distinction; if it did, virtually all psychological thought would be drained of meaning. Besides, there is considerable territory that is not at all gray. Sometimes *amour-propre* is easily identified as vanity, and sometimes, as in the case of Emile, it is easily identified as pride. The following description of Emile's *amour-propre* is a perfect picture of pride.

> He will have the pride to want to do everything he does well, even to do it better than anyone. He will want to be the swiftest at running, the strongest at wrestling, the most competent at working, the most adroit at games of skill. But he will hardly seek advantages which are not clear in themselves and which need to be established by another's judgment, such as being more intelligent than someone else, talking better, being more learned, etc.; still less will he seek those advantages which are not at all connected with one's person, such as being of nobler birth, being esteemed richer, more influential, or more respected, or making an impression by greater pomp. (IV:339)

This psychological snapshot captures Emile at late adolescence. Presumably he will develop new interests and new objects for his pride as he grows older. But if his pride does in fact remain pride and not curdle into vanity, the principle informing it will not change. His sense of self-worth will continue to be based only on praiseworthy achievement. He will continue to pursue excellence only at things whose value is real. As in adolescence, so in maturity "he will hardly seek advantages which are not clear in themselves and which need to be established by another's judgment"; "still less will he seek those advantages which are not at all connected with one's person."[77]

Pride is not without its dangers. Even in Emile it threatens to destroy the work of his education:

> Emile, in considering his rank in the human species and seeing himself so happily placed there, will be tempted to honor his reason for the work of yours and to attribute his happiness to his own merit. He will say to himself, "I am wise, and men are mad." In pitying them, he will despise them; in congratulating himself, he will esteem himself more, and in feeling himself to be happier than them, he will believe himself worthier to be so. This is the error most to be feared, because it is the most difficult to destroy. If he remained in this condition, he would have gained little from all our care. (IV:245)

Pride is not without dangers—but of what sort are the dangers? The danger of which Rousseau speaks is that Emile will be tempted into a false judgment of his own superiority. The "error most to be feared" is an error of attribution: that Emile will attribute to himself things that in fact are the products of his tutor's work. The danger is that he will claim credit for what he has not earned. The danger, in other words, is that his pride will mutate into vanity, for in claiming unearned credit, Emile will be violating the first of the criteria that distinguish pride from vanity. Pride *is* dangerous, but only insofar as it threatens to turn into vanity; it is not dangerous in itself. Indeed, the purest pride, the pride of the *truly* great, far from being dangerous, entails a kind of humility. Such people recognize that they owe their capacity for greatness to fortune: "they are too sensible to be vain about a gift they did not give themselves" (*Emile* IV:245). Moreover, they are keenly conscious of what they still have not achieved: "The more they have, the more they know all that they lack."

There is only one way in which pride can remain pride and yet be dangerous, one way in which pride can be dangerous in itself: it is possible to feel *too much* satisfaction and to claim *too much* recognition for an accomplishment that is one's own and that is praiseworthy. It is possible to love oneself excessively even for one's virtue. Rousseau quietly concedes as much in his discussion of Molière's *Misanthrope* and again in a tale he tells of a young woman

---

77. Sophie's pride, too, although different in some respects from Emile's, is based on real merit: "She has that noble pride based on merit which is conscious of itself, esteems itself, and wants to be honored as it honors itself" (V:439).

whose excessive pride kept her from accepting even worthy suitors.[78] (That even pride can be taken to excess and thereby become dangerous means that we cannot infer from Rousseau's treatment of self-love a simple prescription to encourage pride and discourage vanity. Although Rousseau does generally prefer pride to vanity, he does not endorse any and all instances of pride. Pride is good only when its dimensions are such that it serves a larger purpose, a purpose that is determined by (and varies with) the particular version of the good life that one is pursuing. This point will be developed shortly.)

In the strict sense, all *amour-propre* is unnatural, including pride. Nevertheless, we have seen that "pride is more natural than vanity" (*Corsica* 326). Thus we are not surprised to find a fair amount of pride in Emile and Sophie. Pride is more natural, Rousseau contends, "since it consists in deriving self-esteem from truly estimable goods; whereas vanity, by giving value to that which is valueless, is the work of prejudices which are slow to arise." That is, pride is more natural than vanity in two ways: first, pride is more firmly tied to reality—it arises only where there are "truly estimable goods"; and second, pride appears earlier in the course of man's or society's development—that which is truly estimable can serve as the source of self-esteem far earlier than can "prejudices which are slow to arise."[79]

But the most important sense in which pride is more natural than vanity has to do with its effects. Unlike vanity, pride need not erode the basis of either a good society or a good life. Because it points to an estimable standard, pride can be a shared social passion and even a social bond. Whereas vanity is necessarily individualistic and zero-sum with regard to others, we can and do speak of both family pride and civic pride, prides in which many individuals share and which unite them.[80]

As for pride's relation to a good life for the individual, we need only recall the earlier discussion of the potential benefits of *amour-propre*. *Amour-propre*, we observed, contributes to romantic and familial love and to virtue, especially heroic virtue. What we can now add is that most of the *amour-propre* that deserves our gratitude or admiration is in fact pride. Indeed, *all* of the

---

78. For the discussion of Alcèste, the title character of the *Misanthrope*, see *d'Alembert* 34–45. The story of the prideful young woman appears in *Emile* V:402–5.

79. That pride appeared earlier in human development than vanity is also evident from the *Second Discourse*. "The first stirring of pride" occurred as a result of "the first glance [man] directed upon himself" (144). Vanity, on the other hand, required considerably more mental development: it appeared only when "each one began to look at the others and to want to be looked at himself" (149). Thus vanity could not have appeared until much later in the history of the species. See Kelly, *Rousseau's Exemplary Life*, 99, for more on this and other differences between pride and vanity.

80. See Kelly, *Rousseau's Exemplary Life*, 98–99, for more on this aspect of civic pride.

amour-propre that is good in itself is pride. (Vanity has undoubtedly made con-tributions to our well-being, but only indirectly, as the unwholesome motiva-tion behind inventions or discoveries that have turned out to have beneficial effects: Rousseau does allow for some of this sort of thing, but not—*pace* Man-deville and others—a lot of it.)[81] Pride has a place in the good life, even in Emile's natural version, and not as a begrudged concession. On the contrary, pride, as exemplified by Emile, contributes to the good life by allying itself with *amour de soi* and thus deepening and enlarging existence.

For many who came before Rousseau, most notably those writing from within religious traditions, self-love was synonymous with evil. For Rousseau, of course, this was not the case. Rather than conceive of good versus evil in terms of love of others versus love of self, Rousseau posed the basic moral polarity as good self-love versus bad self-love. (Since every passion and action is moti-vated by self-love, Rousseau could hardly have done otherwise without deny-ing all possibility of good.)

In this, Rousseau has proved to be a major influence on contemporary cul-ture.[82] We today routinely distinguish between good and bad self-love. Ours is a time in which "selfishness" and "egotism" denote vice but self-esteem and self-expression are widely endorsed—and on moral as well as psychological grounds. It is far from clear, however, whether the contemporary popular dis-tinction between good and bad self-love is based on any clear set of under-standings, let alone Rousseau's. When is self-love good? When is it bad? By what objective criteria shall we judge? Too many contemporary voices are either silent or simplistic on this matter. Often the implicit criterion is an inevitably disappointing quantitative one: a certain amount of self-satisfaction

81. Rousseau concedes in the *First Discourse* that vanity has led to a certain amount of useful knowledge and invention. But it has led to far more harm than good. Nor can it serve—nor can any private vice serve—as the basis of a good social order. (See *Narcissus* 104–6.) Rousseau does seem to suggest that vanity could be used to greater advantage than it has been, however. "Vanity is the greatest spring of human conduct" (*Corsica* 325). As such, it could be used by the wise legislator. Vanity could even be used *against vanity*, as it were: Rousseau advises that sumptuary laws could be made effective by the legislator who "make[s] simplicity a point of vanity" (*Corsica* 324).

82. Rousseau, of course, was not the first to defend self-love. Indeed, the celebration of self-love and pride had been central to classical moral philosophy and had been a source of its critique of Christianity (as well as a source of Christianity's critique of it). Yet much of Rousseau's defense of self-love *was* original—most particularly his insistence on the perfect innocence and sufficiency of original self-love and his claim that it is the source of compassion. And it is precisely these elements and not the more stringent classical teaching—nor the more rigorous side of own Rousseau's teach-ing, whose preference for pride over vanity echoes its classical predecessor—that seem to predomi-nate in the contemporary rehabilitation of self-love.

is approved, even encouraged, while "too much" is regarded as unseemly or obnoxious, with the judgment as to how much is the right amount often based on mere fashion. Hardly discussed, meanwhile, is the vast qualitative variety of self-love. Rousseau, by contrast, offers real answers to these questions. His answers are complex and do not correspond to any single polarity, such as *amour de soi* versus *amour-propre* or pride versus vanity. Not only does he not condemn all self-love, he does not even condemn all egoism (at least not if we consider pride a form of egoism).

Yet for all their complexity, Rousseau's answers reduce to a theoretically simple formula. Self-love is good when it extends or deepens existence and bad when it does the opposite (see Chapter 1). Self-love can extend and deepen existence in one of three different ways, as exemplified by the citizen, the uncivilized natural man, and the natural man living in the civil state. What each of these types has in common is an inner wholeness. In each of them self-love is without inner contradiction; it is unmarred by the conflict between nature and society, that is, between inclination and duty (see Chapters 2 and 3). This inner wholeness unites these men as exemplars of the good life. What distinguishes them from one another is the particular character of that wholeness. The citizen's self-love is an exclusively social patriotism; to be sure, he loves himself individually, but he loves himself as a citizen, as a part of a greater whole, and so he suffers no existence-diminishing inner contradiction. The self-love of the uncivilized natural man, whether he be the primitive inhabitant of the state of nature or the exquisitely developed (or "post-civilized") Jean-Jacques, retains its original character and, with it, its original goodness. The self-love of the natural man in the civil state is the most complex. Unlike the other exemplars, Emile has both *amour de soi* and *amour-propre* in his soul. Whereas the other two types "resolve" the contradiction between nature and society by siding with one or the other, Emile manages to reconcile nature and society, *amour de soi* and *amour-propre*, by achieving an alliance between them. All *amour de soi* is by nature good, and all *amour-propre* that is allied with *amour de soi*—and such *amour-propre* is always pride, never vanity—is also good (see the foregoing sections of this chapter). Only such an alliance can reconcile the two forms of self-love. Only such an alliance, in other words, can make naturalness amid civilization a possibility.

For the natural man or woman in the civil state, pride is a good only to the extent that it preserves or protects *amour de soi*. Pride that is satisfying in the moment, but that somehow undermines *amour de soi* or the joyful existence that it represents, has no place in a natural life—*no matter how indirect that undermining might be*. A pride, for example, that alienated a lover or spouse would erode the domestic basis on which civilized naturalness rests—it would undermine *amour de soi* by creating a psychically corrosive social conflict—and so has no place in a natural life. Fortunately, however, nature inclines us toward good pride, toward pride that unites us—at least where "us" refers to men and women. According to Rousseau, male and female pride naturally assume different characters in accordance with the psychological needs of the opposite sex. Male pride will tend of its own nature, without great artifice by parents or tutors, to grow in such directions as will be pleasing to women, and female pride will do the same with respect to men. Indeed, it is just this that makes men and women complementary to one another in more than just the physical sense. The particulars of male and female pride are beyond the scope of the present discussion. I raise the subject only to underscore the decisive importance of consequence, or effect, in determining the goodness or badness of particular cases of *amour-propre*. The relations between the sexes simply present the best context in which to make this point. Nothing about Emile or Sophie is superfluous. Even their *amour-propre* supports—and therefore is part of—their naturalness.

And yet if *amour de soi* is the core of the soul's naturalness and goodness, how much purer must be the soul in which there is only *amour de soi*? How much more natural, how much more full of goodness, must the soul in which there is no *amour-propre* be? We turn now to an examination of just this issue. Would it in fact be better if *amour-propre* could be overcome—if one could possess fully developed human faculties and yet be free of the dangers and limitations of egoism? What is gained in following Jean-Jacques's way rather than Emile's? How accessible is this road? And what, if anything, is lost by traveling it?

Beyond *Amour-Propre*? Prospects and Possibilities

Allan Bloom has interpreted *Emile* as Rousseau's bid to enter the lists against the West's two great and ancient moral-political traditions: the Biblical and the classical. Unlike the prosaic works of other modern philosophy, *Emile* could compete with those traditions on the quasi-aesthetic level of human types. The Biblical and classical traditions, Bloom writes,

> were accompanied by great works of what might be called poetry. This
> poetry depicts great human types who embody visions of the right way

of life, who make that way of life plausible, who excite admiration and emulation. The Bible, on the highest level, gives us prophets and saints; and in the realm of ordinary possibility it gives us the pious man. Homer and Plutarch give us, at the peak, heroes; and, for everyday fare, gentlemen.... With *Emile* Rousseau ... dares to enter into competition with the greatest of the old poets. He sets out to create a human type whose charms can rival those of the saint or the tragic hero—the natural man—and thereby shows that his thought too can comprehend the beautiful in man.[83]

Bloom's interpretation may or may not be an accurate representation of Rousseau's self-understanding in writing *Emile*. But *Emile* is not Rousseau's only book (nor his final offering), and its hero is not Rousseau's only exemplar. Emile is not even Rousseau's only exemplar of naturalness; Jean-Jacques is another. Nor, significantly, is Emile the greater of the two. Thus, if we look at Rousseau's entire corpus and not just at *Emile*, another interpretation, somewhat different from Bloom's, suggests itself. According to this interpretation, Rousseau matches the Biblical and classical traditions by offering two exemplary types, one of which represents the peak of human possibility and the other, the best life available to the man of ordinary gifts. Emile, according to this interpretation, is the latter of the two. Rather than Rousseau's answer to the saint or the tragic hero, as Bloom suggests, Emile is best seen as Rousseau's answer to the Bible's pious man and the Greeks' gentleman. Like those two, Emile belongs to "the realm of ordinary possibility."[84] As for the saint or the tragic hero, Rousseau's answer to them is Jean-Jacques. It is Jean-Jacques whom Rousseau puts forth as the highest human type.

Or, rather, it is Jean-Jacques *at his latest and best* whom Rousseau puts forth as the highest human type. We learned earlier that there is no avoiding *amour-propre* in civilization, and Jean-Jacques was no exception to this rule. *Amour-propre* was born in him as it is born in all social men. Indeed, unlike Emile, he knew *amour-propre*, both as pride and as vanity, at a very young age. What's more, he was to become an author, a choice that usually means—and that did mean even for him—excessive *amour-propre* (*Reveries* VIII:115). What is outstanding about Jean-Jacques is not that he managed to avoid *amour-propre* (he

---

83. Bloom, introduction to Rousseau's *Emile*, 6.

84. "I have assumed for my pupil neither a transcendent genius nor a dull understanding. I have chosen [Emile] from among the ordinary minds in order to show what education can do for man" (IV:245; see also I:52).

didn't) but that he managed to transcend it and return his soul to *amour de soi*—not completely but very considerably.[85]

We have concentrated throughout this chapter on the essential relation between *amour-propre* and the need for self-esteem, or good witness of oneself. The formula that expresses this relation is that *amour-propre* exists only when, to the extent that, and for as long as self-esteem is problematic or contingent. In *Emile* we have seen the truth of the first two ingredients of the formula. In *Jean-Jacques* we see the truth of the third part. Jean-Jacques achieves freedom from *amour-propre* by reaching a state in which self-esteem is no longer problematic.

What is it that makes the need for good witness of oneself, for self-esteem, so problematic? As we discovered earlier, there is a certain impenetrable mystery here—impenetrable at least to those, like Rousseau, who decline to speculate about divine or natural purposes. But if we remain ignorant of ultimate causes, we did discover the proximate and triggering ones. What triggers the transformation of the need for good witness of oneself from a simple and easily satisfied requirement into a chronically complex and difficult one is the development of self-consciousness. Consciousness of oneself as a separate self related to other separate selves prompts, even if it does not fully account for, this vast complication of the human condition. That being so, it will come as no surprise to find that Jean-Jacques has achieved an exceptional kind of consciousness, that he has managed to transcend ordinary self-consciousness (or what Kelly has called "civilized self-consciousness")—again, if not in all circumstances, at least much the time.[86] If it is self-consciousness that complicates the need for self-esteem and thus gives rise to *amour-propre*, it is the overcoming of ordinary self-consciousness that *uncomplicates* the need for self-esteem and thus takes one beyond *amour-propre*.[87] If it is a cognitive step

85. The story of Jean-Jacques's self-love, beginning with the birth of *amour-propre* in early childhood, is recounted in the *Confessions*. As Kelly demonstrates, this work can be read as the story of Jean-Jacques's journey from an unnatural condition in which he was subject to the vicissitudes of *amour-propre* to a condition that is at least partly natural—that is, to a considerable transcendence of *amour-propre*.

But to what extent, exactly, has Jean-Jacques overcome *amour-propre*? During the three quarters of his time that he is left alone and "socializes" only with creations of his imagination, Jean-Jacques is altogether free of *amour-propre*. It is only during the remaining quarter, when he is drawn into the world, that he suffers any *amour-propre*. See *Reveries* VIII:117–18 for a precise statement of the matter. See also *Dialogues* II:106, and Kelly and Masters, introduction to Rousseau's *Dialogues*, xxiv–xxv.

86. See Kelly, *Rousseau's Exemplary Life*, 243.

87. Note that *overcoming* ordinary self-consciousness does not mean *undoing* it. As we shall soon see, and as his autobiographical work makes abundantly clear, Jean-Jacques maintains an extraordinary level of self-awareness).

that initiates the development of *amour-propre*, it is a cognitive step that can take one beyond *amour-propre*. Such is the meaning of Jean-Jacques's story. The way to understand his transcendence of *amour-propre* is thus to examine his exceptional cognitive condition.

We find in Rousseau's autobiographical works a series of experiences in which ordinary or civilized self-consciousness has been overcome. Late in the *Confessions*, for example, Rousseau recounts his exile on the Île de Saint-Pierre. There, separated from the larger world and spending most of his time in solitude, he discovers "the sweetness of inactivity and the contemplative life" (*Confessions* XII:534). The contemplative life described here has little in common with the classical philosophical ideal. The pleasure described is not the pleasure of rigorous inquiry or speculation or even mythmaking but rather the pleasure of intimate and innocent communion with nature. Rather than cite the philosopher, Rousseau invokes two very different other types. What characterizes his distinctive variety of the contemplative life is "the idleness ... of a *child* who is ceaselessly in motion while doing nothing and, at the same time, that of a *dotard* who strays when his arms are at rest" (537; emphasis added). Sometimes his communion with nature comes by way of concentrating on particulars, as when he engages in botany.[88] At other times it comes through "abandon[ing] [him]self to reveries without object"—reveries that bring him so close to nature that he sometimes "crie[s] out with emotion, 'Oh nature, oh my mother'" (539). Whereas most people continue to think about others even when they are alone, Jean-Jacques finds solitude to be liberating. He ceases to be concerned about how he stands with others—which is to say, he ceases to be self-conscious in the ordinary way and thus escapes the grip of *amour-propre*.

It is in the *Reveries*, though, that ordinary self-consciousness is most completely transcended. A number of instances are recounted in which the boundaries of Jean-Jacques's self expand or even dissolve. The communion of the *Confessions* gives way to outright union, with either nature or existence.[89] To be sure, these are peak experiences and do not constitute the sum of Jean-Jacques's inner life; they are not constant. But they do seem to be regular. And

88. For a description of Jean-Jacques's unusual botanical investigations, see *Confessions* XII:537. For an interesting discussion of the nature and implications of Rousseau's botanizing (as it is depicted in the *Reveries*), see Paul A. Cantor, "The Metaphysics of Botany: Rousseau and the New Criticism of Plants," *Southwest Review* 70 (1985): 362–80.

89. Cantor has suggested that Rousseau's step from enthralled admiration of nature to outright union with it marks the birth of Romanticism. For an exploration of Rousseau's relation to subsequent Romantic literature, see *Creature and Creator: Myth-making and English Romanticism* (Cambridge: Cambridge University Press, 1984), 4–25.

the difference between these moments and the time in between, the nonpeak moments, would seem to be mostly a difference of degree, and not so great a difference at that.

In the Fifth Walk we are treated to another description of Jean-Jacques's experience on the Île de Saint-Pierre. This time, however, we are told more about the nature of the experience and of the consciousness that made it possible. What we find is the fading away of the separate-self sense, a transcendence of civilized self-consciousness. Rousseau describes a kind of thoughtless but not unconscious feeling of existence. Far from unconsciousness or regression, this is a state of consciousness that is above and beyond thought and language. Everyday passions and concerns, everything that marks our normal consciousness—including even the sense of time and space—is transcended, making this state the best and the purest, the most godlike, available to man:

> [I]f there is a state in which the soul finds a solid enough base to rest itself on entirely and to gather its whole being into, without needing to recall the past or encroach upon the future; in which time is nothing for it; in which the present lasts forever without, however, making its duration noticed and without any trace of time's passage; without any other sentiment of deprivation or of enjoyment, pleasure or pain, desire or fear, except that alone of our existence, and having this sentiment alone fill it completely; as long as this state lasts, he who finds himself in it can call himself happy, not with an imperfect, poor, and relative happiness such as one finds in the pleasures of life, but with a sufficient, perfect and full happiness which leaves in the soul no emptiness it might feel a need to fill. Such is the state in which I often found myself during my solitary reveries on the île de Saint-Pierre, either lying in my boat as I let it drift with the water or seated on the banks of the tossing lake; or elsewhere, at the edge of a beautiful river or of a brook murmuring over pebbles.
>
> What do we enjoy in such a situation? Nothing external to ourselves, nothing if not ourselves and our own existence. As long as this state lasts, we are sufficient unto ourselves, like God. (68–69)

In the experience described in this passage, nature provides a setting wherein the boundaries of the separate self dissolve. All the particulars (thoughts, passions, and so forth) and even the dimensions of the separate self's existence disappear from consciousness. All that is left—all that the self *is*—is the sentiment of existence.

Other passages tell of related but somewhat different experiences, experiences in which nature not only provides the setting but also serves as the object of identification. Here, as in the experience recounted above, the self dissolves into, or achieves union with, something greater than itself. But that "something greater" is now nature, in all its intricate harmony, rather than existence, which is a much more undifferentiated and abstract thing. The self merges with a whole, but a whole that is known through its many parts and whose attractiveness lies precisely in the harmony between those parts—a whole that is apprehended as a *system*: "I never meditate, I never dream more deliciously than when I forget myself. I feel ecstasies and inexpressible raptures in blending, so to speak, into the system of beings and in making myself one with the whole of nature" (VII:95). (Note here another expression of the principle of soul called conscience: the ecstatic appreciation of nature as a *system* is an example or manifestation of the love of *order*.) Such is the appeal of botany for such a one as Jean-Jacques: "The more sensitive a soul a contemplator has, the more he gives himself up to the ecstasies this harmony arouses in him. A sweet and deep reverie takes possession of his senses then, and through a delicious intoxication he loses himself in the immensity of this beautiful system with which he feels himself one. Then, all particular objects elude him; he sees and feels nothing except in the whole" (VII:92).

It bears repeating that these self-forgettings are presented as moments of transcendence rather than regression.[90] To be sure, there is a sense in which Jean-Jacques seems to return to the condition of the savage. Like the savage, he enjoys psychic balance and harmony and no longer depends on others for the sentiment of his existence. But he also retains a level of awareness and an aesthetic sensibility—not to mention a scientifically trained eye—that the savage lacked.[91] Jean-Jacques continues to possess a highly developed intellectual

90. The experiences described in the *Reveries* bear striking similarities to various accounts of mystical experiences. Religious mystics in particular, both Western and Eastern, have reported many of the same things that Rousseau reports: blissful or ecstatic self-forgetting, the disappearance of an awareness of time, and the sense of union or communion with a greater Being or system. Needless to say, those who have or pursue such experiences interpret them as transcendent rather than regressive. Among those who have professed to examine these claims from the standpoint of science, interpretations are mixed. Strict Freudians have dismissed such experiences as regressions to a relatively undifferentiated ego state. Other psychologists, however, from William James to today's humanistic and transpersonal schools, have argued that what Freud saw as regression to undifferentiatedness should instead be regarded as higher-level integration. For succinct statements of these opposing views, see, respectively, Freud, *Civilization and Its Discontents*, 9–21, and *Standard Edition*, 21:64–73; and Erich Neumann, "Mystical Man," in *The Mystic Vision: Papers from the Eranos Yearbooks*, ed. Joseph Campbell (Princeton: Princeton University Press, 1968).

91. Rousseau's considerable scientific expertise is displayed in his *Dictionnaire des termes d'usage en*

capacity and an aesthetic sensibility that is perhaps more highly developed still. Indeed, he *uses* these capacities in achieving and maintaining his peak experiences, for integral to these experiences is the ability to perceive nature in its unity and diversity and to enjoy it for its complex harmony.[92] Far from regression, Jean-Jacques's experiences suggest that he has added new dimensions or even wholly new capacities to the ordinary complement of mental powers. Thus the ground he shares with the savage is only the first word of Jean-Jacques's story. Each of the two men lacks civilized self-consciousness, but whereas the savage has not yet achieved self-consciousness, Jean-Jacques has gone beyond it even while retaining its positive elements—which is the true meaning of transcendence. (Transcendence entails incorporation of that which has been transcended. As Hegel would put it, "Supercession ... is at once a negating and a preserving.")[93] Doubtless the savage slept well and enjoyed peace of mind, but it is unthinkable that he could have felt the wonder and ecstasy experienced by Jean-Jacques. Jean-Jacques's experiences are "uncivilized," but they are *more* than civilized, and they are achieved by an exquisitely developed soul.

Which raises an important question: to whom is this kind of high-level experience available? Who can transcend *amour-propre?* We know that Rousseau considers it theoretically possible for anyone to become an Emile or a Sophie. As extraordinary as they each become, Emile and Sophie are ordinary in their natural endowments.[94] Does the same thing hold true of Jean-Jacques? Or must some extraordinary conditions obtain, either natural or circumstantial, for those who would follow him?

The answer, in short, is that Jean-Jacques's return to nature required both extraordinary natural gifts and extraordinary circumstances. And while those who follow a path need not always be as outstanding as the one who has discovered it, in this case it seems safe to say that the natural life à la Jean-Jacques remains the potential province of very few.

The essential precondition for achieving Jean-Jacques's version of naturalness is solitude.[95] To suppose that people can live together and yet be free of *amour-propre* is a fantastic notion—literally: the only places where such a life

---

botanique and *Lettres elémentaires sur la botanique à Madame de Lessert* (each of these appears in OC IV).

92. Jean-Jacques is able to derive spiritual benefit from botany only because he has a considerable scientific background in it. This point is explicitly and emphatically made at *Confessions* XII:537.

93. *Phenomenology of Spirit*, section 113, p. 68.

94. "I shall never repeat often enough that I am leaving prodigies aside. Emile is no prodigy, and Sophie is not one either" (V:393).

is imagined are the "ideal world" depicted in the *Dialogues* and (to a lesser degree) Rousseau's "If-I-were-a-rich-man" daydream in *Emile*: fantasies both (*Dialogues* I:9–12; *Emile* IV:344–54). Yet very few are capable of choosing solitude or using it well. Even Jean-Jacques, whose extraordinary sensitivity and inclinations make him uniquely capable of enjoying solitude once he is in it, had to be forced into it. (Persecuted by the authorities and alienated from his former friends, he was effectively pushed to the fringes of society.)[96] And this even though he already knew solitude's value and had had some small tastes of it. How much less likely, then, that many others will choose what even he did not.

To choose solitude is different from fleeing society or being cast out. One must be able to resist the pull of the social passions, even those that are good. To judge from Jean-Jacques's experience—which is the only recourse, as Rousseau makes no pronouncement on this matter—such resistance is beyond most people's strength. It is important to note not only the "assistance" provided him by circumstances but also that he finds contentment in solitude only at a relatively advanced age—a time at which, by his own admission, his social passions have been banked. The goods of the social world may deliver less than the goods found in solitude, but they apparently *seem* to promise more. And indeed, it is far from clear that most people could find much good in solitude even if they were forced into it. Most people are not like Jean-Jacques, after all—they cannot abandon themselves so joyfully to physical nature, and they certainly cannot satisfy their social needs, and especially their sexual needs, through imagination. Add to all this the inconvenient fact that it would be logistically and probably geographically impossible for more than a few to be sustained in lives of rustic idleness and we have a way of life destined to appeal to few and to be realized by even fewer.

This does not render Jean-Jacques irrelevant, however. Like his counterparts in the Bible and in classical literature, he is the peak that defines the terrain below. If his experience is beyond the reach of all but the few (perhaps all but the one), others can at least take some steps in his direction. If the air of solitude is too thin or its slope too steep for them, they can at least make camp in the surrounding foothills. Following the advice offered in the *Lettres morales*, they can retreat into the rustic simplicity of country life and so

95. *Amour-propre* promptly reasserts itself in Jean-Jacques when he ventures out of his solitude—"a foolish *amour-propre* whose complete folly I sense, but which I cannot overcome" (*Reveries* VIII:117–18).
96. See Kelly, *Rousseau's Exemplary Life*, 247–48, on the role of accident in Jean-Jacques's return to nature.

liberate themselves from a good part of their feverish *amour-propre*. Even modest steps in this direction would represent increased naturalness and enlarged existence.

Would it be best to be without *amour-propre?* It would seem so, if not for humanity as a whole, at least for the person capable of achieving this goal. Jean-Jacques, whose singular freedom from *amour-propre* makes him the most natural of men, is held aloft by Rousseau as the highest human type. But overcoming *amour-propre* is not necessary for a good life, or even for a natural life. What the good life requires is an absence of inner conflict and a rough balance between desire and faculty. As we saw in Chapter 1, when these conditions are met, existence is enlarged and life is good. And while this certainly is achieved when *amour-propre* is transcended, it can also be achieved by those in whom *amour-propre* is present—as witness the citizen, whose dominant psychic principle is well-trained (that is, virtuous and patriotic) *amour-propre*, and "the natural man living in the state of society," in whom *amour-propre* is allied with *amour de soi*. What is required for the good life is "only" that self-love be well-ordered.[97] What is required for the natural life is "only" that *amour-propre* be limited and allied with *amour de soi*. Neither the good life in general nor the natural life in particular requires a return to the savage's state of soul. The citizen is obviously far from savagery; Emile, though raised to be a "civilized savage," is far more civilized than savage; and Jean-Jacques, the exemplar of the one variety of the good life that shares the savage's lack of *amour-propre*, has perhaps traveled the farthest of all.

And yet if each of the varieties of the good life is far removed from savage simplicity, each also has something in common with it. Every variety of the good life entails replicating the savage's psychic unity and balance. Sometimes this replication is a matter of maintaining the native state of these qualities (Emile), sometimes a matter of recovering them (Jean-Jacques), and sometimes a matter of artificially re-creating them (the citizen).[98] Thus each of Rousseau's versions of the good life, in addition to manifesting progress beyond

97. It is incorrect to finger *amour-propre* per se as the villain in Rousseau's moral scheme. It is only when *amour-propre* is inflamed or when it produces certain kinds of personal dependence that it becomes destructive of happiness and morality. For more on this point, see Dent, *Rousseau: An Introduction*, 52–67, 70–85, and Melzer, *Natural Goodness of Man*, 70–85. For a systematic treatment of when personal dependence is corrupting and when it is not, see Grant, *Hypocrisy and Integrity*, 163–67.

98. Emile exemplifies maintenance: he never ceases to be natural. Jean-Jacques, on the other hand, exemplifies return: he is alienated from nature at an early age but later returns to nature at a higher level. His combination of progress and return can be compared to climbing a spiral staircase: he ends up directly above where he began.

savagery, also entails replicating it. Savage origins are both transcended and not transcended. It is important to recognize both elements of this truth: to overlook the first part is to mistake Rousseau for a romantic reactionary, while to overlook the second is to cast him, inaccurately, as a simple progressive. The fact is that Rousseau upholds both principles, both progress and replication.

As for which of the two principles has priority, that perhaps is not a fair question: each is upheld with equal consistency and force. There is a sense, however, in which the second principle, the principle of replication, can be said to be foremost in Rousseau's good lives, for it informs the first. That is, progress would not be progress, would not be true progress, if the savage's psychic unity and balance had not been replicated. There can be no good life without significant replication of these qualities of the savage. And if the principle of replication has primacy in all varieties of the good life, its primacy in the natural life, whether Emile's version or Jean-Jacques's, is even more pronounced. In addition to psychic unity and balance, naturalness also requires that *amour de soi* be the leading principle of soul, just as it was for the savage.

The goodness of the good life derives first and foremost from psychic unity and balance, qualities that existed most perfectly in the state of nature. Similarly, the naturalness of the natural life derives from the primacy of *amour de soi* over *amour-propre*, a condition that also obtained most perfectly in the state of nature. What all this means is that the primary goal of those who would pursue one or another of Rousseau's versions of the good life, and especially the natural versions exemplified by Emile and Jean-Jacques, must be the replication of the savage's quality of soul. There are other goals, to be sure, but that is the first one, the one without which the others will be either unattainable or meaningless. However high one aspires to climb, one's aspiration must take its bearings from a being who, among other things, utterly lacked aspiration himself. It is this peculiar combination of high and low, of transcendence and nontranscendence, that gives to Rousseau's vision of human possibilities its uniquely paradoxical character.

5

Critical Reflections on Rousseau's Naturalism

One goal of this book has been to show that nature is more than just a formal standard for Rousseau—to show that naturalness for civilized man entails something more than just an inevitably inferior replication of the savage's goodness and wholeness. It *is* that, but it is also more than that. Emile does bear a certain similarity to the savage. Like the savage, he enjoys a fair degree of psychic integrity and is not the captive of tyrannical *amour-propre*; because of this he is called a natural man, just as the savage is. The same is true of Jean-Jacques. But Emile's and Jean-Jacques's naturalness does not end with this formal similarity to the savage. It also has a substantive dimension that the savage lacked.

The formal dimension of naturalness—the dimension common to all three variants of natural man—is manifest in harmony, or what Rousseau calls order. Everyone whom Rousseau calls natural enjoys a twofold harmony: an interior or psychic harmony, meaning a lack of inner conflict and an equal balance between desires and faculties, and an exterior harmoniousness, a harmonious disposition toward the rest of the world. This harmony—extant in every kind of natural man—is produced and maintained by the preeminence of *amour de soi* in the soul. Each of these characteristics was present in the savage every bit as much as in Emile or Jean-Jacques. Indeed, the savage enjoyed an even more perfect harmony than they do, for he was completely untouched by unnatural influences or circumstances whereas they, for all their success at achieving or maintaining naturalness, are not altogether unaffected by those things. The savage alone was absolutely free of *amour-propre*. At this level, the savage represents the human ideal; Emile and Jean-Jacques only approximate what the savage fully realized. What Emile and Jean-Jacques have that the savage lacked, though—and herein begins the particular substance of post-state-of-nature naturalness—is a love of harmony.

The love of harmony, which Rousseau calls conscience, is what naturalizes those faculties and dispositions that, though not present in the savage, do arise in Emile and Jean-Jacques.[1] (The love of harmony is also the source of Emile's and Jean-Jacques's superiority over the savage, notwithstanding the savage's perfect harmony. Although the savage's harmony was more perfect than Emile's and Jean-Jacques's, theirs is self-conscious and more complex and therefore more impressive and rewarding.) This love of harmony is more than a mere taste or aesthetic preference. It is a principle of soul, and as such it informs the development of all the soul's desires and accounts for everything that is sublime in man. The love of harmony yields a particular psychic arrangement, an arrangement that constitutes the substance of civilized naturalness. This is not to say that every civilized natural man would be exactly alike, that every child reared like Emile would end up indistinguishable from him. Rousseau leaves room for variation among natural men. He quite clearly allows that much of the civilized natural man's character will derive from innate temperament or some other personal circumstance and not just from his education.[2] But there are certain basic characteristics common to every civilized natural man. There is a certain substance that defines civilized naturalness. The investigative yield

---

1. I have on occasion substituted "harmony" for "order." It seems to me that, to contemporary ears, "harmony" comes closer to Rousseau's meaning than the literal "order" (*l'ordre*).

2. Individual variation, evident even among very young children (II:94), becomes increasingly pronounced with age and does not seem to be overcome by a natural education. See, for example, the discussion in *Emile* regarding the choice of a trade, wherein tutors are advised to take into account their pupils' particular genius (III:198–201). See especially IV:226, where Rousseau refers to "the almost infinite division of characters" that begins at adolescence.

of the preceding two chapters, from the sublimation of sexuality to the alliance between a preeminent *amour de soi* and a well-governed *amour-propre*, is the stuff of civilized naturalness generally and not just a description of Emile. And this substance opens an enormous distance between the civilized natural man and his savage forebear. "There is a great difference between the natural man living in the state of nature and the natural man living in the state of society" (*Emile* III:205).

Nevertheless, for all the differences between them, civilized and savage naturalness are also intimately related. Civilized naturalness is fundamentally informed by savage naturalness. Emile is indeed a true descendent of the savage. For although the similarity between the two versions of naturalness is largely formal, what is formal can have—in this case, *does* have—enormous substantive implications. As we have seen, everything that Rousseau calls natural in the civil state is so designated because it meets the formal criterion of promoting or preserving *amour de soi*. This formal criterion determines, if only by process of elimination, what should and should not be considered natural in the civil state. Thus if one of the major themes of this book has been the difference between civilized and savage naturalness, another has been their closeness and, in particular, the sense in which the former takes its bearings from the latter.

It is instructive to look at the passage from which the statement quoted above is drawn. After insisting upon the "great difference between the natural man living in the state of nature and the natural man living in the state of society," Rousseau seems to underscore the point by saying, "Emile is not a savage to be relegated to the desert." But this statement is not as strong as it might at first seem. Rousseau says only that Emile is not a savage to be relegated to the *desert*. He does not say that Emile is no kind of savage at all. Indeed, his next statement is that Emile "is a savage made to inhabit cities." To be sure, it would be unwise to read too much into what might have been intended as nothing more than a loose comparison or metaphor. But even metaphors have meaning, and it is not for nothing that Rousseau calls his Emile a civilized savage. Emile *is* a kind of savage. Although he develops all the faculties and capacities of civilized man, he manages to do so without losing his original goodness. Whereas the rest of us became civilized only by leaving nature's garden, Emile has managed to import the fruits of civilization (and only its fruits) into it. Although he is much more than a savage, he is a savage first and foremost. And therein lies the enormous promise of Rousseau's naturalism, as well as some of its most problematic aspects. First, the promise.

A Return to Wholeness

What is it that Rousseau offers? With his dual-level conception of nature, Rousseau purports to show the way out of the debasement of modern civilization. His dual-level conception allows him to reestablish the naturalness of the sublime and thereby redeem human dignity from the clutches of modern scientific naturalism. Without repudiating the general principles of modern science—indeed, while sharing them—he rescues humanity from the scythe of scientism. Not that the publication of *Emile* would or even could pave the way for a multitude of natural men: Rousseau never believed that any of his theoretical solutions, including the natural education of *Emile*, could be translated into practice. But if it could not bring about the triumph of nature, goodness, and happiness, his philosophical defense of the sublime could at least stem the worst tendencies of modernity and perhaps even point an enlightened few toward something approaching a natural life.

But this rescue of the sublime is only part of Rousseau's intended achievement, and the truncating tendency of modern science is only one of the ills he seeks to address. Each, in fact, is subsumed by Rousseau's larger project. What Rousseau seeks to achieve, most of all, is the restoration of human wholeness —that is, the restoration of the savage's goodness or harmony, both internally and with respect to others. And the means to achieving this, at least in the case of the naturalistic solutions exemplified by Emile and Jean-Jacques, is to undo the severance between nature and human nature or, to put it another way, to renaturalize human nature. (The solution exemplified by the virtuous citizen also entails the restoration of wholeness, but the citizen's wholeness comes about by an artificial replication of original wholeness. For the citizen, and only for the citizen, nature is a merely formal standard.) Establishing the naturalness of the sublime and showing how one might come to experience the sublime is but part, even if the most glorious part, of restoring man's wholeness.

The easiest way to appreciate the meaning of Rousseau's goal is to consider the problem that it purports to solve. Let us recall Rousseau's diagnosis of social man's ills. Social man, as Rousseau portrays him, is torn by inner conflict and tyrannized by excessive desire. In effect, social man suffers from a loss of wholeness, for what are inner conflict and excessive desire if not disruptions of inner or psychic harmony? Inner conflict is the loss or antithesis of inner unity, which is one aspect of psychic harmony, and excessive desire is the antithesis of the equal balance between faculty and desire, between power and will, which is the other aspect of this harmony.[3] Each of Rousseau's theoretical prescriptions aims at recovering this twofold inner wholeness, on the premise that only then would an individual be able to enjoy the sweetness of existence and maintain a benevolent disposition toward others. The promise held out by Rousseau's constructive works, even if it is a promise that Rousseau himself disavowed on practical grounds, is nothing less than that. The *Social Contract* holds out the promise of wholeness through participation in a purposeful and virtuous political community, while *Emile* and the autobiographical writings hold out variations of wholeness through a recovery of naturalness, or through the renaturalization of human nature—or more precisely, at least with regard to *Emile*, through the naturalization of man's second or social nature.

Is this a promise that can be kept? Rousseau thought that it was, but only theoretically. Others, inspired by his writings and less pessimistic than he, would say that wholeness *could* be recovered, although they usually revised the terms of his prescriptions, sometimes beyond all recognition. It is not difficult to interpret much of the romanticism and radicalism of the past two centuries as testimony to faith in the promise held out by Rousseau. Still others, meanwhile, have answered in the negative, arguing either that no such wholeness is possible, at least not in this life, or else that wholeness may indeed be possible but not in the way or through the means that Rousseau suggests.[4] Can wholeness be recovered? Is a return to natural goodness even theoretically possible? It is at least worth noting that the findings of scientific psychology and anthropology have lent a certain credibility, if not to the promise of wholeness then at least to the account of human origins that underlies it. Rousseau's goal is not just wholeness, but *recovered* wholeness. The premise is that man once was (and presumably still is born) whole, or naturally good. And this premise does indeed find some support in the scientific record. Findings from developmental psychology and anthropology suggest, first, that in certain key respects man

---

3. Obviously Rousseau's account of human ills features other things besides these two kinds of lost wholeness. One need only think of personal dependence and untamed *amour-propre*, to name two. But personal dependence and untamed *amour-propre* are more properly thought of as *causes* of social man's "illness" rather than as the illness itself, for although they are enormously important, one does not feel or suffer them in and of themselves. Similarly, the many unhappy symptoms and consequences of lost wholeness—namely, the whole range of human evils, from shame and envy to vanity and contempt to anxiety and hypocrisy to oppression and degradation—are more properly thought of as just that, i.e. symptoms and consequences, rather than as the illness itself. These symptoms and consequences are important, but they are all part of and therefore somewhat incomprehensible apart from the larger phenomenon of lost wholeness.

4. One who argued the latter possibility was Nietzsche, who, while faulting Rousseau for advocating a sentimental understanding of nature, insisted that a kind of natural wholeness, or what he called "totality," nevertheless is possible: "I too speak of a 'return to nature,' although it is not really a going-back but a *going-up*." See *Twilight of the Idols*, trans. R. J. Hollingdale (New York: Penguin Books, 1968), 101–2.

did in fact enjoy an original wholeness (or what Rousseau calls goodness), whether "original" is taken to refer to the infancy of the child born into civilization or to the infancy of the human race; and second, that this wholeness was progressively lost in something like the way Rousseau describes in part 2 of the *Second Discourse*.[5]

But of course the scientific record cannot speak definitively about future possibilities. Even if Rousseau's account of human development proved to be perfectly accurate, we would not know whether the promise held out by his constructive works is realistic. In any case, there is much in Rousseau's own account (leaving the scientific record aside) that speaks *against* the plausibility of the hopes he inspired. We must not forget that Rousseau was profoundly pessimistic regarding the political and even the personal prospects of modern

5. To be sure, not everything about Rousseau's account is borne out by the evidence. Much of it is called into doubt, and some of it—most notably his key assertion that man was originally (and presumably still is born) asocial—has been rather flatly refuted. Nevertheless, the narratives emerging from both developmental psychology and anthropology bear a rough but noticeable resemblance to the shape of the story told in the *Second Discourse*. That shape is one of initial ascent (from the pure state of nature to the epoch of nascent society), in consequence of the advancement of mental faculties, followed by severe decline (all history subsequent to the epoch of nascent society), in consequence of further advancement and especially in consequence of developing self-consciousness. ("Ascent" and "decline" refer to the level of happiness and existence enjoyed by those who lived during these ages.) Neither developmental psychologists nor anthropologists typically speak in terms of "existence" or even "wholeness," but they do report findings that suggest, à la Rousseau, (1) that human beings begin their lives (and began their history) with a certain psychic unity, which in turn kept them from doing great harm to one another, and (2) that this unity and the accompanying relative harmlessness toward one another gave way to anxiety and other psychic ills, along with the accompanying moral ills, precisely as self-consciousness reached critical proportions. None of this can be fully proved, especially where the mental state of prehistoric man is concerned. But the evidence is at least suggestive. And it cannot be gainsaid solely on the grounds that developmental psychology and anthropology undertake their investigations from a Rousseauan point of view: the best researchers in each field have been careful to separate their interpretive biases from their findings. (Nor can it be refuted by anthropological evidence of prehistoric barbarism, namely, massacres, human sacrifice, and the like: the evidence suggests that gruesome behaviors such as these occurred not in *pre*history but in *early* history, that is, after significant mental development had already taken place.)

The record assembled by developmental psychology is available in any number of textbooks. Regarding cognitive development in particular and especially the development of self-consciousness, see Jean Piaget, *The Essential Piaget*, ed. H. Gruber and J. Voneche (New York: Basic Books, 1977). For a comprehensive but nontechnical account of the anthropological record, see Ken Wilber, *Up from Eden: A Transpersonal View of Human Evolution* (Boulder, Colo.: Shambhala Publications, 1981). For analyses of how Rousseau's account of human nature and human origins compares to the scientific record, see Roger D. Masters, "Rousseau and the Rediscovery of Human Nature," in *The Legacy of Rousseau*, ed. Clifford Orwin and Nathan Tarcov (Chicago: University of Chicago Press, 1997), and "Jean-Jacques is Alive and Well: Rousseau and Contemporary Sociobiology," *Daedalus* 107 (summer 1978): 93–105.

man. "Human nature does not go backwards, and one can never return to the times of innocence and equality when one has once left them" (*Dialogues* III:213). Several factors, most of which we have already addressed, speak forcefully against the plausibility of recovering what I have been calling wholeness: first, the potential for *amour-propre* and even for vanity exists by nature; second, this potential is very easily actualized; third, the pleasures of the most noxious expressions of *amour-propre* are extremely addicting from the very first taste; and fourth, the circumstances that triggered the chain of events that eventuated in the historic awakening of *amour-propre* were themselves the products of nature.[6] Indeed, these considerations not only suggest pessimism, or at least sobriety, they also seem to call into question the principle of natural goodness. If natural goodness is so easily lost, if the capacities that made us succumb to temptation are themselves natural, even if only potentially, and if the causes precipitating the actualization of these capacities are also natural, then it becomes at least a little problematic to maintain that man is naturally good and that *amour-propre*, the source of disorder and evil, is not natural. It is of course the latter insistence that makes the former one tenable: it is only by insisting on the unnaturalness of *amour-propre* (in the strict sense) that Rousseau can maintain that man is by nature good or indeed that *everything* natural is good. (Rousseau is able to insist on the unnaturalness of *amour-propre* by defining nature as that and only that which was present and actual in the pure state of nature.) But if defining nature in such a way as to render *amour-propre* unnatural saves the principle of natural goodness, it only accentuates the

---

6. As Rousseau tells it, man in the pure state of nature would have been content to go on living exactly as he was. This proved impossible, however, for he was soon confronted with obstacles that he needed to overcome. It was in overcoming these obstacles that he began to awaken more advanced mental capacities and that he thus inaugurated the process that eventuated in the fall from natural goodness. What were these initial difficulties? Rousseau cites the height of trees, the competition of other animals for food, and the desire of other animals to make him *their* food (SD 142–43). The relevant fact is that *these difficulties were themselves thoroughly natural*, and perfectly ordinary facts of nature at that. Thus one could argue that man was expelled from nature by nature itself. (Indeed, to the extent such difficulties as the height of trees were presumably coeval with human existence, the expulsion can be understood to have begun from the first moment of human existence. To correct the formulation with which I began, man was not *soon* confronted with obstacles, he was *immediately* confronted with them.) Similarly, the difficulties that forced man out of the stage of nascent society were natural, though not quite as ordinary as the heights of trees, for example; Rousseau cites "some fatal accident," by which he presumably means something like a great flood or earthquake, as the precipitating cause (SD 151). I noted in Chapter 2 that the logic of Rousseau's account of the history of the species leaves room for only three options: humanity might have either stayed in the pure state of nature, advanced to and then remained at the stage of nascent society, or developed more or less as it has. As a *practical* matter, however, the third course might have been inevitable. (I am indebted on this matter to David Strom.)

distance between nature and human nature and, therefore, the difficulty of recovering natural wholeness. The more closely we look at it, the more nature seems to recede from our grasp.

Or does it? Certainly the foregoing considerations underscore the improbability of anything like a return to *original* naturalness. (They also underscore the futility of such a return. If our forebears were so easily and perhaps inevitably expelled from the natural state, what reason is there to think that another generation of natural men and women wouldn't likewise be expelled, even assuming, incredibly, that the return could be achieved in the first place?) But they do *not* bear on the probability of a return to nature *at a higher level,* that is, at the level of an Emile or a Jean-Jacques. It is true, as we have observed, that Rousseau's primary understanding of nature is as origins and that, therefore, his understanding of post-state-of-nature naturalness, whether Emile's or Jean-Jacques's, takes its bearings from the savage. But what is borrowed from the savage is a set of principles, principles that at least in theory are compatible with the advanced mental capacities of civilized human beings. With his dual-aspect understanding of nature, Rousseau purports to offer us a standard that is nonhuman in its origins yet accommodating of the highest humanity. He holds out the promise of a wholeness which, while taking its bearings from original wholeness, does not require that we return to our original condition. And so the question of plausibility escapes out of the purview of science and into the realm occupied by the great promises of philosophy and religion.

Thus does Rousseau's erotic promise remain plausible after all. Such a promise, when as attractive as his has proved to be, holds enormous power and is therefore something to be reckoned with. I will thus conclude by leaving aside questions of plausibility in favor of those of desirability and suitability. What risks do we run in pursuing this promise of wholeness? What dangers do we face, if any, in adopting Rousseau's nonteleological nature as our lodestar? And what might it cost us in terms of precluded possibilities?

The Perils of Rousseau's Naturalism: Some Concluding Reflections

Rousseau's readers will decide for themselves—or, more likely, will simply discover for themselves—whether they find his vision compelling. One's basic response to his portrait of natural goodness and to the prospect of renewed wholeness is at least as much a personal and aesthetic matter as a rational one. It was not critical reason that inspired the romantic and revolutionary fervor of those who were most deeply stirred by Rousseau, nor does it seem likely that it was critical reason that provoked the often visceral dislike of Rousseau among opponents of Romanticism and revolution. Indeed, it is hard to imagine that anyone's first response to Rousseau would be based solely or even predominantly on critical reflection. Certainly Rousseau did not mean for it to be: from the first, his rhetoric was skillfully aimed at the heart. He understood that his various portraits of the good life would pass through the senses and sensibilities of his readers before reaching their rational faculties. But if critical reason has little to do with our initial response to Rousseau, it certainly can say something about the implications of his vision, about the necessary trade-offs and potential dangers.

All moral and political visions carry costs and dangers, all notions of the Good preclude other notions of the Good, and all moral and political understandings are subject to misreading and abuse. Among the potentially troublesome implications of Rousseau's vision, two in particular—or rather two sets of implications—seem worthy of note. Each derives from Rousseau's reliance upon a nonteleological conception of nature.

Rousseau's Subjectivism and Its Consequences

As we have seen, nature serves as more than just a formal standard for Rousseau. While all good lives meet the formal standard (that is, replicate the savage's psychic unity and equal balance between desires and faculties), Emile and Jean-Jacques, Rousseau's two post-state-of-nature natural men, also have a substantive dimension to their naturalness: they not only replicate the savage's wholeness but also develop and live according to the natural love of order that Rousseau calls conscience. And yet if Rousseau's nature is more than a formal standard, it turns out that there is at least one way—one troubling way—in which it seems to act like one.

Like a merely formal standard, Rousseau's nonteleological nature allows for multiple solutions to the problem of the good life. This in itself is neither conceptually problematic nor troubling in its implications; indeed, one might see it as a major virtue. What is potentially troubling, however, is that which makes this multiplicity possible. The reason Rousseau can approve equally of denatured citizenship and the naturalness of Emile is that his nonteleological standard is essentially psychological and, therefore, subjective. When Rousseau endorses or condemns a way of life, he does so on the basis of the state of soul that it requires or engenders. The citizen and the natural man are affirmed because they each enjoy considerable psychic integrity, which in turn allows them to experience a high degree of existence and leads them to behave well toward others. The bourgeois is condemned on the basis of the same psychological standard: because he lacks psychic integrity (he is internally divided and basely appetitive) and so is petty both morally and in terms of the degree of existence he enjoys. It is only because Rousseau's basic standard is psychological that he can endorse such disparate versions of the good life as the citizen's, Emile's, and Jean-Jacques's. Now, it is possible that Rousseau's understanding of the relation between psychological state and behavior is entirely correct and that psychic integrity does always produce desirable behavior. But even if that is the case, there is something inherently difficult and perhaps also dangerous about such a subjective standard. What makes it difficult is how impractical it can be in real-life situations. What is dangerous about it is the room it opens up for bad faith.

One who would orient his behavior and his moral striving by a standard as subjective as Rousseau's may find that standard has little to say to him about many or even most of life's difficult choices. As noted earlier, none of Rousseau's constructive works includes a code of conduct or even a catalog of basic virtues. Instead they provide what might be called metamoral principles—principles that, if implemented, would purportedly yield good behavior. Perhaps it is unfair to fault Rousseau for this. Why should anyone be faulted for failing to say everything? Why should a moral philosopher be found deficient for failing to be a moral legislator—especially when he has never claimed to be one? But perhaps Rousseau does deserve criticism in this regard, for the ethos he encourages is psychologically rather than behaviorally oriented. He advocates, if only by implication, an approach to moral life that is concerned more with what one *is* than with what one *does,* on the understanding that the latter derives from the former. And such an approach, however true its basic understanding of the relation between character and behavior might be, may often prove inadequate and even irrelevant to moral questions immediately at hand. When one is faced with an immediate question of what to do, it will be of little use to know what one should be. In the face of difficult choices, it is moral counsel, and not psychotherapy, that is most urgently needed. Moreover —and now we come to the potentially dangerous part—this psychological orientation provides an all-too-easy escape from the demands of right behavior.

An emphasis on what one is rather than on what one does makes the supposed intention of an act, rather than the act itself, the object of moral judgment, for it is intention that normally provides the most direct reflection of what one is. And this focus, to the extent that it crowds out consideration of the effects of the act and the nature of the act itself, can easily lend itself to a kind of moral laziness or bad faith. Surely it is easier to justify questionable actions when the standard of justification is intention rather than effect and when the means of determining whether the act is justified is self-examination rather than objective analysis. And surely this emphasis on good intentions over good effects makes it easier to excuse questionable actions, not only after the fact but also before. None of this is to say that Rousseau's nonteleological conception of nature and his consequent adoption of a psychologically oriented moral standard creates a danger where none had existed previously. Moral sophistry, whether in anticipation of a questionable act or after the act has been committed, is all too great a temptation under any moral regime. But the temptation would seem to grow greater as one enters the more lawyer-friendly court of subjective self-examination. And if we doubt that this danger exists, we have a portrait of it from Rousseau himself.

Let us briefly consider some episodes from the *Confessions*. What we find, at least in the parts of the book that precede the hero's return to nature, is a flawed being who is full of excuses for his bad actions.[7] Rousseau neither denies the wrongness of many of his actions nor attempts to justify them, but he does repeatedly absolve himself of responsibility for them.[8] He attributes them to something other than his true self, as when he abandons his friend Le Maître in the latter's hour of need. This, he tells us, was one of those "times when I am so little like myself that I would be taken for another man of a completely opposite character" (III:107). In other instances he pleads good intentions, as he does with regard to placing his children in a foundling home: "I shuddered at giving them over to that poorly brought up family to be brought up even worse by them. The risks from the education of the foundling hospital were much less" (IX:349). At other times he simply excuses bad actions on the grounds that if he hadn't committed them, someone else would have. Such is

---

7. A cautionary note: Although the *Confessions* is presented as autobiography, we should be careful about criticizing Rousseau *the author* for actions attributed to Rousseau *the character*. There is some question as to the factual accuracy of the episodes recounted. We should even be careful about criticizing Rousseau the author for what we might find objectionable in Rousseau *the narrator*, who after all is also one of the book's characters. Hartle argues that Rousseau the author intends for us to be bothered by the narrator's attempts at self-justification. "His 'excusing' is part of the portrait," she writes, "and Rousseau *intends* that there be such responses [namely, objections by his readers]. This is the way we are: excusing (ourselves) and judging (others)" (*The Modern Self*, 31; emphasis in the original). Thus it may be that Rousseau means to illustrate the very danger I am outlining here.

8. "I do not fear that the reader will ever forget that I am making my confessions and thereby believe that I am making my apology" (VII:234).

his excuse for accepting money from Madame de Warens despite knowing of her financial difficulties: "I can swear that I would have suffered all retrench-ments ... with joy, if Mamma had truly profited from these savings; but certain that whatever I refused myself passed over to some rogues, I abused her desire to be obliging in order to share with them, and like the dog who came back from the slaughterhouse, I carried off my bit of the piece that I had been unable to save" (V:180). What is most telling in this passage is Rousseau's distinction between himself and the "rogues." Rousseau, who partakes of Madame's indulgence, is himself not a rogue. Why not? Apparently because he would have *preferred* to have done otherwise. One's moral stature, it would seem, is determined not by what one does—nor even, in this case, by one's immediate intentions—but by one's abstract preference, for it is such prefer-ences or wishes that best reflect one's true self. It is only on such grounds as these that Rousseau can claim, even after making all these confessions, that he is "taking everything into account, the best of men" (X:433).

Rousseau's is not the only moral orientation to leave room for exculpatory sophistry. No moral code is invulnerable to bad faith. Some moral systems, however, might be more vulnerable than others. (Perhaps one criterion of a great moral system is the recognition of and response to this danger.) And it certainly seems possible that, with its subjective basis, Rousseau's moral orien-tation creates more room for bad faith, more space within which the person might elude the demands of moral accountability.

This is perhaps the most compelling criticism that might be leveled against Rousseau's moral subjectivism. But there is another line of criticism, based on the danger of another (albeit related) kind of bad faith. We have observed that Rousseau's moral thought concentrates much more on what one is than on what one does. If there is a single moral imperative in Rousseau's work, it is the imperative to follow nature, to *be* natural. This imperative takes precedence even over Rousseau's own version of the golden rule, for it is good character—specifically, it is a natural character—that will best ensure adherence to that or any other worthwhile rule. But how can this imperative be translated into reality? The best way, and the only way that Rousseau explicitly advises, is to adopt a more natural way of life—for example, to leave large cities and the demands of city life for rustic simplicity. (This and other such measures are endorsed in the *Lettres morales*, the nearest thing to a natural handbook that Rousseau ever wrote.) But it is not difficult to imagine another way in which one might attempt to realize the imperative to be natural, a way that is perhaps exemplified (again) by Rousseau himself. When the subjective goal of being natural supplants adherence to objective rules or principles as the focus of one's moral striving, the danger exists that one's efforts will be aimed chiefly at feeling good, that is, feeling like a good person. One may be more concerned with impressing oneself with one's own goodness than with actually doing good.

Rousseau acknowledges something like this danger in the *Letter to d'Alembert*, where he criticizes theatergoers for imagining that, by virtue of having sympathized with (enacted) suffering or having felt indignation at (enacted) injustice, they have discharged their moral duty. The same people who congratulate themselves for their moral responses in the theater are apt to find a way to do the same thing in the real world. Which means either that they will be satisfied with themselves merely for having the right emotions and thus not act at all, or that they will act according to the requirements of their self-satisfaction rather than the more uncomfortable demands of the situation. The latter would be no danger at all if doing the right thing always meant doing the thing that feels best. But sometimes the right thing does not feel best. Sometimes one is faced with choosing the lesser of two evils or with a need to exercise "tough love," neither of which is apt to appeal to those for whom clean hands and an untroubled heart are the highest moral values.

The Denial of *Amour-Propre*'s Naturalness and the Consequences for Our Moral Lives

Rousseau's denial of original sociability is not quite as radical, and therefore not quite as erroneous, as it might seem. Rousseau does allow for the possibility of cooperative interaction in the pure state of nature. He only denies that that interaction would have been in any way distinctively human, and in this he is not contradicted by the anthropological record.[9] Rousseau's position, however, is not merely an anthropological claim; it is also a philosophical one. He asserts not only that humans were originally asocial but also that they are (therefore) *naturally* so. And from this, from the equation of the original with the natural, arises some enormously important consequences.

The immediate effect of denying the naturalness of sociability is to deny the

9. That Rousseau allows for the possibility of cooperation for the sake of meeting basic needs is evident from the following statement in the *Second Discourse*: "it is impossible to imagine why, in that primitive state, a man would sooner have need of another man than a monkey or a wolf of its fellow creature" (126). Rousseau does not deny the possibility of cooperation; he only denies that cooperation among early humans was essentially different from that among other animals. As Masters puts it, "Rousseau's rejection of sociability refers to what we call human culture rather than to what a biologist would describe as social behavior" ("Jean-Jacques is Alive and Well," 99–100).

naturalness of *amour-propre*. *Amour-propre* had no place in the soul of primitive man; therefore, it is unnatural. That is the position taken in the *Second Discourse*. In *Emile* and elsewhere, to be sure, Rousseau allows for a second level of naturalness, and at that level *amour-propre* can indeed be considered natural, at least in the sense that it has a place in the civilized natural man's soul. But we have seen that that second level of naturalness is indeed secondary —that it takes its bearings from original naturalness—and that, in order to qualify as natural, *amour-propre* must serve *amour de soi*.

The savage is the primordial man in more ways than one. He not only preceded the civilized natural man, he also fundamentally informs him. That this is the case—that the most perfect exemplar of naturalness had no *amour-propre*—is bound to have repercussions. In short, even though Rousseau concedes that *amour-propre* is inevitable in every civilized person, and even though he concedes that it can be the source of virtue and other good things, the fact that he considers *amour-propre* unnatural in the strict sense would seem to render it perpetually suspect. From the start of his career Rousseau identified *amour-propre* as the chief source of our ills. That alone would seem to produce a cautious attitude toward it. Add to that the designation of unnatural—in a philosophical system that holds nature to be absolutely good and everything else (that is, man) to be rather perverse—and *amour-propre* becomes *extremely* suspect, so much so that Rousseau's most impassioned moral rhetoric is reserved for warning of its evil effects.

Now, to render a thing suspect—to decree, as it were, that it is to be treated with something analogous to judicial "strict scrutiny"—is not to condemn the thing. Indeed, Rousseau not only allows for *amour-propre* in Emile's soul, he pointedly suggests that the young man *needs* it: he needs *amour-propre* (well governed, of course) so that he might develop virtue and nobility, and even for the sake of a more intense and successful romance. Nevertheless, rendering *amour-propre* suspect by denying it the sanction of primary naturalness must surely have consequences. It must inevitably influence a whole range of moral stances or attitudes. And although not all of the potential consequences are troubling—Emile is in no way morally deficient, and he is constructed on the understanding that *amour-propre* is unnatural in the primary sense—some of them are. There are at least two ways in which denying natural status to *amour-propre* might produce unfortunate results in our moral lives. First, it can lead to adoption of an unrealistically high moral standard—one by which most people fail most of the time—and so to a very harsh assessment of one's fellows. This in turn translates into pessimism and can also lead to misanthropy and to either intolerance or resignation. Second, denying the naturalness of *amour-propre* can produce a constricting moral atmosphere, one in which the attempt to delay or limit *amour-propre*'s development can lead to its distortion and in which some of *amour-propre*'s loftiest potentials are dampened.

A Standard Beyond Reach

To deny that any *amour-propre* is natural in the primary sense and to deny that the great majority of *amour-propre*, including all vanity, is natural even in the secondary or civil sense is to construct a standard against which most people will fail most of the time—and fail dismally, at that. As we saw in the preceding chapter, most feeling and behavior derives from less than ideal sources. The consequences of such a high failure rate are significant. To start with, one who holds so high a standard is apt to take a very dim view of his fellows. He is apt to condemn them rather roundly. Whether he does so with passion or with resignation will depend on his general disposition. A person with a more fiery temperament is apt to become a loud and scathing critic and is likely to earn the reputation of an angry prophet or a misanthrope (it is interesting to note that Rousseau himself has been seen as both of these things). A person with a more subdued temperament, on the other hand, is apt to manifest disapproval of others in somber resignation. But whichever route is taken, constructive moral action is not likely to be the result: angry prophets may be morally impassioned, but unless they are able to invoke an angry God, their passion is not likely to inspire reform; and since neither the misanthrope nor the resigned man expects any good from others, neither is apt even to attempt to elicit any. Nor is it clear that we should *want* constructive action to be carried out on the basis of such a standard. A standard that invalidates most of what we do and feel is an inhuman standard, at least when not tempered by compassion, and an inhuman standard is apt to produce inhumane results. Action based on such a standard is apt to be harsh. In the event that it is backed by revolutionary fervor and state power, such action is likely to prove utterly pitiless, somewhat (to reach for the nearest example) in the manner of Robespierre and the guillotine.

Another, related effect of holding people to an unrealistically high standard is pessimism. Although some of Rousseau's readers drew wildly romantic or revolutionary inspiration from his books, Rousseau himself was profoundly pessimistic about the moral or political improvement of his species. He thought that people were motivated most of the time by vanity, and where vanity is the leading passion, he believed, there is, and would continue to be, only moral blight. Thus neither virtue, nor goodness, nor happiness, nor political freedom was likely to be extended in future years. If anything, the future figured to be even worse than the present.[10]

There is no way to prove that Rousseau's estimation of the moral quality of modern men was wrong. We cannot prove either that his contemporaries were better than he believed them to be or that we, their descendants, are morally better than he foretold. But it *is* possible to establish that much of Rousseau's pessimism, insofar as it was expressed in specific, empirically verifiable predictions, was unjustified. Rousseau was simply wrong, for example, in predicting that patriotism could not exist in large or undemocratic states (this was refuted by the explosion of nationalism in the nineteenth and twentieth centuries) and in his more general prediction that Europe would slide into poverty, despotism, and susceptibility to conquest (this has been demonstrably refuted by the West's extraordinary prosperity and considerable political success).[11] And while these errors may prove nothing more than that Rousseau misread the future in certain respects, it may be that they betray a deeper error, an error in his philosophical system.

Rousseau's pessimism seems to have derived from a combination of two beliefs: first, that most of what most people do is, and will likely continue to be, motivated by *amour-propre*; and second, that the character of most people's *amour-propre* is rather bad and so precludes social progress. If Rousseau's pessimism was demonstrably unjustified, and it was, then the error must lie in one of these beliefs. Which one? Probably not the first: it is difficult to argue with Rousseau's estimation of the predominance of *amour-propre*, either in his time or in ours. It is difficult to contest that most of what most people do is motivated, at least in significant part, by the desire for recognition. Indeed, it is difficult to dispute that what Rousseau calls vanity figures significantly among most people's motives, though perhaps not as largely as Rousseau suggests. His error, therefore, must lie in the second belief: that most *amour-propre* is of such bad character that no social improvement can be expected. *If Rousseau underestimated the political potential of the modern world, it is because he overestimated the evil effects of our amour-propre.* There is no reason to suppose that human nature is any better today than it was in the eighteenth century or that we educate *amour-propre* very differently than it was educated then. We are certainly no less interdependent today than people were then—that is to say, our

---

10. Rousseau tells us that the things that make us discontent in our present state "foretell even greater discontents for [our] unhappy posterity" (*SD* 104).

11. For more on Rousseau's pessimism and its refutation by subsequent history, see Melzer, *Natural Goodness of Man*, 265–71, 288–90. My own brief account is indebted to Melzer's more comprehensive one.

amour-propre is probably of much the same quality as the *amour-propre* Rousseau observed in his contemporaries—yet somehow we enjoy political and economic successes that Rousseau thought could not be had under those circumstances.

Taking this inquiry a step further, if Rousseau was wrong about the necessary *implications* of *amour-propre*, it may be that he also misjudged the *character* of *amour-propre* as it is manifest in most people. Perhaps, for example, he overestimated the ratio of vanity to pride in most people's souls. True, it is not difficult to find vanity in most people, but perhaps, as Adam Smith suggests, vanity is often accompanied by pride.[12] Or perhaps Rousseau simply overstated the evil of vanity. Undoubtedly vanity, as Rousseau defines it, is a vice, and undoubtedly it is capable of the greatest evils. But perhaps it is not without a redeeming feature, just as hypocrisy, vanity's close cousin (both hypocrisy and vanity seek to exploit the distinction between being and seeming), is not without a redeeming feature. Like hypocrisy, vanity can be seen as a tribute paid to virtue. But in fact, vanity's tribute to virtue is greater than hypocrisy's because it is, or at least can be, more sincere. Hypocrisy is the way of the cynic, who pays tribute to virtue merely for personal gain. Vanity, on the other hand, often reflects a person's sincere desire not just for praise but for praiseworthiness as well. Undeserving people who seek praise might wish they deserved it—they might very well understand that deserved praise is better and more meaningful than undeserved praise—in which case vanity would seem more a weakness than a calculated evil. Such vanity is the tribute paid to virtue by the would-be virtuous person. That is why vanity can sometimes seem innocent and why it can actually presage virtue. Many who settle for undeserved praise would rather deserve it, and some will end up doing just that, much as the child who plays at being a hero sometimes goes on to become one.

If Rousseau does misjudge the character and effects of *amour-propre* as it is manifest in most people, as now seems possible, why does he do so? Some might argue that his error reflects merely a disposition to find fault, a disposition arising either from natural temperament, harsh personal experience, or a misanthropic spirit. None of these explanations would be fair, however, nor need we even look for personal explanations. The explanation, rather, may lie among the basic premises of Rousseau's system. There is a dualism underlying Rousseau's philosophy: that which is natural is wholly good, and that which is

---

12. Smith alerts us to the possibility that vanity and pride are not mutually exclusive, that they can coexist in the same soul. "The proud man is often vain," he writes, "and the vain man is often proud." See *The Theory of Moral Sentiments*, part VI, section 3, paragraph 33 (New York: Oxford University Press, 1976), 259.

unnatural or estranged from nature is bad.[13] *Amour-propre*, as it manifests itself in most people, falls into the latter category; it is estranged from nature. Hence it is bad, and therefore we, in whom it reigns, are also bad. And so Rousseau sees in us little potential for good and much inclination to evil.

Now, if Rousseau was wrong in the ways I have suggested—if he was erroneously pessimistic, if his pessimism reflected an overestimation of *amour-propre*'s evil effects, and if this overestimation arose from an overly grim assessment of the character of most *amour-propre*, that is, if most people's *amour-propre* is better than Rousseau thought—then he must have erred in one more way. And herein must lie his most basic error. Either Rousseau was wrong to believe that what is unnatural must be wholly bad, or else most people's *amour-propre* is not unnatural, or at least not *as* unnatural as he thought. Of the two possibilities, the first would be more difficult to establish: the goodness of nature and the badness of unnaturalness could always be maintained by simply designating all good things natural and all bad things unnatural. The second possibility, on the other hand, is not so difficult to argue. In fact, a certain amount of suggestive empirical evidence supports the proposition that *amour-propre* is not unnatural.[14] But it is not in empirical evidence that we will find the most compelling argument against *amour-propre*'s supposed unnaturalness. The most compelling argument of all, from the perspective of political philosophy, is neither sociobiological nor anthropological, but rather moral and political: denying *amour-propre* natural status has serious and troubling consequences, of which an unrealistic standard of behavior and the resulting pessimism are only the first.

The Risk of Delegitimating Longing and Aspiration

The immediate consequence of considering all *amour-propre* unnatural in the strict sense and most *amour-propre* unnatural in any sense is to render *amour-propre* as such suspect. Even if some *amour-propre* is endorsed and even celebrated, as a practical matter it is enormously difficult to know whether particular instances of *amour-propre* fall into the good category or the bad category.[15]

13. "Everything is good as it leaves the hands of the Author of things; everything degenerates in the hands of man" (*Emile* I:37).

14. It turns out that something akin to *amour-propre* can be found among certain animals. Certain species, especially social vertebrates, exhibit territoriality as well as a kind of natural deference in recognition of social hierarchies, or "pecking orders." See Masters, "Rediscovery of Human Nature," esp. 117, 137n. 17, and *Political Philosophy of Rousseau*, 431; Melzer, *Natural Goodness of Man*, 51n. 3; and George Maclay and Humphrey Knipe, *The Dominant Man* (New York: Dell Publishing, 1972).

15. The theoretical distinction between good and bad *amour-propre* is one thing; making a

The consequence of this difficulty is a general attitude of extreme, perhaps excessive, caution regarding *amour-propre*. Rousseau's primary emphasis is on discouraging bad varieties of *amour-propre* rather than encouraging good varieties. Recall the litany of urgent warnings against foresight, reading, imagination, and other things that can awaken *amour-propre* too early in the life of the child and thus ruin his character. Recall, too, the singular harshness of the tutor's response to Emile's first display of vanity and the severe warnings against the danger of excessive pride even in early manhood.[16] As we observed in Chapter 1 and at the conclusion of Chapter 4, the negative component of the good life is given priority by Rousseau.

Nor is it only *amour-propre* as such that is rendered suspect. All manner of passions and strivings that are associated with or are expressions of *amour-propre* also become suspect. The greater the magnitude of the *amour-propre* they express, the greater the caution with which Rousseau regards them. It is as if *amour-propre* is a potent drug, one that can do great good but that also is highly addictive and highly destructive when abused. Of course, all forms of such a drug are to be regarded with caution. And the most extreme caution is to be directed toward the purest forms of the drug—which means, in the case of *amour-propre*, toward longing and aspiration.

Rousseau of course does not simply condemn longing and aspiration. Indeed, he often celebrates them. The whole charm of Emile as a young man is his innocent but intense longing for his beloved, a longing that is even suffused with religious passion. And Rousseau speaks wistfully of the many moments of intense longing, and he mentions proudly the abundant instances of noble aspiration that have marked his own life. But if he agrees that longing and aspiration are among the highest expressions of humanity, he also sees them as its most dangerous expressions. And, as with *amour-propre* generally, it is the *danger* of longing and aspiration, more than their promise, that seems to determine Rousseau's approach to them. Everything that is true of Rousseau's general stance toward *amour-propre* is especially true, intensely true, of his approach to longing and aspiration. Just as caution wins out in his stance toward *amour-propre*, so extreme caution wins out in his approach to

---

practical judgment of something this subjective is another—especially if, as Adam Smith suggests, the good and bad versions are often intermingled in the same instances.

16. Regarding the warnings against foresight, reading and imagination, see "Beyond Happiness ..." in Chapter 1 above. For the story of Emile's first display of vanity and the humiliation the tutor arranges in response to it, see *Emile* III:173–75. Regarding the danger of excessive pride, even in one who has been as wholesomely educated as Emile, see "How Much *Amour-Propre* ..." in Chapter 4 above.

longing and aspiration. The reasons for this caution are not unfamiliar to us. First, although there are both good and bad varieties of longing and aspiration, it is very difficult as a practical matter to know which kind one is presented with in a particular instance. This we have already discussed.[17] And in any event, the best thing one can do to encourage good varieties of longing and aspiration is to discourage the bad ones. Encourage the good without preventing the bad and you will end up with bad, as the dismal record of traditional moral education attests; prevent the bad, however, and you will have gone a long way toward promoting the good. Thus the top priority of a moral education must be to prevent the bad. The question, of course, is whether this supposition is valid. If it is, Rousseau's caution is eminently justified. But if it is not—if he is wrong to assume that a cautious approach toward longing and aspiration is the way to discourage the bad versions and support the good ones—then a significant part of his natural education is rendered highly questionable.

Rousseau is very careful and specific in his injunctions regarding longing and aspiration. Rather than condemn them in blanket terms (as he sometimes seems to condemn *amour-propre*), he merely delimits their permissible content.[18] The limits he prescribes, moreover, would seem to be entirely unobjectionable. We are advised to respect the boundaries that our humanity has imposed on us. Who could argue with that? Let us look at two such pieces of advice from *Emile*, the first of which was given directly to the young man; the second, directly to us.

> I have only one precept to give you, and it comprehends all the others. Be a man. Restrain your heart within the limits of your condition. Study and know these limits. However narrow they may be, a man is not unhappy as long as he closes himself up within them. He is unhappy only when he wants to go out beyond them. (V:445–46)

> O man, draw your existence up within yourself, and you will no longer be miserable. Remain in the place which nature assigns to you in the chain of being. Nothing will be able to make you leave it. Do not rebel

17. This practical difficulty is a result of the subjective nature of Rousseau's standard. Thus his cautious approach to longing and aspiration derives not only from the denial of natural status to *amour-propre* but also from the subjectivism discussed earlier.

18. As we saw in the previous chapter, his apparent blanket condemnations of *amour-propre* are deliberate overstatements for the sake of rhetorical effect. See "The Birth of *Amour-Propre*" in Chapter 4 above.

against the hard law of necessity; and do not exhaust your strength by your will to resist that law—strength which heaven gave you not for extending or prolonging your existence but only for preserving it as heaven pleases and for as long as heaven pleases. Your freedom and your power extend only as far as your natural strength, and not beyond. All the rest is only slavery, illusion, and deception. (II:83)

Underlying the limits that Rousseau prescribes for longing and aspiration is the belief that strength, happiness, and goodness depend upon respecting them. These goods are easily lost by dint of overreaching, and most especially by the desire to be something other than what one is. Whether one's desire is to be another, more fortunate human being or to be more than a human being, the result is weakness, unhappiness, and vice. If Emile "just once prefers to be someone other than himself," Rousseau warns, "were this other Socrates, were it Cato—everything has failed. He who begins to become alien to himself does not take long to forget himself entirely" (IV:243). And if wanting to be one of those excellent men is destructive, the desire to be more than human is even more so: "how much it is to be feared that by dint of trying to raise ourselves above our nature, we may relapse beneath it" (*Bordes* 113–14). This is one of the chief lessons Emile derives from his study of history: "He will be afflicted at seeing his brothers tear one another apart for the sake of dreams and turn into ferocious animals because they do not know how to be satisfied with being men" (IV:242). "Be[ing] a man" would seem to express the appropriate limit of legitimate aspiration. Anything higher is apt to end in misery and degradation. In any case, the goal is itself a high one. To be a man means to be an Emile, with all the virtues and fine feeling—all the wholeness—the young man ultimately achieves. It does not mean what is usually meant by the phrase "only human." And drawing one's "existence up within [one]self," far from being egocentrism, is the first and most important step toward reaching that goal.

But are these limits really as benign as they sound? Certainly some of them are. It would be ludicrous to argue against respecting "the limits of [our] condition" or to suggest that we should "rebel against the hard law of necessity." But not all of Rousseau's advice is so obviously salutary. His admonition against emulating others, for example—the basis of his excluding books from Emile's early childhood—flies in the face of traditional principles of education, as Rousseau well knows. And the most basic of all his governing principles, the principle that it is poisonous to a natural education for a child to want to be more than he or she is—or for *any* of us to want to be more than we are—is also questionable.[19] Indeed, Rousseau's principle contradicts the intuitive belief of many who share his desire to encourage the right kind of longing and aspiration. Many of us have a deep-seated sense that the desire to be more than one is, is both natural and valuable and that a certain dissatisfaction with oneself is one of the surest prods to nobility—and that, consequently, to discourage this desire would be to risk moral and psychological distortion. Rousseau of course would consider this deep-seated sense an illfounded prejudice, and he might in fact be right. But a prejudice as venerable as this one, which has roots in the founding documents of Western religion and philosophy, at least deserves a hearing.

Rousseau's concern with preventing the wrong kinds of longing and aspiration is great, but no greater than that which finds expression in countless other sources, beginning with the Bible. From Genesis, wherein man and woman are enjoined from eating a certain fruit lest they become "as God," and on through the books of the Prophets and beyond, human beings are commanded to walk humbly with God—they are told to respect the limits of their condition. Not only self-deification but arrogance of any dimension is forbidden. But even as the Bible condemns one version of ontological aspiration (that is, the aspiration to be more than one is, or to reach a higher level of being), it actually commands another. Men and women are told that they have been created in God's image, and that they should be "as God." "You shall be holy," says God to his people through Moses, "*for I, the Lord your God, am holy*" (Leviticus 19:2). Nor is it only the Bible that distinguishes among different versions of ontological aspiration. We need only think of Plato, who recognizes that the difference between one version of this desire and another is the difference between the worst of men and the best. The tyrant is a product of the desire to be godlike, but so is the philosopher.[20] In words not so different from those of Leviticus, Plato's Socrates advises: "we ought to fly away from earth to heaven as quickly as we can; and to fly away is to become like God, as far as this is possible; and to become like him, is to become holy, just, and wise" (*Theaetetus*,

19. It should be noted that Rousseau's strictures against emulation and the desire to reach beyond oneself is applied only to natural men and women and to those being educated to become such. The education appropriate to *citizens* seems to include, and even make great use of, just these things. See chapter 4 of Rousseau's *Considerations on the Government of Poland* (in *Political Writings*, ed. and trans. Frederick Watkins [Madison: University of Wisconsin Press, 1986]) for an account of the latter sort of education.

20. One of the major themes of the *Republic* is the psychological kinship between the tyrant and the philosopher. As far apart as they are—and, morally, they are as far apart as any two individuals can be—they are both exemplars of an intense eros, which is why the young potential philosopher (a Glaucon) is also a potential tyrant and may find himself drawn equally to these opposite poles.

176). Thus do the two fonts of Western culture dispute Rousseau's blanket condemnation of the desire to be more than one is.

It might seem at first that the difference between these ancient sources and Rousseau is largely semantic. The meaning of the biblical and Socratic imperative to be godlike seems not very different from the meaning of Rousseau's own imperative, "be a man." Emile, after all, who exemplifies that imperative, is just and wise and even holy, at least in the sense that one supposes Rousseau might use the term. But the semantic difference reflects a fundamental difference of outlook between the ancient approaches and Rousseau's. Even if the heights occupied by Emile (or Jean-Jacques) are as elevated as those occupied by the biblical and Socratic ideals—even if to "be a man" as Rousseau intends it is as high a thing as what the Bible or Plato means by being godlike—there is a world of difference between Rousseau's understanding of how we might ascend those heights and the biblical and classical understandings. For the writers of the Bible and for Plato, and for all who belong to either or both of the traditions they founded, one essential requirement of scaling the heights is to *want* to be more than one is. One must want to transcend the all-too-human tendencies toward complacency and compromise. One's aspiration must partake of a superhuman dimension. Without that, one is doomed never to transcend the bad aspects of our nature. (Here we see the source of the disagreement between Rousseau and those other traditions. For Rousseau, there is no need to transcend any of our natural tendencies because there *are* no bad aspects to our nature.)

To want to be "as God" in the wrong way, in an egocentric way, is the greatest of evils, or at least the cause of them, for both the biblical and the classical traditions. But to have no transcendent aspiration, to rest content with being "like the nations," is not much better. Indeed, the latter may be no better and even no different in the end from the former: they who do not have the desire to be godlike (or godly) in a good way may in the end fall prey to the desire to be godlike in a bad way. To put it in religious terms, those who do not aspire to godliness will be inclined to idolatry, especially self-deification. Or, to put it in the terms of Socratic philosophy, eros that is not educated to pursue the Good risks being seduced by false goods, and the most erotic and potentially philosophical individuals are apt to become the most dangerously tyrannical. It may well be, in other words, that the basic choice for human beings, especially for the greatest human beings, is not *whether* to seek to be more than one is but rather *how* to seek to be more than one is.

Rousseau not only considers the desire to be more than one is dangerous, he also considers it unnatural and hence avoidable, at least in principle. Others, however, might look around and come to a different conclusion. We notice, for example, that children especially, but not only children, frequently exhibit this desire by emulating those whom they admire. And even when emulation is muted, ontological aspiration is frequently the predominant theme of our thoughts, so much so that it would seem to have a presumptive claim to inevitability and even naturalness. This is not an insignificant issue. The question of whether it is natural for people to be dissatisfied with the limits of humanity is of decisive practical importance. If in fact it *is* natural—if, in the words of a recent philosopher, man naturally "experiences an ontological privation"—then to overlook this dissatisfaction would be to risk real moral and spiritual damage.[21] Emile's tutor makes sure that the desire to be more than he is never appears in his pupil. But if *Emile* should prove unrealistic in this regard—if this desire is in fact inevitable—then what we need is a principle by which to govern such desire, and Rousseau does not offer one. Without such a principle, this most basic and consequential of aspirations would go uneducated, leaving it either unsatisfied, or ill-directed, or both. There is a considerable irony in this. One of Rousseau's fundamental criticisms of liberal theory is that it does not take adequate account of *amour-propre*—that, in trying to discourage fanaticism and vainglory, liberal theory neglects to educate this most stubbornly important part of social man's nature, leaving it to sour into petty vanity. But if Rousseau is wrong in assuming that the aspiration to be more than one is simply bad and avoidable, then he has exposed himself to a similar criticism. He, too, might be faulted, if not for neglecting to educate the whole of *amour-propre*, at least with failing to educate a major part of it.

It is ironic and perhaps a little unfair to conclude our inquiry here. Far from wanting to discourage longing and aspiration, after all, Rousseau sought to validate and even inspire them. One of his major purposes, as we have seen, was to find a natural basis for the sublime so that he might rescue it from the spiritual scythe of modern philosophy. Where other political philosophers seemed to want to bank the flames of grand passion and to replace them with smaller and more manageable fires, Rousseau sought to show that a soul that

21. The philosopher is Walter Kaufmann. The culminating sections of his *Critique of Religion and Philosophy* (Princeton: Princeton University Press, 1958) are a meditation on this theme and the central place it has occupied in the best of religion and philosophy. In section 98, "Man's Ontological Interest," Kaufmann argues that, in addition to physiological and psychological needs, "Man also experiences an *ontological* privation, whether he is aware of it or not: he needs to rise above that whole level of being which is defined by his psychological and physiological needs and their satisfaction; he needs to love and create" (423; emphasis in the original).

burns bright need not be destructive, as long as its fire is kindled properly. Emile is one such soul: his love for Sophie is a magnificent passion but also a noble and orderly one. Jean-Jacques is another: although at his peak he transcends desire, his reveries seem to me a kind of consummation nonetheless; and they certainly have inspired longing in many readers. It is not for nothing that Rousseau is looked upon as a founder of Romanticism. The question we are left to consider, though, is whether this first purpose wasn't at least partially subverted by the overzealous pursuit of a second and related purpose. In his effort to instruct us as to the good governance of *amour-propre*—in his effort to point us toward restored wholeness—Rousseau delegitimated much longing and aspiration. The question is whether in doing so, he didn't deprive the soul of the very fuel that powers its quest for the sublime.

References

Aristotle. *Nicomachean Ethics*. Trans. Martin Ostwald. Indianapolis: Bobbs-Merrill Library of Liberal Arts, 1962.

———. *The Politics*. Trans. Carnes Lord. Chicago: University of Chicago Press, 1984.

Bacon, Francis. Preface to *Magna Instauratio*. In *Instauratio Magna with New Atlantis*, ed. A. B. Gough. Oxford: Blackwell, 1915.

Bates, Louise, et al. *The Gesell Institute's Child from One to Six*. New York: Harper and Row, 1979.

Belloc, Hillaire. *The French Revolution*. London: Oxford University Press, 1911.

Bloom, Allan. Introduction to *Emile, or on Education*, by Jean-Jacques Rousseau. Trans. Bloom. New York: Basic Books, 1979.

———. *Love and Friendship*. New York: Simon and Schuster, 1993.

Blum, Carol. *Rousseau and the Republic of Virtue*. Ithaca: Cornell University Press, 1986.

Burke, Edmund. *Reflections on the Revolution in France*. London: J. M. Dent, 1910.

Cameron, David. *The Social Thought of Rousseau and Burke*. London: Weidenfeld and Nicolson, 1973.

Cantor, Paul A. *Creature and Creator: Myth-making and English Romanticism*. Cambridge: Cambridge University Press, 1984.

————. "The Metaphysics of Botany: Rousseau and the New Criticism of Plants." *Southwest Review* 70 (1985): 362–80.

Cassirer, Ernst. *The Question of Jean-Jacques Rousseau*. Ed. and trans. Peter Gay. Bloomington: Indiana University Press, 1954.

————. *Rousseau, Kant, and Goethe*. Trans. James Gutmann, Paul Oskar Kristeller, and John Herman Randall Jr. New York: Harper and Row, 1963.

Chapman, John W. *Rousseau: Totalitarian or Liberal?* New York: AMS Press, 1956.

Charvet, John. "Individual Identity and Social Consciousness in Rousseau's Philosophy." In *Hobbes and Rousseau: A Collection of Critical Essays*, ed. Maurice Cranston and Richard S. Peters. Garden City, N.Y.: Doubleday, 1972.

————. *The Social Problem in the Philosophy of Rousseau*. New York: Cambridge University Press, 1974.

Cobban, Alfred. *Rousseau and the Modern State*. London: Allen Unwin, 1934.

Cranston, Maurice. *The Noble Savage: Jean-Jacques Rousseau, 1754–1762*. Chicago: University of Chicago Press, 1991.

Crocker, Lester G. *Rousseau's Social Contract: An Interpretive Essay*. Cleveland: Case Western Reserve University Press, 1968.

Cropsey, Joseph. *Political Philosophy and the Issues of Politics*. Chicago: University of Chicago Press, 1977.

Davis, Michael. *The Politics of Philosophy: A Commentary on Aristotle's Politics*. Lanham, Md.: Rowman and Littlefield, 1996.

Dent, N. J. H. *Rousseau: An Introduction to His Psychological, Social, and Political Theory*. New York: Basil Blackwell, 1988.

————. *A Rousseau Dictionary*. Cambridge, Mass.: Blackwell Publishers, 1992.

Derathé, Robert. *Le rationalisme de Jean-Jacques Rousseau*. Paris: Presses Universitaires de France, 1948.

Dodge, Guy H., ed. *Jean-Jacques Rousseau: Authoritarian Libertarian?* Lexington, Mass.: D. C. Heath, 1971.

Ellenburg, Stephen. *Rousseau's Political Philosophy: An Interpretation from Within*. Ithaca: Cornell University Press, 1976.

Freud, Sigmund. *Civilization and Its Discontents*. Ed. and trans. James Strachey. New York: W. W. Norton, 1961.

————. *The Standard Edition of the Complete Psychological Works of Sigmund Freud*. Ed. and trans. James Strachey, in collaboration with Anna Freud and Alan Tyson. London: Hogarth Press, 1957.

Fukuyama, Francis. *The End of History and the Last Man*. New York: Avon Books, 1992.

Gesell, Arnold, and Frances Ilg. *The Child from Five to Ten*. New York: Harper and Row, 1946.

Goldschmidt, Victor. *Anthropologie et politique*. Paris: Librairie Philosophique J. Urin, 1974.

Gossman, Lionel. "Time and History in Rousseau." *Studies on Voltaire and the Eighteenth Century* 30 (1964): 311–49.

Gourevitch, Victor. "Rousseau's Pure State of Nature." *Interpretation* 16, no. 1 (1988): 23–59.

Grant, Ruth W. *Hypocrisy and Integrity: Machiavelli, Rousseau, and the Ethics of Politics*. Chicago: University of Chicago Press, 1997.

Grimsley, Ronald. *The Philosophy of Rousseau*. London: Oxford University Press, 1973.

————. "Rousseau and His Reader: The Technique of Persuasion in Emile." In *Rousseau*

After 200 Years: Proceedings of the Cambridge Bicentennial Colloquium, ed. R. A. Leigh. New York: Cambridge University Press, 1982.

———. "Rousseau and the Problem of Happiness." In *Hobbes and Rousseau: A Collection of Critical Essays*, ed. Maurice Cranston and Richard S. Peters. Garden City, N.Y.: Doubleday, 1972.

Gurvitch, Georges. *L'idée du droit social. Notion et système du droit social. Histoire doctrinal depuis le XVIIe siècle jusqu'à la fin du XIXe siècle*. Paris: Libraire du Receuil Sirey, 1932.

Hartle, Ann. *The Modern Self in Rousseau's Confessions: A Reply to St. Augustine*. Notre Dame: University of Notre Dame Press, 1983.

Hegel, G. W. F. *The Phenomenology of Spirit*. Trans. A. V. Miller. New York: Oxford University Press, 1977.

Hendel, Charles W. *Jean-Jacques Rousseau: Moralist*. 2 vols. Indianapolis: Bobbs-Merrill, 1934.

Hobbes, Thomas. *Epistle to the Reader*. Vol. 1 of *The English Works of Thomas Hobbes*, ed. Sir William Molesworth. 11 vols. London, 1839–45.

———. *Leviathan*. Indianapolis: Bobbs-Merrill, 1958.

Horowitz, Asher. *Rousseau, Nature, and History*. Toronto: University of Toronto Press, 1987.

Kass, Leon. *The Hungry Soul: Eating and the Perfecting of Our Nature*. New York: Free Press, 1994.

Kaufmann, Walter. *Critique of Religion and Philosophy*. Princeton: Princeton University Press, 1958.

———. *Nietzsche: Philosopher, Psychologist, Antichrist*. 4th ed. Princeton: Princeton University Press, 1974.

Kelly, Christopher. *Rousseau's Exemplary Life: The Confessions as Political Philosophy*. Ithaca: Cornell University Press, 1987.

Kelly, Christopher, and Roger D. Masters. Introduction to *The Collected Writings of Rousseau*, ed. Masters and Kelly, vol. 1. Hanover, N.H.: University Press of New England, 1990.

Knott, Lorna Dawson. "The Transpolitical Moral Education in Rousseau's *Emile*." Paper presented at the annual meeting of the American Political Science Association, Washington, D.C., 1997.

Kojève, Alexandre. *Introduction to the Reading of Hegel*. New York: Basic Books, 1969.

Levine, Andrew. *The Politics of Autonomy: A Kantian Reading of Rousseau's Social Contract*. Amherst: University of Massachusetts Press, 1976.

Locke, John. "Second Treatise of Government." In *Two Treatises of Government*, ed. Peter Laslett. New York: New American Library, 1960.

MacAdam, J. I. "The *Discourse on Inequality* and the *Social Contract*." *Philosophy* 47, no. 182 (1972): 308–21.

Machiavelli, Niccolò. *The Prince*. Trans. Harvey C. Mansfield Jr. Chicago: University of Chicago Press, 1985.

Maclay, George, and Humphrey Knipe. *The Dominant Man*. New York: Dell Publishing, 1972.

Maine, Henry Sumner. *Ancient Law*. London: Everyman's Library, J. M. Dent, 1917.

Mason, John Hope, ed. *The Indispensable Rousseau*. New York: Quartet Books, 1979.

Masson, Pierre-Maurice. *La religion de J.-J. Rousseau*. 3 vols. Paris: Plon, 1916.

Masters, Roger D. "Jean-Jacques is Alive and Well: Rousseau and Contemporary Sociobiology." *Daedalus* 107 (summer 1978): 93–105.

———. *The Political Philosophy of Rousseau*. Princeton: Princeton University Press, 1968.

————. "Rousseau and the Rediscovery of Human Nature." In *The Legacy of Rousseau*, ed. Clifford Orwin and Nathan Tarcov. Chicago: University of Chicago Press, 1997.

Melzer, Arthur M. *The Natural Goodness of Man: On the System of Rousseau's Thought*. Chicago: University of Chicago Press, 1990.

Morgenstern, Mira. *Rousseau and the Politics of Ambiguity: Self, Culture, and Society*. University Park: Pennsylvania State University Press, 1996.

Neumann, Erich. "Mystical Man." In *The Mystic Vision: Papers from the Eranos Yearbooks*, ed. Joseph Campbell. Princeton: Princeton University Press, 1968.

Nichols, Mary P. *Citizens and Statesmen: A Study of Aristotle's Politics*. Lanham, Md.: Rowman and Littlefield, 1992.

Nietzsche, Friedrich. *Twilight of the Idols*. Trans. R. J. Hollingdale. New York: Penguin Books, 1968.

Osborn, Annie. *Rousseau and Burke*. New York: Russell and Russell, 1940.

Piaget, Jean. *The Essential Piaget*. Ed. H. Gruber and J. Voneche. New York: Basic Books, 1977.

Plamenatz, John. *Man and Society*. 2 vols. London: Longman Group, 1963.

Plato. *Gorgias*. In *Collected Dialogues*, ed. Edith Hamilton and Huntington Cairns. Princeton: Princeton University Press, 1961.

————. *The Republic of Plato*. Trans. Allan Bloom. New York: Basic Books, 1968.

————. *Symposium*. Trans. Alexander Nehamas and Paul Woodruff. Indianapolis: Hackett, 1989.

————. *Theaetetus*. In *Collected Dialogues*, ed. Edith Hamilton and Huntington Cairns. Princeton: Princeton University Press, 1961.

Plattner, Marc F. *Rousseau's State of Nature: An Interpretation of the Discourse on Inequality*. DeKalb: Northern Illinois University Press, 1979.

Poulet, Georges. "Le sentiment de l'existence et le repos." In *Reappraisals of Rousseau*, ed. Simon Harvey et al. Manchester: Manchester University Press, 1980.

Riesman, David. *The Lonely Crowd*. New Haven: Yale University Press, 1950.

Riley, Patrick. *The General Will Before Rousseau: The Transformation of the Divine into the Civic*. Princeton: Princeton University Press, 1986.

Rousseau, Jean-Jacques. *The Confessions*. In *The Collected Writings of Rousseau*, trans. Christopher Kelly, ed. Christopher Kelly, Roger D. Masters, and Peter G. Stillman, vol. 5. Hanover, N.H.: University Press of New England, 1995.

————. *Considerations on the Government of Poland*. In *Political Writings*, ed. and trans. Frederick Watkins. Madison: University of Wisconsin Press, 1986.

————. *Constitutional Project for Corsica*. In *Political Writings*, ed. and trans. Frederick Watkins. Madison: University of Wisconsin Press, 1986.

————. *Correspondence générale de J. J. Rousseau*. Ed. Th. Dufour and P. P. Plan. 24 vols. Paris: Armand Colin, 1924–34.

————. *Discourse on Political Economy*. In *On the Social Contract with Geneva Manuscript and Political Economy*, ed. Roger D. Masters, trans. Judith R. Masters. New York: St. Martin's Press, 1978.

————. *Discourse on the Origin of Inequality*. In *The First and Second Discourses*, ed. Roger D. Masters, trans. Roger D. Masters and Judith R. Masters. New York: St. Martin's Press, 1964.

————. *Discourse on the Sciences and the Arts*. In *The First and Second Discourses*, ed. Roger D. Masters, trans. Roger D. Masters and Judith R. Masters. New York: St. Martin's Press, 1964.

————. *Emile, or on Education.* Trans. Allan Bloom. New York: Basic Books, 1979.

————. *Essay on the Origin of Languages.* In *The First and Second Discourses Together with the Replies to Critics and Essay on the Origin of Languages,* ed. and trans. Victor Gourevitch. New York: Harper and Row, 1986.

————. *First Discourse.* In *The First and Second Discourses,* trans. Roger D. Masters and Judith R. Masters. New York: St. Martin's Press, 1964.

————. *Fragments politiques.* In *Oeuvres complètes,* vol. 3. Published under the direction of Bernard Gagnebin and Marcel Raymond. Paris: Gallimard, Bibliothèque de la Pleiade, 1959–69.

————. *Jean-Jacques entre Socrate et Caton.* Ed. Claude Pichois and René Pintard. Paris: José Corti, 1972.

————. *Jean-Jacques Rousseau citoyen de Genève à Christophe de Beaumont, archevêque de Paris.* In *Oeuvres complètes,* vol. 4. Published under the direction of Bernard Gagnebin and Marcel Raymond. Paris: Gallimard, Bibliothèque de la Pleiade, 1959–69.

————. *Julie, or the New Heloise.* Trans. Philip Stewart and Jean Vaché. In *The Collected Writings of Rousseau,* ed. Roger D. Masters and Christopher Kelly, vol. 6. Hanover, N.H.: University Press of New England, 1997.

————. *Last Reply by J.-J. Rousseau of Geneva.* In *The First and Second Discourses Together with the Replies to Critics and Essay on the Origin of Languages,* ed. and trans. Victor Gourevitch. New York: Harper and Row, 1986.

————. *Letter to M. d'Alembert on the Theater.* In *Politics and the Arts,* trans. Allan Bloom. Ithaca: Cornell University Press, Agora Editions, 1968.

————. *Lettres morales.* In *Oeuvres complètes,* vol. 4. Published under the direction of Bernard Gagnebin and Marcel Raymond. Paris: Gallimard, Bibliothèque de la Pleiade, 1959–69.

————. *Oeuvres complètes.* 4 vols. Published under the direction of Bernard Gagnebin and Marcel Raymond. Paris: Gallimard, Bibliothèque de la Pleiade, 1959–69.

————. *Preface of a Second Letter to Bordes.* In *The First and Second Discourses Together with the Replies to Critics and Essay on the Origin of Languages,* ed. and trans. Victor Gourevitch. New York: Harper and Row, 1990.

————. *Preface to Narcissus.* In *The First and Second Discourses Together with the Replies to Critics and Essay on the Origin of Languages,* ed. and trans. Victor Gourevitch. New York: Harper and Row, 1990.

————. *Reveries of the Solitary Walker.* Trans. Charles E. Butterworth. Indianapolis: Hackett, 1992.

————. *Rousseau, Judge of Jean-Jacques: Dialogues.* Trans. Judith R. Bush, Christopher Kelly, and Roger D. Masters. In *The Collected Writings of Rousseau,* ed. Masters and Kelly, vol. 1. Hanover, N.H.: University Press of New England, 1990.

————. *Second Discourse.* In *The First and Second Discourses,* trans. Roger D. Masters and Judith R. Masters. New York: St. Martin's Press, 1964.

————. *On the Social Contract.* In *On the Social Contract with Geneva Manuscript and Political Economy,* ed. Roger D. Masters, trans. Judith R. Masters. New York: St. Martin's Press, 1978.

Salkever, Stephen G. "Rousseau and the Concept of Happiness." *Politics* 11 (fall 1978): 27–45.

Santas, Gerasimos. *Plato and Freud: Two Theories of Love.* New York: Basil Blackwell, 1988.

Schama, Simon. *Citizens: A Chronicle of the French Revolution.* New York: Alfred A. Knopf, 1989.

Schwartz, Joel. *The Sexual Politics of Jean-Jacques Rousseau*. Chicago: University of Chicago Press, 1984.

Scott, John T. "The Theodicy of the *Second Discourse*: The 'Pure State of Nature' and Rousseau's Political Thought." *American Political Science Review* 86 (September 1992): 696–711.

Shklar, Judith. *Men and Citizens: A Study of Rousseau's Social Theory*. Cambridge: Cambridge University Press, 1969.

Skillen, Anthony. "Rousseau and the Fall of Social Man." *Philosophy* 60 (1985): 105–21.

Smith, Adam. *The Theory of Moral Sentiments*. New York: Oxford University Press, 1976.

Starobinski, Jean. *Jean-Jacques Rousseau: Transparency and Obstruction*. Trans. Arthur Goldhammer. Chicago: University of Chicago Press, 1988.

Strauss, Leo. "On the Intention of Rousseau." In *Hobbes and Rousseau: A Collection of Critical Essays*, ed. Maurice Cranston and Richard S. Peters. Garden City, N.Y.: Doubleday, 1972.

——. *An Introduction to Political Philosophy*. Detroit: Wayne State University Press, 1989.

——. *Natural Right and History*. Chicago: University of Chicago Press, 1950.

Strong, Tracy B. *Jean-Jacques Rousseau: The Politics of the Ordinary*. Thousand Oaks, Calif.: Sage Publications, 1994.

Taine, Hippolyte A. *Les origines de la France contemporaine: L'anciene regime*. Paris: Libraire Hachette, 1876.

Talmon, Jacob L. *The Rise of Totalitarian Democracy*. New York: Frederick A. Praeger, 1952.

Tocqueville, Alexis de. *Democracy in America*. Ed. J. P. Mayer. Trans. George Lawrence. Garden City, N.Y.: Anchor Books, 1969.

Vico, Giambattista. *The New Science of Giambattista Vico (Scienza nuova)*. Trans. T. G. Bergin and M. H. Fisch. Ithaca: Cornell University Press, 1948.

Wilber, Ken. *Up from Eden: A Transpersonal View of Human Evolution*. Boulder, Colo.: Shambhala Publications, 1981.

Wokler, Robert. *Rousseau*. New York: Oxford University Press, 1995.

Index